Ten Years Of Upper Canada In Peace And War, 1805-1815: Being The Ridout Letters, With Annotations By Matilda Edgar. Also An Appendix Of The Narrative Of The Captivity Among The Shawanese Indians, In 1788, Of Thos. Ridout, Afterwards Surveyor-general...

Lady Matilda Ridout Edgar, Thomas Ridout

This is a curated and comprehensive collection of the most important works covering matters related to national security, diplomacy, defense, war, strategy, and tactics. The collection spans centuries of thought and experience, and includes the latest analysis of international threats, both conventional and asymmetric. It also includes riveting first person accounts of historic battles and wars.

Some of the books in this Series are reproductions of historical works preserved by some of the leading libraries in the world. As with any reproduction of a historical artifact, some of these books contain missing or blurred pages, poor pictures, errant marks, etc. We believe these books are essential to this collection and the study of war, and have therefore brought them back into print, despite these imperfections.

We hope you enjoy the unmatched breadth and depth of this collection, from the historical to the just-published works.

yours ever

Thos Gt Ridout

Deputy Assistant-Commissary-General during the War of 1812,
Cashier of the Bank of Upper Canada from 1822 to 1861.

Born 10th October, 1792.   Died 29th July, 1861.

Deputy Assistant-Commissary General
Cashier of the Bank of Upper Canada from 1822 to 1861.

Born 10th October, 1792.   Died 29th July, 1861.

TEN YEARS

OF

UPPER CANADA

IN PEACE AND WAR,

1805-1815;

BEING

THE RIDOUT LETTERS

WITH ANNOTATIONS

BY

(Ridout) Lady

MATILDA ^ EDGAR.

⸻

ALSO

AN APPENDIX

OF

The Narrative of the Captivity among the Shawanese Indians, in 1788, of Thos. Ridout, afterwards Surveyor-General of Upper Canada: and a Vocabulary, Compiled by him, of the Shawanese Language.

⸻

TORONTO:

WILLIAM BRIGGS.

1890.

CONTENTS.

CHAPTER IV.

VOYAGE TO ENGLAND, 1811.

CHAPTER V.

GOSSIP FROM LONDON, 1811.

CONTENTS.

CHAPTER VI.

AMUSEMENTS IN LONDON—NEWS FROM YORK, 1811-12.

CHAPTER VII.

A CANADIAN AT OXFORD, 1812.

CONTENTS.

CHAPTER VIII.

LONDON AND WOOLWICH.

CHAPTER IX.

FIRST NOTES OF THE WAR, 1812.

CHAPTER X.

OPENING OF FIRST CAMPAIGN—MICHILLIMACKINAC—DETROIT, 1812.

CONTENTS.

CONTENTS.

CONTENTS.

CONTENTS.

Contents.

CONTENTS.

APPENDIX.

INTRODUCTION.

PARTLY to interest the members of a family, and partly for the sake of preserving, for future historians of Canada, some additional records of a memorable time, the publication of these letters was taken in hand. If the explanatory notes have grown to a modest volume, it is because it is thought that the reader may, perhaps, share the absorbing interest the writer felt in tracing the historical bearing of the incidents referred to in the letters. They range over a period from 1805 to 1815, and give a faithful picture of an epoch of Canadian History, which, overshadowed as it was at the time by the great events then passing in Europe, has now a deeper significance for us Canadians than the contemporary triumphs of Salamanca and Waterloo.

The earlier letters are simple ones, written by school-boys to their father, with his replies; but so small was society in Upper Canada, that almost all the names mentioned are, in some way or other, interwoven with its history.

The letters from England in 1811, and 1812 are placed in the collection because they relate to the state of affairs there, and bring vividly before us the condition of both England and Canada, just prior to the declaration of war by the United States. The pictures these letters give of the times in which they are written are the impressions of a youth striving to chronicle for father and mother, in distant Canada, events of the great world beyond the sea.

We see London in the days of the Regency, when Napoleon ruled Europe, and Wellington was earning his first laurels, when Siddons still reigned at Drury Lane, and Scott and Byron walked through London streets.

Now and then flit across the pages the names of the great personages of the day, and Vauxhall is lighted up at a birthday fete for the Duke of Clarence, and the little Princess Charlotte drives through Kensington Gardens on a Sunday afternoon; and there are a Lord Mayor's show, and a Mansion House ball, and many other festivities, which, to a young Canadian whose life had been spent in "Little York," seemed very wonderful. We are told, too, of the famine and distress that then prevailed in England from the stoppage of the trade of the country, and of the smothered discontent of the people at the Ministry of the day, whose "Orders in Council," they thought, had caused the trouble.

Then the scene changes, and the next letters are full of details of battles fought and hardships endured, when Canada was a battle-field, and the whole land from the St. Clair to Quebec was in peril.

There is so much to be proud of in the war of 1812, that its events cannot be too strongly dwelt upon; not in order to stir up old animosities, nor to revive a spirit of antagonism towards our kin beyond the border, but to inspire every Canadian with a feeling of pride in his country, and of grateful admiration for those who saved the land in its hour of need.

As we have reached the last decade of our century, it is well to look back on those footprints stained with blood, that marked its beginning. The shores of Lake Erie, of Huron, and of Ontario, the banks of the Niagara and the St. Lawrence, are full of associations for those who have followed the fortunes of the little band of heroes, that for three years held the frontier against enormous odds. Every home in the land gave husband, or brother, or son, to the country's service, and had it not been for the martial spirit aroused in the people, the efforts of the small body of regular soldiers then in Canada, would have been useless.

It is not intended in this chronicle to give a minute history of the war, which would include many other gallant fights on land and sea.

The public events, described in the letters, form the thread of the story, and lead us on from scene to scene, in the tangled web of the drama of " The Three Years' War."

The details given in the letters are the more valuable, because, of that time there are but few contemporary records preserved. There was no daily paper then, no local reporter to picture each passing event. There are but few survivors now of those who bore a part in the gallant deeds, and bitter trials, that distinguished the first years of this century in Canada.

> " Here is the land,
> Shaggy with wood,
> With its old valley,
> Mound, and flood,
> But the heritors !
> Fled like the flood's foam."

Introduction.

It has been a labour of love to collect these memorials of an honoured father. Perhaps their publication may lead other descendants of the pioneers of this country to search in dusty boxes, and ancient desks, for other records of these "days that are no more."

TEN YEARS OF UPPER CANADA.

CHAPTER I.

A HUNDRED YEARS AGO.

"The great eventful Present hides the Past; but through the din
Of its loud life, hints and echoes from the life behind steal in."

THOMAS RIDOUT, to or by whom the greater part of
these letters was written, settled with his family in
York, now Toronto, in 1797, and was therefore identi-
fied with the place from its earliest years. He was an
Englishman by birth, from Sherbourne, Dorsetshire,
where his forefathers had lived peaceful and unevent-
ful lives. An elder brother of his had emigrated to
Maryland in the old colonial days, had acquired a large
property there, and also held an important position
in the Government of that State. To this brother,
Thomas, then twenty years of age, was sent in the year
1774. Of perils by land and perils by sea, during the
stormy days of the Revolution, the young man had
his full share, and a quaint account of his many adventures is still preserved in his own handwriting.

The obnoxious " tea duty " was still unrepealed, and
in Boston and other colonial ports, scenes of riot and

2

violence occurred whenever a tea cargo arrived. Mr. Ridout's first danger on landing arose from the " tea duty," and is told in his diary in the following language :—

I took leave of my parents for the last time and embarked in the Downs, the 4th September, 1774, for New York, where I arrived after seven weeks' passage. In this vessel went also, as passenger, the merchant who had shipped, a few weeks before, some tea to Annapolis, in Maryland, against the express rules of the Convention, then sitting at Annapolis. His anxiety on his arrival was, I perceived, very great, but two days passing away, and hearing no news of his tea, he flattered himself that all things were well. The arrival of the post, however, undeceived him. He learned that his tea and vessel had been burnt by an enraged populace, and that in consequence of it his life was in danger. In an hour's time New York was in quest of him. He escaped, but I was in danger of feeling the effects his indiscretion, to say no worse of it; for having, since our arrival, been always in his company, and lodging together, I was by many looked on as an accomplice, and, as such, was forbidden entrance to the house where I lodged. A gentleman, Hugh Wallace, who was a member of the King's Council, and an acquaintance of my brother, hearing of my arrival, protected me, and by his attentions I was secured from insult.

His Maryland brother provided him with capital to engage in trade with the West Indies and France; sugar, tobacco and wine were his merchandise, and Sindbad the Sailor's ventures were scarcely more exciting; for on the high seas between the years 1775 and 1785, each trading vessel had to run the gauntlet of privateers bent on capturing prizes, and many a time an exciting chase helped to break the monotony of a sea voyage. In the year 1787, he set off from his brother's house in Annapolis, Maryland, on a journey to the western settlements of Kentucky. On the way, however, he and his party were taken prisoners by a party of Shawanese Indians on the Ohio, and most of his companions were slain. His life was spared, either on account of an extraordinary liking with which he inspired one of his savage captors, who thenceforward became his protector, or because he was the bearer of letters of introduction from General Washington to General Scott, from Colonel Lee to General St. Clair; and to other well-known men in the western settlement.[*] These letters, which were examined by the Indian interpreters, may have caused the Indians to expect a ransom.

It is not the place here to describe Mr. Ridout's adventures;[†] suffice it to say, that, after a captivity of four months, he was brought to Detroit, then an English garrison. Here the officers of the 53rd regiment received him as a brother, clothed him, filled his purse, and as the regiment was about leaving for Montreal, they invited him to accompany them thither. On the way they stopped at Fort Erie and Niagara, and at the latter place were hospitably entertained by Colonel

[*] The originals of these letters are now in possession of his grandson, Thomas Ridout, C.E., Ottawa.

[†] See Appendix for his own narrative of his Indian captivity.

Hunter, of the 60th, who commanded a battalion there. This officer was afterwards Lieutenant-Governor of Upper Canada and Commander-in-chief of the forces in both Canadas.

They arrived in Montreal about the middle of July, 1788, and Mr. Ridout was kindly received, as his old journal relates, by Sir John Johnson, Captain Grant, and Lord Dorchester, then Governor-General, residing at Quebec. A hundred years ago Montreal was both a lively and hospitable place, as witness the cards of invitations to dinners, hops and assemblies which are still extant. The " engaging stranger," as Mr. Ridout is named in a Montreal *Gazette* of August 21st, 1788, soon determined to cast his lot in Canada. On the 26th of May, 1789, he married Mary Campbell, daughter of Alexander Campbell, a U. E. Loyalist, settled at the Bay of Quinte. Soon after he received an appointment in the Commissariat Department and removed to Newark, now Niagara.

As an example of what offices were held by one person in those early days, the following list is given of Mr. Ridout's different employments :—

1792—In the Commissary Department under Lieutenant-Governor Simcoe.

1793—In the Surveyor-General's Office ; D. W. Smith then being Surveyor-General.

In 1794—Public Notary.

In 1794—Sergeant-at-Arms to the House of Assembly.

In 1796—Registrar of County of York.

In 1797—Removed to York, seat of Government.

In 1799—Appointed Captain of York Militia.

In 1800—Clerk of the Peace for Home District, Clerk of the District Court.

1799 to 1800—Joint Acting Surveyor-General with Mr. Chewett.

Again from 1802 to 1805—Joint Acting Surveyor-General with Mr. Chewett.

1807—Joint Acting Surveyor-General, on suspension of Mr. Wyatt, who had been appointed Surveyor-General in 1805, and was dismissed by Lieutenant-Governor Gore.

1810—Surveyor-General of Upper Canada.

1811—Commissioner on Claims to Land.

1812—Elected Member of Parliament for West Riding of York; Member of Corporation for Management of Clergy Reserves; Member of Board for General Superintendence of Education.

1823—Member of Board of Claims for Losses during war.

1824—Called to seat in Legislative Council, Upper Canada.

1827—Member of original Board of King's College, Upper Canada.

Mr. Ridout was, therefore, closely associated with the early history of Upper Canada, and his letters may well take their place among the few records we have of those primitive days.

The scene opens at York in 1805, when Mr. Francis Gore was Lieutenant-Governor. Mr. Strachan's school had just been opened at Cornwall, and there Mr. Ridout's eldest son, George, was sent in 1805, and his second son, Thomas Gibbs, in 1806. A father's love placed their boyish letters carefully away, and in fair round hand each tells its little tale.

York, at this date, is thus described by a traveller, showing what strides it had made in the ten years since Governor Simcoe selected it for the seat of Government :—

A long and narrow peninsula, distinguished by the appellation of Gibraltar Point, forms and embraces the harbor, securing it from the storms of the lake, and rendering it the safest of any around the coast of that sea of fresh water. Stores and block-houses are constructed near the extremity of this point. A spot called the garrison stands on the bank of the mainland opposite this point, and consists only of a wooden block-house and some small cottages of the same material, little superior to temporary huts. The house in which the Lieutenant-Governor resides is likewise formed of wood in the figure of a half-square of one story in height, with galleries in the centre. It is sufficiently commodious for the present state of the Province, and is erected upon a bank of the lake near the mouth of Toronto Bay. The town, according to the plan, is projected to extend to a mile and a half in length, from the bottom of the harbor along its banks. Many houses are already completed, some of which display a considerable degree of taste. The advancement of this place to its present condition has been effected within the lapse of six or seven years; and persons who have formerly travelled in this part of the country are impressed with sentiments of wonder on beholding a town, which may be termed handsome, reared as if by enchantment in the midst of a wilderness. Two buildings of brick, at the eastern extremity of the town, which were designed as wings to a centre, are occupied as Chambers for the Upper and Lower House of Assembly. The scene from this part of the basin is agreeable and diversified. A block-house situated on a wooden bank forms the nearest object; part of the town, points of land clothed with spreading oak-trees gradually receding from the eye one behind another, until terminated by the buildings of the garrison and the spot on which the Governor's residence is placed, compose the objects on the right. The left side of the view comprehends the long peninsula which encloses this sheet of water, beautiful on account of its placidity and rotundity of form; the distant lake, which appears only bounded by the sky, terminates the whole.*

See Heriot's "Travels through the Canadas, 1807."

CHAPTER II.

LITTLE YORK—CORNWALL SCHOOL, 1805-1809.

THE first letter, dated Cornwall, 17th September, 1805, is from George Ridout to his brother, and says :—

I have been eight days on my journey from York and was frightened a little coming down the rapids. Mr. Strachan has received me, I stay at Mr. Vankoughnet's.

The next letter is from Thomas G. Ridout to his brother at Cornwall, and mentions festivities in York during the winter of 1805-1806.

YORK, 19th January, 1806.

DEAR GEORGE,—We received yesterday your letter of the 8th January. There is to be a ball given by President Grant on Monday, the 20th. There have been three balls given this winter, to two of which papa and mamma have been. Whilst they are gone Basil stays to take care of the house and amuses the children with stories until 11 or 12 o'clock. The reason why papa and mamma did not go to the last ball was that Basil got drunk, and did not come, so mamma would not go, because she was afraid of leaving the house alone. I send this letter to you by a man named McFee, who is going through to Cornwall, and sets off the day after to-morrow. I should like to know how you and Sam. Jarvis and John Macaulay and John Robinson agree. There has been very little carioling hitherto, but I hope there will be, as it is snowing pretty well to-day.

The word "carioling" seems to have been generally used, where we in Canada would now speak of "sleighing."

The "John Robinson" mentioned became the distinguished Sir John Beverley Robinson, Chief Justice of Upper Canada.

It is rather amusing to read now of assemblies and balls, considering the limited society and sparse population of the little town.   However, even as far back as 1798, old invitations still remain to testify to the social qualities of the early inhabitants of York.   Official dinners took place at an earlier hour than nowadays, as the following card shows :—

THURSDAY, 28*th June*, 1798.

The President requests Mr. Ridout's company to dinner to-morrow (Friday), at 4 o'clock.

"The President" was doubtless Hon. Peter Russell, on whom devolved the government of Canada on the recall of General Simcoe in 1796, and who continued administrator until the arrival of General Hunter, in 1799.

The following is another card of that early period :—

SUNDAY, 28*th January*.

Major Shank requests the honour of Mr. Ridout's company to Dinner and the Hop on Thursday next.

A third invitation runs thus :—

The officers of the Queen's Rangers request the honour of Mr. Ridout's company to a Ball on Friday evening next, at the Canvas House.

Wednesday Morning, 11th *December*, 1799.

This "Canvas House" once belonged to the celebrated Captain Cook, and was bought by Lieutenant-Governor Simcoe at the sale in England of the unfortunate mariner's effects. When Governor Simcoe selected York as the capital, the canvas tent became his temporary residence. It is not quite certain where it was placed, but its site was probably to the west of the town, near the old Garrison Creek. It is thus described by a well-known writer, Colonel Bouchette :—

Frail as was its substance, it was rendered exceedingly comfortable, and soon became as distinguished for the social and urbane hospitality of its venerated and gracious host, as for the peculiarity of its structure.

From George Ridout to his Parents :—

Cornwall, 27th *January*, 1806.

We intend to send these letters by Mr. Steele, who is going to-morrow morning, and who comes down every winter to see his son Abraham. We have three or four new scholars, all of them are bigger than Mr. Strachan. There is one who has come from Kingston, his name is Wm. Grant. Mr. Steele had promised all the boys who came from Kingston a ride, but unfortunately the cariole got broke. We came on pretty well in Sallust and we have begun Euclid. Mr. Strachan has given us books. Washburne and I have one between us. The Euclid we have is Simson's. Tom comes on well in his ciphering and book-keeping, and is at the head of his reading class, which is a large one, consisting of twelve or fourteen boys. He seems to be a great favourite of Mr. Strachan's, of which some of the boys are jealous. He always has his tasks very well and never tries to find excuses for any, as some of them do. Mr. Strachan asked us to-night whether Tom had rather be called Tom than Tam, as he generally calls him. Tom told him which, and Mr. Strachan laughed, and when he laughs he laughs heartily. It has been very cold lately and ice has come in great quantities down the river, it has raised the water eight or ten feet. Mrs. Chewett was not buried at St. Regis as we thought she was, but back at the River au Raisin. William and James stay at Mr. Wilkinson's, who has three or four boarders.

From George Ridout to his Brother :—

CORNWALL, 24*th February*, 1806.

I received your letter of the 18th January on the 12th of this month, but have had no opportunity to answer it until this morning, when there is a Scotchman going to York, by whom I am writing. We have had a mild winter here, and the river has not been stopped with ice. I hear that Mr. Weekes has been making great work. There has been a report here that D'Arcy Boulton and Jos. Willcocks were going to fight a duel, but Mr. Willcocks was afraid. I would like to hear whether it was true. We have had church three or four times in our new church, and I understand that yours is only clap-boarded. The first pew went for £30, Halifax cy., and the second for £24, Halifax cy., and the whole amounts to £500, Halifax cy.

The next letter is from the father, and mentions an item of political news.

YORK, *27th November,* 1806.

MY DEAR BOYS,—This is to you both, by an opportunity I have just met with of a man going to the Bay of Quinte and from thence to Kingston, for I do not apprehend we shall have any more opportunities for Kingston by water this season. The election for a member in the place of Mr. Weekes will come about the Christmas holidays. Mr. Thorpe, Captain Fulton and young D'Arcy Boulton are the present known candidates. The Parliament is to meet on the second of February next.

The new election spoken of in this letter was occasioned by the death of Mr. Weekes, who was killed in a duel with Mr. Dickson, of Niagara, in 1806. The East Riding of York, Durham and Simcoe, was rather unfortunate in the tragical fate of its members, the one who preceded Mr. Weekes having gone down with the vessel *Speedy,* sunk in Lake Ontario, with all on board, in 1804. The Mr. Thorpe mentioned as a candidate, was Judge Thorpe, one of the puisne Judges of Upper Canada. By becoming a champion of the people he fell under the displeasure of Lieutenant-Governor Gore and the Government party. According to their code no criticism was to be permitted on their acts, however unjust and tyrannical they might be. The complaints of the people found expression in memorials from the grand juries to Judge Thorpe—the "Radical Judge," as he was called—to be by him laid before the Governor. In the election spoken of in the letter Mr. Thorpe was successful, and with his election came the dawn of party politics in Upper Canada, and an organized Opposition. He was not, however, long allowed to hold his seat. Soon after his election, the Governor procured his recall to Great Britain, where he sued Mr. Gore for libel and obtained a verdict. He, however, never returned to Canada, and his subsequent history was a sad one. As a sort of recompense for his unjust recall, he was appointed Chief Justice of Sierra Leone. In that unhealthy climate his health broke down, and he returned to England bearing with him a petition from the people to the Ministry for the redress of certain grievances in that colony. For this second championship of the oppressed, his appointment as Chief Justice was cancelled, and he was left to pass the remainder of his days in poverty and obscurity.

The next letters from Cornwall school shew that the course of study there was rather a severe one, and the boys had to sit up very late to prepare their lessons.

CORNWALL, 10th *January*, 1807.

MY DEAR PARENTS,—I am afraid you may be angry with us for not writing for so long a time, but there have been no opportunities. I come on middling well, and am going into book-keeping on Monday. I got a quire of paper to-day from Mr. Strachan, to make my book. Mr. Strachan has not struck me yet, nor has he been angry. We have finished our grammar and are learning it by heart every morning. It is very cold weather here and excellent sleighing, and very fine skating for the boys who have skates. It is snowing very fast now. We had about a week's play at Christmas and now and then half-days, but very seldom. The boys say that Mr. Strachan is going down to Quebec to see the Bishop in June, and that the vacation will be then. The boys had a frolic upon the ice yesterday with three pecks of apples which Stanton bought, and after his apples were gone they were as bad as ever teasing him. We stay up every night till about twelve or one o'clock and we have got so used to it that we don't mind it. We repeat four problems a week, and I am two from head. The day after New Year's Judge Anderson invited sixteen of the boys down there, and George and I were of them. He threw about a bushel of apples to scramble for now and then, and I got as many as I could carry, and half a bushel of hickory nuts; and they had a dance, and all the boys danced except Robert Anderson, his grandson, and I. George danced very well.

I am, my dear parents,

Your affectionate son,

THOMAS G. RIDOUT.

A letter from Cornwall school on the 18th January, 1807, says :—

Since I have been in book-keeping I have had to stay up until two o'clock in the morning. Sam Jarvis learns his lessons well, and he and Stanton are almost always head of their class.

The following letter from Mr. Ridout, York, to his

sons continues the story of Mr. Thorpe's election, and also mentions Mr. Wyatt's return to England. This Mr. Wyatt had been appointed Surveyor-General in 1806, and had fallen under the displeasure of Lieutenant-Governor Gore about the same time that Mr. Thorpe did. Some say it was because of his advocacy of Mr. Thorpe's cause, another reason assigned is that he disapproved of some irregular purchase of land from the Indians. However it might be, he was dismissed and returned to England.

Mr. Ridout to his son, George :—

YORK, 18*th February*, 1807.

I have received by Mr. Sherwood your letters of the 12th, 18th and 27th January, together with one from Mr. Strachan, who speaks highly of your and your brother's good conduct and progress in education, than which nothing can afford me greater pleasure. Mr. St. George sets off to-morrow for New York, and I have commissioned him to buy a Euclid for you. I shall not send your book that you left behind. If Mr. Strachan asks for it, tell him where it is, and if absolutely necessary, I will send it at the opening of communication by water. I have the pleasure to inform you that I am much in favor with the Governor. He has given me a new commission of Sergeant-at-Arms, so that I can execute that office by deputy. Mr. Wyatt and his wife set out for England about a fortnight ago by way of New York. There have been great differences between them, insomuch that he has frequently tied her hands to the bed-posts, and confined her in the cellar, with other harsh treatment. Mr. Thorpe has hitherto retained his seat in the House, but since Mr. Sherwood's arrival I understand that the right of a judge to sit therein will be again debated. Mr. Abraham Nelles and his wife, formerly Miss Kitty Ball, have been at our house these five days. I write this at the table of the House of Assembly, intending to send it by the post or a Mr. Roxborough, a merchant of Montreal, who both intended setting out to-day, but the weather is so exceedingly stormy with snow, rain and wind that I apprehend neither will move.

An item of American news now comes:

Mr. Burr, it is said, is gone from Kentucky to New Orleans, with 5000 or 6000 men. Political disputes in the States runs very high. You have, no doubt, heard of Bonaparte's success in Europe. Time is big with great events, but the mind who takes reason for its guide and places its dependence on an all-wise Providence is prepared for all events which the Creator of the universe is pleased to send.

Aaron Burr, an ex-Vice-President of the United States, had formed a plan to seize the territory west of the Alleghanies, and to establish there an independent empire, of which New Orleans was to be the capital, and himself the chief. He was arrested in February, 1807, and tried on a charge of treason. Though acquitted, his escape was so narrow, and his fears of renewed prosecution so great, that he sailed for Europe under an assumed name and remained there for several years in exile and poverty. As to Napoleon Bonaparte's successes, he had at the time (1807), just succeeded in bestowing the crown of Holland on his brother Louis, and the crown of Naples on his brother Joseph. He had won the battle of Jena, and entered Berlin, whence he had issued his famous "Decrees" against British commerce, hoping to ruin England by shutting out her ships from every port.

From Thomas G. Ridout, to his Father :—

CORNWALL, 16*th June*, 1807.

Mr. Strachan is building a new school-house, about 40 feet by 30. It is to be arched, and there are twelve windows in it. In the meantime he keeps school in the church. I am now in the surveying class, and Mr. Strachan gives us a figure to work every night. We have made ourselves quadrants out of cherry-wood, which cost us two shillings to be made smooth, and we are now in Euclid, 6th book, which is the furthest Mr. Strachan teaches his boys. He knows to the 12th. We are now making preparations for the examination, which will be five weeks from to-day. Some have to make their own speeches, and I among the number. The question is, Whether general History or Biography is the most useful? Mr. Strachan has now been married nearly two months, he lives in great style, and keeps three servants. He is a great friend to the poor, and spends his money as fast as he gets it. He is very passionate.

These letters from school at Cornwall recall the form of Mr. Strachan, afterwards Anglican Bishop of the Province of Upper Canada, who at that time, 1807, had been about three years installed at Cornwall, and who lived to see some of the boys he ruled over become the foremost men of the Province.

3

Mr. Strachan was born at Aberdeen, on the 12th of April, 1778, and was educated at the grammar school and university of that place. In 1797, he commenced to teach in the little village of King's Kettle. At this time he received the offer, through Hon. Richard Cartwright and Robert Hamilton, to proceed to Canada to organize and take charge of a college, which Governor Simcoe had determined to establish at York, the seat of government in Upper Canada. Unfortunately, when the young Scotchman arrived in Canada in the winter of 1799, Governor Simcoe had left the Province, and the scheme was, for the time, dropped. Mr. Strachan, much disappointed, remained in Kingston as tutor to Mr. Cartwright's children. Here he lived for three years, and then decided to enter the English Church, and was ordained priest on the 3rd June, 1804, by Dr. Mountain, first Bishop of Quebec, and appointed to the mission of Cornwall. In 1807, he married Ann, widow of James McGill, a lady of considerable fortune. Through his long life, and he lived until he was nearly ninety, Dr. Strachan watched over his boys. Many of them were married by him ; a kind pat on the head greeted their children as he passed them on the street, and every year, at stated times, all of his old pupils within reach were gathered round his hospitable board.

Among the papers of Mr. Ridout was the following census of the Home District, which possesses much interest :—

Numbers of Inhabitants returned by the Town Clerks of the Home District, Province of Upper Canada, taken in March, 1809:

TOWNSHIP.	Men.	Women.	Males under 16 years.	Females under 16 years.	TOTAL.
Town of York......	195	162	137	83	577
Township of York.	175	126	167	150	618
Scarborough........	34	24	44	38	140
Etobicoke	32	27	34	44	137
Pickering	40	35	51	54	180
Whitby...........	63	43	42	45	193
Markham.........	294	234	320	263	1111
Vaughan..........	75	60	99	99	333
Whitechurch and Uxbridge........	123	127	258	218	726
East Gwillimbury.	79	69	149	128	425
West Gwillimbury.	13	12	29	20	74
North Gwillimbury	16	15	18	24	73
King.............	45	30	58	42	175
Toronto	37	26	65	47	185
Trafalgar.........	55	45	71	62	233
Nelson and East Flamboro'	80	70	75	70	295
West Flamboro'.....	55	52	109	98	314
Beverley..........	26	23	55	37	141
Block No. 2, G. R...	64	48	71	58	241
Number in 1809 ...	1501	1228	1852	1590	6171
Number in 1805 ...	1080	870	985	849	3784
Increase...........	421	358	867	741	2387

CHAPTER III.

LITTLE YORK, MONTREAL AND QUEBEC, 1809-1811.

IN October, 1809, Mr. Ridout obtained leave of absence, and set out on a visit to his friends in England, which country he had left more than thirty years before. His two eldest sons, George and Thomas, had now left school, and were in charge of their father's office during his absence. George was then in his nineteenth year, and Thomas just seventeen.

From Thomas to his Father :—

YORK, *15th October,* 1809.

MY DEAR FATHER,—It was with the greatest pleasure we received your letter from Kingston by Doctor Glennon. Your tender charge to me respecting my little brothers and sisters I will affectionately fulfil, and the responsible offices you left to my charge will be my pride to execute with diligence, care and punctuality. The Acts I put on board of Kendrick's, with a box of the honey peaches for Mr. Markland; they are very fine. Winter is coming on very fast, the leaves begin to fall, and the wild geese fly over the town to the southward. We begin to gather in our apples and our other winter store.

I remain, honoured Father,

Your affectionate Son,

THOMAS G. RIDOUT.

A letter dated the 1st November, 1809, announcing the father's safe arrival in Quebec, reached York on the 28th of the same month, brought by a " Mr. Cumming," who, it is mentioned, " will travel by land as all travellers do now." That same November, 1809, the first steamer was placed on the St Lawrence, viz; the steamer *Accommodation*, built by Mr. John Molson, of Montreal.

The voyage to England in 1809 is chronicled in a letter from Portsmouth, and is worthy of notice, as being a remarkably short passage for those days, just a month.

Mr. Ridout writes :—

17th December, 1809.

We sailed from Quebec on the 15th November, under convoy of the *Mermaid*, Frigate, in company with twenty other vessels, but the weather was so severe before we got out of the St. Lawrence that we separated from the frigate in the Gulf. We had a snow storm from the north-east, the wind then shifted to the north-west, and blew very heavy, which carried us to sea. We have not experienced the least misfortune or accident. The *Everetta* is the best vessel I have seen. We were becalmed a morning on the Grand Bank of Newfoundland, and caught sixty-two cod fish. Yesterday we dined on board on a dish of beef steaks, " Quebec beef." We have crossed the ocean *alone*, without a *company*.

This is italicized as a great event at a time when crossing the ocean meant peril both to life and liberty.

From George Ridout to his Father in England :—

YORK, *6th February*, 1810.

A few days ago we received your letters dated the 9th November, from Quebec. The enclosed packet for the Governor I took up the next day. As he was very busy at his own house, I gave it to Mr. Stanton, acqainting him of the length of time it had been coming, he then sent the letter to the Governor with what I had said. I thought it proper to state this, as you had mentioned in your letter to me, that you had enclosed to him one of the same pamphlets you sent us, copies of which had reached this several weeks before. For some time, no business but the Governor's was allowed to be attended to ; different occurrences which have taken place under the respective Governors and Presidents, are the subject of these proceedings ; it is thought that Messrs. Thorpe and Wyatt have had some hand in this. About two weeks after we wrote our last letter, Tom and I were taken ill of the same fever, which you may recollect proved so fatal in Whitchurch, and a day or two afterwards, Sally and Horace were attacked. We were much reduced. Had it not been for Dr. Baldwin's skill and attention, good nursing and pretty good constitutions, I think it would have gone very hard with us. They have subscribed £200 in York towards a library. Bring me, if in your power, Commyn's Digest.

The pamphlet mentioned in the letter, and of which we shall hear further, was, no doubt, the one issued by Mr. J. Mills Jackson, and entitled, " A View of the Political Situation of the Province," and considered libellous, as all such criticisms were, by the Governor and his party.

From Thomas G. Ridout to his Father in England:—

YORK, 18*th February*, 1810.

You must not charge us with neglect in not writing since the 14th December, as that neglect was caused by a fever which attacked George and me the same day, and continued from 30th December till about 20th January. Under Dr. Baldwin's care, and my mother's, we recovered, and are now heartier than ever. The House of Assembly met here on the 1st inst. There does not seem to be so much spirit for opposition in them as there has been. Jos. Willcocks is greatly curbed by the watch which is kept over his publications and speeches. There are no assemblies here this winter, but now and then a party ball is given in private houses, for they are divided into two parties. Nancy and Sam went to the Governor's ball. We were too ill to go.

From George Ridout to his Father in England:—

YORK, 11*th March*, 1810.

This packet we send by New York. Nothing very material has occurred since I wrote you last. The Parliament met the 1st February, and is not yet prorogued, although expected to be in a few days. An address of the House of Assembly to the Governor respecting the pamphlet, signed John M. Jackson, declaring it to be a scandalous and libellous publication, pleases the Governor, and is no doubt a great satisfaction to him. It has had a no less contrary effect upon Jos. Willcocks. When the question was put whether it was a libel or not, Willcocks and Rogers were the only two dissenting members, but when the ayes and nays were called for, they thought proper to rise. Tom has been writing in the Lower House of Assembly from eight in the morning till ten at night, and Mr. Boulton has been so good as to allow me to stay at home while the session lasts, by which means the Registry Office has never been closed. From four o'clock in the afternoon till ten I write in the House of Assembly.

The Jos. Willcocks, whose name appears in this letter, was another turbulent spirit, who, when Judge Thorpe was recalled, succeeded him in the representation of the East Riding of York in the House of Assembly.

Mr. Willcocks had been Sheriff of the Home District, but had been dismissed from his office for daring to express his opinions. He was then returned to the Legislature, but was impeached for breach of privilege, and was cast into the common jail, the offence charged being that on September 17th, 1808, Willcocks said members had been bribed by twelve hundred acres of land each in the October previous, by the Governor. He was accused of saying this in in his paper, the *Guardian*, and on the public streets. After his release from jail, he was returned as member again, and continued to lead the Opposition.

The Rogers mentioned was D. McGregor Rogers, who had sat in the House of Assembly since 1799, and was in 1810 member for Northumberland. He also was on the people's side, as opposed to the Government; but being more moderate in expressing his views, he did not get into such trouble as his friends Judge Thorpe and Willcocks.

A little further news of Mr. Willcocks comes in the next letter.

From Thomas G. Ridout to his Father in England:—

YORK, 12*th March,* 1810.

MY DEAR FATHER,—Three months have now passed since we received any news concerning you, but your great distance from us authorizes that time in some measure. The House of Assembly is to be prorogued to-morrow; it has been a profitable session for us, as I wrote in the Lower House a month, night and day, and have earned ninety-two dollars. George wrote in the evenings and will get forty-five dollars. There has been a severe stroke given to Mr. Willcocks and his party this session, as Mr. Jackson's pamphlet was brought before the House of Assembly, by Mr. Mc-Lean of Kingston, and considered as a gross libel against this country, government and people, and they sent an address to the Governor to that purpose, desiring him at the same time to let the Government in England be acquainted with the same, for the purpose of doing away any ill impression that it might occasion there.

The next letter in the packet is one from Mr. D. W. Smith to Mr. Ridout. This Mr. Smith, afterwards Sir D. W. Smith, was the son of Colonel Smith of the 5th regiment, commandant at Fort Niagara in the time of Governor Simcoe. The son served as ensign and lieutenant in the same regiment, but left the profession of arms for the study of the law in Upper Canada. He was called to the bar there, and with the rapid promotion usual at that time, was accorded precedence as Deputy-Judge, was appointed Surveyor-General of Lands in Upper Canada, a trustee for the Six Nations, one of the Executive Council, became a member of the three first Parliaments, and Speaker of the House in two of them. For these services he was created a baronet in 1821. At the date of the letter he had been for some years residing in England, but evidently his ambition was to return to Canada as Lieutenant-Governor.

The letter is dated, Alnwick, 11th April, 1810, and after some business details, goes on to say:—

There is a rumour that Governor Gore is coming home, but it seems rather with a view of returning to Canada. The Duke has said to me that, if he should not return, and I wish to go out, he will ask the appointment as a special favor to himself; but he rather advises me to wait, as he is not with the present administration, and might, therefore, meet with a refusal. Dickson left me on Friday night last, and is at the Turk's Head Coffee House, near Somerset Place.

The "Duke" was probably the Duke of Northumberland, whose estates Mr. Smith administered.

Mr. Ridout returned safely from England in 1810, more fortunate than his fellow-townsmen, Mr. Small and Mr. D'Arcy Boulton, the Solicitor-General for Upper Canada, who had sailed in the ship *Minerva*, and were taken prisoners by a French privateer, and carried off to France, where they remained prisoners of war, at Verdun, until 1815.

In June, 1811, Thomas Gibbs Ridout set out for England, by way of Montreal and Quebec, on a visit to his father's relatives, and with the intention of remaining in that country if prospects of business were good. At that time he was not quite nineteen years of age, but his letters show an observant mind, and that the training of Mr. Strachan's school had not been without good results.

With the usual economy of the time in the matter of postage, the youth was evidently charged with many letters, both public and private, to deliver in Quebec, and also in London, England, which commission he seems to have faithfully fulfilled. Henry John Boulton, son of Mr. D'Arcy Boulton, set out from York at the same time, his intention being to study law in Lincoln's Inn, and also to endeavour to procure his father's release from captivity.

The account of the capture of Messrs. Small and Boulton is given in a letter from Henry John Boulton to his brother D'Arcy, in York.

He says that his father writes from Cambray on the 11th of April, 1811 :—

That he is quite recovered from his wounds, and he is treated with respect proportioned to his rank. His expenses are about five shillings per diem.

On the 15th July, 1811, the prisoner writes from Verdun, in France, to his son Henry, who, in a letter to York, gives the following account of the engagement at sea, which cost Mr. Boulton and Mr. Small their liberty and kept them in durance vile for three years, until the close of the European war in 1815 :—

Now for the engagement, which was a very gallant though unsuccessful one. When the privateer

first came in sight the *Minerva* hoisted the English
colours, but the privateer hoisted none till she came
within close gun shot, when she up with the French
colours, and gave the *Minerva* a broadside, which was
instantly returned, and carried away their bowsprit,
with a chain shot.   The engagement lasted an hour
and a half, during which the *Minerva* was boarded
three times, but they repulsed them as often ; but the
rigging being much cut, they could not manage the
ship, and the privateer succeeded in getting a grappling
into the *Minerva*, and boarded it with such superior
numbers, that they were obliged to give it up, sword in
hand.   The *Minerva* mounted four four-pounders, two
six-pounders, with fourteen men, including the passengers and the cabin boy.   The *Grand Duke of Bey*,
the privateer, fourteen twelve-pounders, and ninety
men, all well armed with musketry.   Papa and Woolink
were captains of the two sixes, and, as papa says, gave
them little respite.   Mr. Woolink told me that after the
first shot, he felt no more anxiety for his safety than
if he had been playing cards, and that he and papa were
laughing all the time.   Small was a little blue, but
fired away with a musket, and said nothing.   The
Grand Duke of Bey has taken fifty-six prizes, and is
the finest privateer in the French service.   Papa was
wounded, in boarding, with a sabre, in the forehead,
which was very severe, and Woolink was afraid it had
dished him ; but he has, thank God, lived to tell the
story, and how many French rascals he fixed for it.
He being very active in the engagement, was supposed
to be the captain by the privateer, and was dragged
on board alone.   He had the precaution to save his
money, but his box was left in the *Minerva*. Small
lost all his money ; a sailor coming up, and giving
him his choice of giving it up or having his brains
blown out, he chose the former.   Small and Woolink opened papa's box after the hurry of the battle
was over, and threw overboard all his public papers.

To their great joy, the *Minerva*, going into Calais, ran aground, and was lost, cargo and all.

Mr. Henry John Boulton afterwards became Attorney-General for Upper Canada, and also held the position of Chief Justice of Newfoundland for five years. He returned to Toronto in 1838, and afterwards represented Niagara, and also Norfolk, in Parliament. His second son, George D'Arcy Boulton, Q.C., practised law in Toronto, and married the eldest daughter of Mr. T. G. Ridout.

The first letter from Montreal sounds the first note of the coming war, and mentions the name of a commander, who was destined soon to take a prominent part in it.

From Thomas Gibbs Ridout to his Father at York:—

MONTREAL, *3rd July*, 1811.

There is great talk here of war with the Americans. The British are provisioning Quebec and Halifax, the 41st regiment are continually out on the parade, marching, forming, filing. They are 800 strong. I went on the parade yesterday afternoon, looking at them. The men made a very fine appearance, but I thought the officers almost too young. Colonel Sheaffe commands. I have been over the whole town, the streets are full of people. The great bell of the French church roused me out of bed this morning before four. I went to both markets, and found hundreds of people there at that hour, with everything for sale; ripe cherries, and currants and beans. On inquiring my way through the town, not one in ten could speak a word of English, and I hear French jabbered in every house. Henry Boulton stays at Holmes' tavern, and will not be ready to go with me.

From Thomas G. Ridout to his Brother at York :—

QUEBEC, *5th July*, 1811.

After a journey of nine days, I arrived at this place, which far surpassed my opinion of it.   There are near two hundred sail lying in the river, they form a forest of three or four deep for six miles.   I came from Montreal for nineteen shillings, including provisions, which were nothing but a bit of ham and a loaf of bread. We were shockingly crowded in the boat, there being ten passengers with their baggage, the crew, and 12 barrels of potash.   I only delivered Mr. Stuart's and Macaulay's letters.   I am to breakfast and dine with Dr. Macaulay on Sunday.   He inquired a great deal about you and his friends at York.   John is now a first lieutenant at Cadiz, and expects after that to go to the East Indies.   James is at Annapolis, New Brunswick.   George has been taking me round part of the ramparts this afternoon.   There are great works going on now, round towers and half-moons are building in front of all the gates, and the double wall is continued down through the Quebec suburbs.   They are in great expectation here of war with the Yankees, and the works are accordingly carried on with great industry.   There are two or three additional regiments expected from England.   Montreal is nothing to compare with Quebec in regard to bustle, business or anything else.   Consider what the loading and unloading of two hundred sail must make !   In coming to anchor, we passed close under the stern of the *Everetta*.   She is the prettiest vessel here.   I saw Captain Patterson on the deck.   The quays and lower streets are completely covered and crowded with bales and men. One half of the crews of the ships look to be made up of boys between nine and fourteen years old, nice, smart little fellows.   I was at the market this morning, it was well supplied with everything, particularly strawberries, of which I dare say there were ten or twelve bushels, nice fresh butter on leaves, gooseberries and cakes of all kinds.　Better mutton and beef than at Montreal.

From Thomas G. Ridout to his Father at York :—

QUEBEC, *6th July*, 1811.

This morning I set out to find Mr. Gray,* I at last found him on the street in company with Colonel Mc-Donell.　He asked me if I was going to England, and said he would get me a passage.　After reading the Governor's letter he seemed pleased, and said that a friend of his is now here who commands the best ship in the port, and who shortly sails with his lady for England, the ship being fitted up and provided in the best manner, he says, will be just what the Governor meant for me.　I am, however, to go on Monday at half after eleven to Colonel McDonell, and with him in his carriage to Mr. Gray's country-seat, and spend the day.　Mr. Gray will then settle how I am to go, as the fleet does not sail till the 20th.　The two letters for the Commander-in-Chief, I left with General Drummond's *aide-de-camp* at the castle.　There is a gentleman here from New York who says that New York is not to compare with this place for active business. About five hundred men are at work upon the fortifications every day.　Another round tower is building back of the Quebec suburbs, it is said they are to be connected by walls and batteries.　There are also half-moons built in front of each land-gate.　It is too extravagant to send letters by post, all one would wish.

From Thomas G. Ridout, Quebec, to his Brother at York, 9th July :—

We sail to-night.　The transport I go in is a very fine copper-bottomed ship, carries six guns, and muskets for the invalids, and passengers and sailors, so that we are almost as safe as the frigate, or even safer, as

---

* Mr. Gray was at that time Deputy Quarter-Master-General.

she has orders to take us under particular care so that we will keep in company during the voyage. Get papa to write to Dr. Macaulay for the civilities he has shown me. Betsy and Mary are very fine, lively and sensible girls. George is a good Greek scholar.

From Thomas G. Ridout to his Father at York:—

QUEBEC, *9th July*, 1811.

This evening I embark on board a government transport called, the *Sea Nymph*, Captain Robert Smith, bound for Portsmouth. In the cabin there are three ladies (one of them widow of Major Andrews, who died at Niagara).

Yesterday, at the mess, the officers talked as if they wished and expected war. Colonel Shank has his regiment under very bad discipline. There was a press-gang came up from the frigate last night and pressed fifteen fine seaman, all English. I saw the poor fellows marched into the boat by a party of soldiers.

From Thomas G. Ridout to his Father at York:—

OFF THE BRANDY POTTS, *15th July*, 1811.

As I informed you in my last, we embarked on the 9th, but owing to an easterly storm, which lasted from the 9th to the 14th, we did not weigh anchor until yesterday morning at five o'clock, and have just now (noon) got to the Brandy Potts, where the *Primrose* lies with about twenty sail of merchantmen, and twenty-two more are in sight; so that we'll have a fleet of near fifty sail. The *Sea Nymph* is a very fine ship and has been a transport these nine years, and is well accommodated for carrying troops. We have on board forty-two invalids, sixteen seamen, six soldiers' wives, four ladies, two servant-women, nine children, captain, mate and boy, and three gentlemen— total, eighty-four. But we are not in the least crowded, and have plenty of provisions for two months, and fifty-five tons of good water. Every morning the rations and water are delivered out. I am allowed a ration, which consists of pork, beef, peas, oatmeal, sugar, rum, rice, flour, butter and English cheese. The cabin stores are also plentiful, which cost us £10 apiece at Quebec. In the morning we have a dish of burgee with butter, after that two or three cups of chocolate, coffee or tea, with biscuit and butter; at twelve, some biscuit and cheese; for dinner, beef, fowls, potatoes, pease-pudding and plum-pudding, cheese, porter, Madeira and port, with pickles; in the evening, coffee, and cakes and preserves, and at bed-time, wine and water. There are forty or fifty fowls, two sheep, three pigs; therefore, I think, we'll do very well.

When we left Quebec there were some 250 sail lying in the river. Henry Boulton is in company with us on board the brig *Salus*, Captain Vicker, bound for Liverpool. The fleet looks beautiful. We are all at anchor, waiting for those in sight, who are coming up fast. We carry six eighteen-pounders, and have about sixty men on board, seventeen of whom are artillerymen, and can manage the guns; plenty of muskets in good order, and ammunition, therefore it will not be a common privateer that can take us. The *Primrose* has us under her particular care.

I gave Governor Gore's letters to General Gore, to General Drummond's *aide-de-camp*. I am so prejudiced in favour of York, that I think it the neatest and prettiest place I have yet seen, and St. George's house by much the best and handsomest.

The handsomest house in the York of 1811 is still to be seen in the Toronto of 1890, on the corner of King and Frederick Streets. It is now occupied as the Canada Company's office.

4

From Thomas Ridout to his son Thomas in England :—

YORK, UPPER CANADA, 16th *July*, 1811.

We have received your letters of the 29th June, from Kingston ; 3rd July, from Montreal. The letters came to hand on the evening of the 14th inst. The Governor sent yesterday a message to your mother that you had set out from Montreal, and he informed me that he had hopes you would get on board the sloop of war that was at Quebec. It is not likely that this will reach you before you leave Quebec ; indeed, I conclude that you are now on your way down the river, and with a fair wind pursuing your voyage. May it, my dear son, be a fortunate one. The Governor, I am persuaded, interests himself in your welfare. Make Mr. Watson and Mr. Oldham your friends. Consult Mr. Prince in all things. He, after your uncle, will feel most interested in your welfare. I shall write to Mr. Prince, in a day or two, to endeavour to send hither a gentleman for the school, etc.

There was at that time great difficulty in obtaining both a schoolmaster and a parson for Little York, Mr. Stuart having resigned his post in the District School.

From Thomas Ridout to his son Thomas in England :—

YORK, UPPER CANADA, 31st *July*, 1811.

We received on the 27th the letters you wrote at Quebec on the 9th inst. I shall write immediately to Mr. Gray and Dr. Macaulay to thank them for their civilities to you. It has blown a heavy gale of wind from the north-east all the last night, attended with rain, and the gale continues. John is only waiting its motions to embark on board the *Lady Gore*, for Kingston. Mr. St. George and many others go in her. Mrs. Allan returned a day or two ago from Kingston. She speaks of your civilities to her. John Robinson returned hither with Mrs. Allan. Whether he remains here or not, I know not. George is much pleased in his transfer to Mr. McDonell's office. No accounts from Mr. Boulton since you left us. Mr. Firth is about to return to England with his family. He applied to the Governor for leave of absence, but as he did not obtain it, he has, it seems, made up his mind to surrender his appointment, and a sale of all his effects is to commence on the 12th proximo. We learn that Mr. Miles Jackson arrived in the *Everetta* at Quebec, and is daily expected here. No doubt he will attempt to sow discontent, if not sedition, but he will do well to be cautious and circumspect.

During the last week much grain has been cut on Yonge Street, and housed, as the weather was fine. The harvest promised to be exceedingly abundant. I have written to Mr. Adams, the Colonial Agent, who lives in St. James' Place, St. James' Street, near the Palace, with reference to my draft. Mr. Allan has not been able to give me the cash as yet. There is not any in the receiving chest, so that none of the Government accounts due the 20th June last have been paid, nor any warrants have issued from the Lieutenant-Governor's office. My accounts of the department, amounting to upwards of £800, for the last year, passed the audit on Monday last, but I know not when they will be paid. Mr. Selby, however, says he expects money from Quebec. My fee accounts to 30th June only amount to £21, owing to Mr. Jarvis being without parchment for his patents till two days ago, when he received £40 worth. I have, since you left us, received a very kind letter from Mr. Smith. Pray send him Mr. Cartwright's pamphlet, with the two last Acts of the Legislature. As Mr. Stuart has resigned the District School, I have informed Mr. Cameron and Mr. Small, two others of the Trustees, of my intention to write Mr. Prince for a gentleman qualified, and I have mentioned my intention to the Governor, and they all approve of it. A young gentleman who had taken orders, if he could obtain the £50 per annum given by the Society for the Propagation of the Gospel, with the school, which you know is worth £100 per annum, and the good expectation of a parish here, would I hope, be induced to come hither. I enclose copy of my letter to Mr. Adams, which I request you will deliver yourself.

In another letter from George Ridout to his brother, dated York, July 31st, 1811, a few familiar names are mentioned.

Allan McLean has been here almost since you left us. He is as great a coxscomb as ever. I almost forgot to tell you that Mr. Firth is going home, and intends selling off everything here, consequently he never intends to return. He asked leave of absence, which was refused. Archy McLean does not know what is to become of him. Mr. Firth for the hundred guineas was to board him, etc., during his clerkship. John Robinson returned here two or three days ago. If they do not all come to McDonell's office, I know not what they will do. I am the only one at present settled among them all.

The " Archy McLean " of this letter was afterwards Chief Justice of Upper Canada.

CHAPTER IV.

VOYAGE TO ENGLAND, 1811.

From Thomas G. Ridout to his Father in York:—

PLYMOUTH, 10*th August*, 1811.

AFTER a very pleasant passage of twenty-seven days, I arrived here this morning, being only seventeen days from Cape Ray to the Lizard. The three ladies in the cabin did not agree three days together, neither did the captain and officers; but as I took neither side, I continued on the best terms with both parties. We sailed before the wind from Quebec to Plymouth Sound, and beat in from the Eddystone. We parted convoy in thick fog on the Banks of Newfoundland and crossed the ocean alone, being the first sailer in the fleet. We frequently ran one hundred and fifty and one hundred and ninety miles a day. The only ship of war on the seas was the *Comet*, which we met on the Banks, and the second I saw was the *Boyne*, in Plymouth Sound, of ninety-eight guns. There are also in the Sound ready for sea four seventy-fours, fourteen large frigates, and twelve sloops of war. Admiral Calder commands the *Boyne*. I also saw the grand repeating ship, the *St. Salvador*, of one hundred and twenty guns, a Spanish prize; she lies in the inner basin, with about thirty sail of the line and fifty frigates, being all of them prizes from the French, Russians, Spaniards, Dutch and Danes. There is also on the stocks in the dockyard, the *Union*, of ninety-eight guns, several seventy-fours, and a great many frigates. There was a reinforcement of horse and foot sent to Lisbon from Portsmouth three days ago, in two hundred sail of transports, to recruit Lord Wellington's army, which now suffers exceedingly in men, they having taught the French to fight obstinate battles. The transports carry out British troops and bring home French prisoners; there are now two hundred and twenty thousand in England, about one hundred thousand in this place and neighbourhood.

I have seen the London papers to the 8th, which say the King is so deranged that he refuses all nourishment, and say that he'll starve himself to put an end to his sufferings; and it is suspected that the physicians are obliged to use him as all others in his mind are, to compel him to eat. I am in dread of the war with America, which is daily expected here, seventeen Americans being condemned the other day in this port. The French have taken but one merchantman these three months. As I have before written, our ship put in here for convoy, and none sailing before the 13th, determined me to go ashore and ride to London. The distance is two hundred and fifteen miles, and I have taken the outside of the stage, which starts to-morrow morning at eight o'clock for Exeter. On Monday, the 12th inst., at four in the afternoon, I shall be in London. I am full of hope and fear in regard to my own fortune in that city. I cannot express my feelings when I saw the native country of my dear father, the beautiful and enchanting appearance of which description can give but a faint idea of.

Plymouth is a very curious place. The entrance into the Sound is between the Ram's Head and Moor Stone, about a mile broad; you then go round a great rock or island, on which there are three hundred and sixty-five guns; to your right, or east, is the town of Plymouth; round a basin, in front is Stonehouse, where the Governor resides, who is General England, and where all the public offices are. What a climate this must be, for the men and women, boys and girls have universally such a ruddy complexion, which appears remarkable to an American like me.

From Thomas G. Ridout to his brother George in York:—

LONDON, *22nd August*, 1811.

My letter from Plymouth, you have, I hope, received long before this, giving an account of our voyage. On the 14th July we left Quebec, Cape Ray on 23rd, saw England 9th August, and landed at Plymouth 10th August. I took a place on the stage-coach for myself and trunk. Plymouth is 220 miles from London, therefore I would see a great part of the west of England. On Sunday morning, at eight o'clock, I took my seat alongside the coachman, from whom I got a great deal of information. We then drove out of Plymouth, and passed Lord Burlington's estate, and immediately got into the most highly-cultivated country in the world. The road throughout Devonshire is very narrow, except on Brinkdown and Dartmoor, being only wide enough for two carriages, and seems to be dug out of the ground, running between two high hedges of twelve or fourteen feet in height.

In the course of the day we passed several noblemen's and gentlemen's seats, through the large towns of Ashburton and Chudleigh, and forty other towns, besides upwards of thirty villages; passed over the River Teign, about as large as the Don, and came in sight of the Channel, and below us, at the distance of five miles, was the city of Exeter, lying in a most delightful vale, forty-four miles from Plymouth. I saw the two towers of its ancient cathedral rising above the town, besides innumerable spires and turrets throughout the city. It seemed situate in the midst of a forest or wood. The hedges hereabouts were planted with rows of trees. At a small distance on the right, but on a hill, stood an ancient, once strong, but now mouldering castle, with ivy growing from its battlements and towers, called Courtney Castle, surrounded with a deep ditch and wall, covering a great extent of ground, built in a square form, with two great towers. The windows were high from the ground and very narrow. There was a large wood or forest, surrounding the castle, of elms and oak. At five we got into Exeter, passed the River Exe, and drove up to Phillips' Hotel, opposite the cathedral.

Next morning, being Monday the 12th, at three o'clock we left Exeter, and breakfasted at a large brick town or city, called Axminster. We soon after got into Dorsetshire and passed over Liddon Down, on which were 100,000 sheep feeding. We now began to get into a high, dry, flint and chalk country, as this part of Dorset has very little meadow or pasture, but great fields of wheat. I saw one field, belonging to a gentleman, of 5,000 acres of wheat. At noon we came alongside the Channel, and passed Lyme Regis and the Isle of Portland; also crossed the Roman military highway, running from Lyme Regis to Bristol. It was wide enough for two carriages, with a bank of earth about eight feet high on each side. We passed a large Danish camp on Liddon Down, and two large square Roman camps with deep ditches. At four we dined at the ancient Roman city of Dorchester, which we entered through a double row of oaks a mile long. In twenty minutes we left Dorchester, and passed at six o'clock another Roman military highway, leading in a straight direction from Poole to London. In the evening passed the division betweeen Dorset and Wilts, being the ancient division thrown up by the Saxons between these two kingdoms. We passed through Salisbury, and saw that most beautiful and lofty spire.

Tuesday, the 13th, we were passing from seven to eleven over Bagshot Heath; to our left was Windsor Park. We crossed the Thames at Staines. Saw Windsor Castle, with the royal flag flying; thence over Hounslow Heath, and got within eight miles of Hyde Park Corner, when, from the number of people, the carriages going and coming, the closeness of the houses and the paved road, I could hardly think I was not in London, for it is one long street, excepting two small breaks. At last, we entered the city through a great iron gate and frame, with many lamps upon it. Then to see the height and regularity of the houses! The lower stories are nothing but glass on both sides the street, the houses being in the front supported by iron posts, and the windows filled with the most curious cut-glass. The footways were covered with people; you see four or five abreast continually turning the corners of the streets, without ceasing one moment. I was very much tired, being two days and a night in the coach without sleeping. You would be surprised at the nicety with which every one dresses here, therefore, to appear in the fashion, I have got an entire new suit of clothes in the London cut (very different from the York), a pair of boots and London hat.

The next day, Wednesday, I walked through London four or five hours, delivering papa's and the Governor's letters. Thursday night John took me to the Court of Chancery in Lincoln's Inn, where I saw the Lord Chancellor, who is Speaker of the House of Lords, and a multitude of lawyers, and heard a great deal of fine speaking.

Friday, dined with Mr. Watson, who is very civil to me; he said that Governor Gore is coming home. At nine I left his house, No. 5 Saville Row, Bond Street, and came from there to Paternoster Row, a distance of two and a half miles, without missing my way. The lamps in the street and on the bridges make a most beautiful appearance, and when you are at the end of a long street it looks like a stream of fire.

On Saturday, I dined with John and George, at Mr. Hamilton's country house, at Clapton, near Hackney. On Sunday, I went to the Prince's chapel, where Mr. Prince read the lessons most admirably, beyond anything I ever heard, and his son Tom preached a most

excellent sermon. I dined, and spent the evening
with that most friendly family, and was invited by
Mrs. Prince to go with her to Vauxhall, on Wednesday
evening, the 22nd August. Accordingly, on Wednesday I dined and drank tea at Mr. Prince's, and at eight
o'clock, in company with Mrs. P. and Betsy, her son
Tom, the clergyman, and Philip, got into a Hackney
coach, and drove to the gardens.

Then follows a description of Vauxhall in 1811.

As you enter you see before you a long arched gallery
open on the right side to the square ; on the left, boxes
for entertainments. The gallery is about fifteen feet
high and twenty wide, and surrounds a very large
square closed on two sides. On the arched ceiling are
hung the lamps upon chains, which cross the roof
backward and forward. They are made of coloured
glass, yellow, blue and red, and are only two or three
inches apart. These little lamps are hung in festoons
of about eight feet sweep. The square is full of large
elm and poplar trees, which are joined together by
festoons of lamps, as close as they can hang, and
coloured. In the midst of the square is the orchestra,
about thirty-five feet in height, and eighteen wide,
which looks like one blaze of fire, from the infinite
number of lamps with which it is entirely covered. It is
made in the form of a temple ; the cupola was sur-
mounted by a crown made of lamps, " Duke of
Clarence " underneath, this being his birthday, with
the anchor, he being an admiral. The front of the orchestra was open, and in the second story were about
twenty-five capital performers.

In the intervals, a little boy sang in the most wonderful manner, also a Mrs. Bland and Miss Ferrer,
both famous singers. We had also martial music
from the Duke of York's band.

We walked out one side of the square, and came
into a great temple, which glittered with lamps.

The walls were surrounded with flags of different nations. In the middle hung three large lustres ; the lamps, blue, red and yellow. The temple was surrounded with paintings, and avenues branched from it with long beads of lamps, terminated by a dark wood through which you could see some fantastical fairy lights. We walked along, and presently came to three or four large trees in a dark corner, under which sat a company of gypsies, smoking their pipes, with two or three children, and a jackass feeding. Before them was a fire with a pot boiling, and it was only by the fire-light we could see them. It was a very complete deception.

Going a little farther, we came to a hermitage, where sat by a table an old hermit reading, his cat by the fire. Then to the cascade, which is another deception. We went down a dark avenue through crowds—it being supposed there were six thousand in the gardens—and we came to where the most astonishing fireworks were displayed. At! half-past twelve we left this fairy ground.

From Thomas G. Ridout to his Father in York.

LONDON, 23rd August, 1811.

I arrived in this wonderful city on the 13th inst, after a journey of forty-four days. Next day I delivered the letters to Mr. Watson, Woldham, Colonel Derby, Franklin, Hoddinot, Mr. Hamilton, by all of whom I was well received, and was by Mr. Watson invited to dinner. I also called on Mr. Selby, of the South Sea House, and delivered his father's and your letters. On Friday I went to the Magdalene, and was received by that real and best friend of yours, Mr. Prince, like a son who had been long away. Their son Tom, who is now in orders, is secretary to the Duke of Brunswick, and tutor to his children. Mr. Prince treated me on Wednesday night, being the Duke of Clarence's birthday, to a sight of Vauxhall, which

I have very imperfectly described to George. Mr. Amyatt will not be in town this week, so I shall keep his letter till then.

I am sorry to tell you there is a general stagnation of commerce, all entrance into Europe being completely shut up; there never was known a time to compare to the present, nearly all the foreign traders becoming bankrupt, or about a tenth of their former trade. But if a war takes place between France and Russia, which is very likely, the great trade formerly carried on with Russia will then revive, and merchants' counting-houses will not look as solitary as they do at present. Neither will the Royal Exchange be as deserted, for there are not above two or three hundred gentlemen now transacting business there. The West India merchants are nearly ruined, having no sale on the continent for their immense quantity of colonial produce, which is now accumulating in their warehouses.

Mr. Edmundson and I have just come down from St. Paul's, we were both up into the ball, which is really frightful to think of, though I did not mind it then. The ball and cross stand upon eight iron legs about as thick as my wrist, and before we could get up into the ball, we had to climb up those legs, by notches cut in them, so that by slipping through a person would have been precipitated four hundred and four feet. From there I saw the immense cities of London, Westminster, Southwark—and, indeed, nothing but one mass of buildings as far as the eye could reach. The deep ditches of streets with the moving black in them and the red-tiled houses. We saw Lord Nelson's tomb in the vaults of St. Paul's. It is immediately under the dome, and his body is in the tomb or coffin of black marble, which Wolsey had made for himself. Collingwood lay alongside of him.

I have seen Henry Boulton. I arrived here a week before him. He seems to be mighty busy with Lord

Liverpool, Mr. Amyatt, and other great men, about getting his father from France.

John, the other night, took me to the Lyceum. I have not yet seen the wild beasts at Exeter 'Change, but frequently hear the lions roar on going past. The King is very ill, and is expected to die every day. There are six of Dr. Willis' men who are appointed to beat him, but they are not allowed to see any one. He is entirely deranged, and talked the other day for twenty-two hours without ceasing. The Prince Regent is in great favor with the people, and it is expected will keep a splendid court.

Sometime ago, Lord Grosvenor, another nobleman and several gentlemen decamped for the continent. They were obliged to fly for their lives, being connected with the infamous Vere Street gang.

Three men were hung at Newgate yesterday morning; every day two or three robbers or forgers are taken up. One of the clerks of the Bank of England was hung the other day for forgery. Henry Boulton has lost his watch already. To-day (I shall never be done writing about what I have seen) I saw from the top of St. Paul's Mr. Sadler and another gentleman ascend in a balloon. They went through the clouds over Hackney.

From Surveyor-General Ridout to his son Thomas in England:—

YORK, UPPER CANADA, 11*th September*, 1811.

I was at the Governor's this morning, when he informed me that the Hon. Captain Gore, 100th regiment, would set out for Quebec to-morrow morning, and embark in a frigate immediately for England, and that he would take charge of, and deliver to you, a letter from me. Captain Gore coming in at the same time, the Governor introduced me to him, and he is so obliging as to take charge of this. The Governor, with whom you appear to be much in favour, spoke very handsomely of you to Captain Gore. I have already informed you how much the Governor was pleased with your letters from Quebec and the Brandy Potts. The Duke of Manchester returned hither yesterday from Lake Huron, by way of Lake Simcoe and Yonge Street. I saw him this morning at the Governor's. He sets out to-morrow, if the weather permits, in company with Major Halton, to Quebec, and probably the Governor will accompany his Grace thither, whence he (the Duke) embarks for England.

I have given instructions to Mr. Wilmott to lay off a road from Kempenfeldt Bay, on Lake Simcoe, to Lake Huron, into lots, and a village at each extremity of the road, which I hope will be executed by Christmas.

Having wrote last week to Markle that George would be with him as to-day, your brother accordingly set out yesterday on Dolphin, intending to be with Mr. Markle this morning, and from thence goes to Niagara, where the Court opens on Monday next, the 16th instant, and where they expect to sit for a week. We have had a great deal of hot weather this summer. Many days, the week before last, the thermometer was at ninety-two to ninety-four. It now threatens a storm from the east.

Mrs. Gough, Hetty Robinson, and Hugh McLean died about ten days ago ; the Rev. John Stuart at about the same time, and on the 4th instant Dr. Gamble was buried. Mr. James Cartwright is extremely ill. Mr. Whitlow not yet returned. As the congregation of Kingston wish that our Mr. Stuart might succeed his father as their pastor, it is probable he will remove thither. I have not yet seen Jackson.* He had the folly or assurance to pay a visit to the Governor—surely with no good intent—but His

* This was Mr. Mills Jackson, who afterwards settled on Lake Simcoe, and Jackson's Point still bears his name.

Excellency signified his wish not to see him again. I have written Dr. Macaulay and Mr. Gray, thanking them for their kind attention to you. Fail not, my dear boy, to pay your respects occasionally to those gentlemen for whom the Governor has been so kind as to give you letters.

His Excellency possesses a warm and generous heart, and I am well persuaded will not neglect those whom he has once taken by the hand without very good reason. Men of his warmth of temper are of generous minds, they may sometimes be imposed upon, but never do things by halves. I am extremely anxious, my dear son, for your prosperity, and that you should be esteemed and beloved by the praiseworthy. I was about to give you more admonition, and yours is a soil on which all the virtues will thrive. I shall therefore transcribe from a book of memoranda, written by me many years ago, "A father's advice to his son about to travel." I believe they are the words of your favourite Shakespeare :

"Give thy thoughts no tongue,
Nor any unproportioned thought his act ;
Be thou familiar, but by no means vulgar
The friends thou hast, and their adoption tried,
Grapple them to thy soul with hooks of steel.
But do not dull thy palm with entertainment
Of each new-hatch'd, unfledg'd comrade.   Beware
Of entrance to a quarrel ; but, being in,
Bear it, that th' opposéd may beware of thee.
Give every man thine ear, but few thy voice ;
Take each man's censure, but reserve thy judgment.
Costly thy habit as thy purse can buy,
But not expressed in fancy ; rich, not gaudy ;
For th' apparel oft proclaims the man.   .   .
Neither a borrower nor a lender be,
For loan oft loses both itself and friend,
And borrowing dulls the edge of husbandry.
This above all, to *thine own self be true*,
And it must follow, as the night the day,
Thou can'st not then be false to any man."

Mr. Firth goes from here in a day or two, and to his care I intend committing a packet for Quebec, enclosing one to Mr. Amyatt, etc. Nancy and Mary intend writing to you by the October fleet. You see, my dear boy, that I write to you as though you were arrived in the land of safety. The public papers will inform you of the public news. Three parties of Indians, west of Lake Michigan, have come hither this summer. The Governor has only seen one party of them. A party of the St. Regis Indians are now here respecting their lands, on which subject I am directed, with Mr. Selby, to see them to-morrow. No money has yet arrived from Quebec, so that we are distressed for want of it. Government bills are discounted at twenty per cent.

CHAPTER V.

GOSSIP FROM LONDON, 1811.

From Thomas G .Ridout to his Brother in York:—

LONDON, *26th September,* 1811.

I PROMISED to tell you how the poor Canadian felt when London saw him. After riding all the morning of the 13th ult. over Bagshot Heath, we arrived at the River Thames, at a large brick town called Staines. Here the river is not larger than the Don. It is twenty miles from London; from thence we saw Windsor Castle, and the royal flag flying. Next, entered upon Hounslow Heath, over which we rattled, and presently came to a long street, eight miles from Hyde Park Corner, and drove through a multitude of waggons, coaches and people in crowds. We drove through Hyde Park gate in high style, with six fine horses, into Piccadilly.

The houses are four or five stories high on each side, built of a brown kind of brick; the lower stories of the houses are nothing but a long glass frame, from one street to another, and so throughout the city, on both sides, and of the largest kind of glass, and the houses are supported by iron posts. The sides of the streets are paved with large, square, flat stones, and posts on each side to keep the carriages off; the middle with thick, oblong stones, and rounding, like our stones, but rather muddy. In the middle of the streets stood a long line of Hackney coaches waiting for employment; on each side of them was a long row of coaches, waggons, carts and gigs, one going down and the other coming up. The footways were crowded with the

5

London bucks and ladies, dressed in the neatest manner ; chimney sweeps, coalheavers, porters ; fish and fruit women, with their stalls and wheel-barrows ; men, women, butcher's trays, dog-carts, and children, and old blind fiddlers—racket and riot, jostling, insomuch that I wished myself in the woods again. The throng was so great that sometimes there was a general stop. At last, I landed somewhere in Fleet Street. . .

Merchants have either become bankrupt, or retired, while they could, from business. Their clerks are all discharged, and gone into the army or country. Those merchants who formerly kept ten or fifteen clerks, now have but two or three. There are now many thousands half-starved, discharged clerks, skulking about London ; in every street you see, " A counting-house to let."

The foreign trade is almost destroyed, the Custom House duties are reduced upwards of one half. Of such dreadful power are Bonaparte's orders or edicts, which have of late been enforced in the strictest manner all over the continent, that it has almost ruined the commerce of England. The East India Company have their great warehouses filled with the most valuable goods, spoiling and wasting, as England is the only part of Europe that consumes for them. Tea and coffee are as cheap here as at York. As for the West India Company, they are going fast ; for besides their own immense warehouses, they have hired additional ones to the cost of £42,000, which are all filled with their overplus produce.

The Royal Exchange is miserably attended ; no foreigners, but about a dozen Hamburgers, very few Americans. Another thing, there is no coin, or very little, in circulation ; most of the guineas have been sold to the French at the rate of 26s. sterling apiece. There is now a law against selling guineas, but as long as the Government keep the value at 21s., while the real value is 26s., they will continue to be sold, and sent out of the country.   The silver is no longer the king's coin, but is coined by the Bank of England into 5s., 3s. and eighteen-penny pieces, with these words on, " Bank of England token;" 5s. passes for 5s. 6d., of such value is gold and silver, though it is only a Spanish dollar stamped over.   All payments are made in bank notes, these tokens and signs being only for change.   Neither will the bank give you coin for their own notes, they having a law in their favour to that purpose.

Such a time as this was never known in England. It is the universal murmur.   Whilst the British army in Portugal are supported at the rate of £35,000 per diem, which is near thirteen millions a year, this country is groaning under intolerable taxes, and a debt which it would take a mountain of gold to pay off.   It is now upwards of £700,000,000; but such a spring has been given to all public works that it will require something very extraordinary to make them lie by.

Two or three times a month either a ship of the line or a frigate is launched.   All His Majesty's ships are very badly manned, though pressing of seamen was never carried on in such a tyrannical manner before.

I had a bit of an adventure in that line myself, which you shall have.   When I left Plymouth on board the coach, I was dressed in my blue coat, blue trousers and black silk handkerchief. When we came to a town called Plympton, and were passing through a turnpike gate, we spied a boatswain and his gang bearing down upon us.   We accordingly stopped, they demanded if we had passes.   The three Danes presently showed theirs— " All's well."   But being dressed as a sailor, I expected something.   The boatswain then hailed me. " Where is your pass ? " " I have none," I answered. " Come down here."   Down I came from the top, and stood before his tremendous majesty, the boatswain, and about fifteen of his old weather-beaten courtiers. " What ship are you from ? " " The *Sea Nymph*." " Very well; where did you sail from?" "Canada." "Aye, aye, we knows where Candia is. It is in the East Indies. You were second mate or boatswain's mate, I suppose?" "Neither." "Then you must be before the mast?" "No." "Come, come, my lad, you can't sheer off; you must go with us before the Admiral, on board the *St. Salvador*, in Plymouth Sound (130 guns)." I then opened my trunk, and showed them the Governor's letters. "Oh, sir, we are sorry for detaining you." "Yes," said the old coachman, "you may beg my pardon for detaining me this half-hour."

From Thomas G. Ridout to his Sister :—

LONDON, 26th September, 1811.

I am now in the land of caps and bonnets, kings and queens, dukes, rogues and princes; but I am away from mother, father, brothers, sisters, home and delight, old Towser, Dolphin and all. The sea when it rolls mountains high, and the gale whistling through the rigging, seems more at rest than the famed city of London, bustling and rattling crowds in all directions. The other day, when the balloon ascended, there were no less than 200,000 people on Hackney Green. One can never stop in the streets to look at anything.

From Thomas G. Ridout to his Brother in York :—

LONDON, 7th October, 1811.

Last month we had a famous fair in West Smithfield, called Bartholomew fair, which was kept up for four days and three nights without ceasing, by about thirty thousand of the greatest blackguards in London. I squeezed myself through it three or four times. The people were as close as a bundle of sticks. There were stages erected, plays acted, all sorts of wild beast shows, bands of music, dancers, and swinging and riding machines. Altogether it was a complete tumult.

Last Sunday Mr. Edmundson and I took a walk up the Thames to see the Royal Gardens of Kew and Richmond. They are of great extent, laid out in long, shaded, laurel walks, leading to elegant Chinese, Roman and Grecian temples. Dark groves of oak, pine and beech, small plots of grass surrounded by orange and olive trees, tulips, and every beautiful flower. On one side of the garden is the Royal Palace of Kew, built by George III., in the style of an ancient castle; on the other, in the midst of a wood, rises a lofty Chinese pagoda of twelve stories, each story having a separate roof, such as you see on cups and saucers.

After strolling about from temple to temple, and grove to castle, for two hours, I was very glad to bear away for dinner to the house of a gentleman of the name of Manning. We did not leave until late, and passed through London town at twelve o'clock.

Here's a girl rolling her wheel-barrow along, crying, " Who'll buy my nice walnuts, two shillings a hundred walnuts, very fine wa-alnuts." An old Negro with a powdered head and white waistcoat has just come through London yard with a pan of coals and a dish on top, with sausages, crying, " Hot, hot, hot." Now comes the croaking of a string of Jews, " Clo'es, clo'es, any old clo'es !" followed by some little sweeps with their brush, scraper and bag of soot, crying in shrill voices, " Sweep, sweep, ho! " I must not write any more nonsense.

From Thomas G. Ridout to his Father:—

LONDON, 10*th October*, 1811.

(*Not received until 22nd June*, 1812.)

I had the very great pleasure of receiving your letter of 31st July, on the 7th, also yours of the 11th August and 14th July. Concerning myself, I have not much to say at present. I don't think it likely that I shall get any employment for a while. The Government offices are filled with clerks and trade is

at a total stand.   In July and August, the merchants
made a desperate effort to get off their goods, and loaded
eight hundred ships, which they sent to the Baltic for
Russia, Sweden and Prussia, under an insurance of
forty per cent.   Some were lost on the seas, others
taken by privateers, and the remainder got into ports,
where they were immediately seized and condemned.
In consequence, most of the insurers at Lloyd's have
failed, along with many rich and reputable houses.

Mr. Laroche has allowed me to attend his compting
house, and learn the nature of business.   I do nothing,
but learn a good deal.   I have been with one of his
clerks to the London and West India docks, the warehouses of which are filled with goods, and likely so to
remain.   Coffee, which last year sold for one hundred
shillings and one hundred and twenty shillings per
cwt., sells now with difficulty at thirty-five and forty
shillings.   Whenever trade is mentioned, serious
countenances and a shrug of the shoulders follow.
I. & W. Jacobs failed for £375,000, and divide about
five shillings in the pound.

Last Saturday, at a dinner, I got acquainted with a
gentleman who is Secretary to the lottery office, and
lives in Somerset House.   To-morrow he has promised
to show me how they cut the lottery tickets, and on
Tuesday next will let me see them drawn.   This week
he'll take me throughout Westminster Abbey, on Sunday to Foundling Chapel, and then back to his house
to dinner; he is a very respectable old gentleman.

I think that Mr. Firth will repent leaving Canada,
where, if he had remained a few months longer, the
Governor would have left him without a master.   That
Mr. Jackson will endeavor to be elected a member, I
think is very probable, his friends being the blackguards,
and yours the decent farmers.   I am very much afraid
(though it is no honor to my country) that he will
carry a great majority.

The present times are more trying to England than

you can imagine. The trade with Europe is completely destroyed; even smuggling is discontinued, as Bonaparte punishes that with immediate death. Brandy is now from forty-five shillings to fifty shillings per gallon. I attended, with Mr. Laroche, the commercial sale. Not one lot in ten can be disposed of, and that at a price none but those in the greatest need would think of, even for damaged goods. The non-importation law of America will be severely felt here; and, in short, poor trade is hobbled and crippled at all points of the compass.

The proceedings of the Government and armies you know better than I can tell you. The Prince Regent is much liked, though it is thought he is very indolent, which arises from his infirmities, and they are great. The present ministry, it is thought, will remain in power, as there are very few of the Prince's friends who are not much fitter for the bottle and a pack of hounds than the affairs of a nation.

From the threatening appearances of the Catholics in Ireland, Government have wisely and quietly drawn the militia from that country, and supplied their places by a good breed of English militia. The French prisoners are also scattered throughout the inland towns. I am very much surprised at Mr. Firth's coming to England from such an appointment. Archy McLean and Sam Jarvis must find it difficult to get such another place. John Robinson is likewise adrift; and as if fortune had a mind to sport with and tease Mr. Strachan's flock settled at York, there is not one, excepting Robert Stanton, who has escaped her sometime vexatious and unlooked-for turns.

I have seen Henry Boulton but once or twice, he seems delighted with England. From the present rigorous state of affairs, there is not the least likelihood of Mr. Boulton's release. I believe that Henry receives promises in abundance from the great men, but that's all they are able to give.

From George Ridout to his Brother in England :—

YORK, *19th October*, 1811.

A great many extraordinary circumstances have taken place since you left this miserable hole, part of which you will hear before you receive this. Among other things, Governor Gore has leave of absence for a year, of which he has availed himself in embarking for England with his family. Most probably he is re-called, as he has remained the usual time of five years. He promises to see both you and uncle John. Mr. Firth has gone also. This place is therefore wanting in a Lieutenant-Governor, Puisne Judge, and Attorney-General. Three very high and important places to be vacant at one time very rarely happens. I had almost forgotten that of Solicitor-General also. Poor Boulton has not yet been heard of, at least by D'Arcy. He received a letter from Mr. Franklin yesterday, which he showed to papa; it contained nothing satisfactory, Mr. Franklin neither being able to tell whether he was alive or not, or, if alive, where he was. D'Arcy is very much distressed about his father. I think we ought to be very thankful that our father should have arrived safe, after encountering so many dangers and difficulties.

I do not believe that there are two thousand dollars in the town. But I have heard that the *Earl of Moira*, which sailed from this place to-day, will return with some, which has come up and is now at Kingston. Mr. Strachan is appointed rector of this place, in the stead of Mr. Stuart, who goes to Kingston in the room of his father. We have reason to rejoice at the exchange, as thereby we can send John, Horace and Charles to school here at less expense, exclusive, too, of the difference in the characters of the two men; one sociable and cheerful, the other haughty, sullen and austere.

John McDonnell is appointed Attorney-General for the time being, in the room of Mr. Firth. Old Kendrick is dead of the dropsy. Jackson is now here, engaged in mercantile pursuits, distillery, etc. Johnson has made a great many recruits here; among ye rest, Colonel Graham's son, Bill Crawford, old Mary Williams' son, etc. General Brock is President, and commands ye forces of Upper Canada. Ye 41st regiment is now here, ye 100th at Three Rivers.

From Thomas G. Ridout to his Father in York.

LONDON, *8th November,* 1811.

By the ship *Orient,* which sails to-morrow for New York, my uncle and I send these letters. Your letters of the 26th August I received 18th October. They are called flying ones, for never before had they arrived under three months. You, no doubt, hear that things are getting worse every day. Trade is now at the foot of the hill

From Thomas G. Ridout to his Mother in York:—

19th December, 1811.

When I first entered this great city, I was as sad and melancholy as a fish upon the sand, going through streets where I thought nothing but confusion, distraction and ignorance governed; meeting one hundred thousand people I had never seen before, wondering how these people lived, and how any regular business could be carried on in such a tumultuous place. With all these ideas in my head, I rode on the stage through London, not knowing a single person in this great place. Thus was I situated when the coach stopped on Fleet Street—all one to me where, for I knew not the difference between that and Barbican's Lane. The coachman then said I could not go until my fare from Exeter was paid, as my name was not entered; I told him I'd rather stay in the coach a whole day than pay twice. At last he let me go, though I now believe it was only a trick to cheat me out of something; and I got a porter to carry my trunk to Paternoster Row, whom I followed through crowds, step by step, minding nothing else, to the door.

Now I know London as well as York, and everything seems to go on with the regularity of clockwork, and I begin to know many merchants and others. You can't think what honourable company I have been in. On the 19th November uncle and I went in the carriage to Sydenham, and dined with Mr. Mariot, a member of Parliament, a great merchant and agent for the island of Trinidad. On the 27th, we were all invited to Mr. Evans', another rich merchant, and American agent in London. There was a large party of twenty-two gentlemen, and among them the American Plenipotentiary to the court of France, just returned from that court and now American Minister in London—Mr. Russel.

The moment I cast my eyes on him, I told John, "There's a Yankee, for a dollar." He talked very highly of Bonaparte, of the splendour of his court, the regularity and order maintained in France, and many curious things relating to Bonaparte. What must you think of the jewellers in London, when Bony's new crown about six months ago was made, and the jewels set by a famous goldsmith and jeweller in Ludgate Hill.

At Mr. Marston's I have dined twice with the Accomptant-General of the Bank of England. The kindness to me of the Princes is beyond everything. Tom is a wonderful clever fellow, I believe I told you that he is secretary to the Duke of Brunswick, and tutor to his two children, who, after the Princess Charlotte, are next heirs to the crown. He preaches alternately at St James' Church in Piccadilly, and the Magdalene. At St. James' to a congregation of five thousand, consisting of most of the nobility and gentry of that end of the town.

The Duke of Brunswick mentioned is the one who fell at the battle of Waterloo.

From Thomas G. Ridout to his Father in York :—

LONDON, 18*th December*, 1811.

It is now upwards of two months since I heard from home, which has almost worn out my patience, but I now begin to look for the Governor daily, from whom I hope to receive your letters. I am chiefly employed at the London and West India Docks, in shipping, landing, and warehousing goods, consisting of Brazil and West India sugars, cottons, East and West India coffees, hides, tallow, logwood, etc. The East India Company sell nothing but at public auction in their house, where they have a very handsome room, with the statues of the Governor-Generals and great men standing in niches around the room. At one end sits a director; before him, inside a railing, five clerks; at the two outer corners of the table, in pulpits, stand two auctioneers. Before them, on seats raised one above the other, almost to the top of the room, are seated the merchants and brokers. The auctioneer on the right puts up the lot, upon which the price is immediately bidden, as quick as thought; and the one on the left in a few moments sings out the buyer and the highest price, so that in the course of ten minutes they may sell twenty chests of mace, etc. The Director sits as judge. Should any difference arise between the bidders, his decision settles to whom the lot is sold. He is always addressed with great respect, hats in hand, and with a low bow.

I am afraid my stories are too long and minute to afford you any pleasure, but I know that M. and G. will be much amused at many things I write, however well-known to you, and my stock of London manners, shows and wonders is not yet spun out. Almost every day I see something remarkable. Previous to the sale a clerk and I went through the several India warehouses, to draw samples of the coffee, cotton, sugar, etc., and I was astonished to see the immense quantities of goods stored. This has been a busy day for us, as we ship to Malta on to-morrow 150,000 pounds West India coffee, and 100,000 pounds Brazil cotton, from whence it will be smuggled into Italy; the exports to Malta being now very great, and for no other purpose than smuggling. The Americans have the most beautiful ships in the river. The Portuguese, from Brazil, are the largest traders, excepting Indiamen.

On account of the scarcity of wheat, the distilling of spirits from grain will in a short time be stopped, which will cause the great quantity of West India sugar now lying in warehouses to be in part sold to the distillers, benefiting both the King's customs and the West India merchants, whose trade before was almost ruined, and even in this will be very little benefited. The quantity of tobacco on hand in the city of London alone, amounts to 30,000,000 pounds weight, enough to give a good quid to the whole world.

I have frequently been in the Bank of England, the clerks of which, every Sunday morning, parade in Moorfields to the number of nine hundred, calling themselves the Bank Volunteers. They are dressed in uniform, and seem to know little besides putting on their clothes and carrying a gun. The Bank still continues to issue their notes without bounds, along with a little silver or base metal for change, theirs being the only current money seen in the kingdom, so that Threadneedle rags and bank tokens are now in the place of good old guineas.

I was at Woolwich and Deptford the other day, and went to Colonel Pilkington's house, as he desired me, unluckily, he was in London, but Mrs. P. received me very politely, and I was invited to dinner, but on account of the stage, I could not stop. However, that I should not go away disappointed, she got a Captain of the Engineers to go about with me. The first place I went to was the Grand Arsenal and Foundry, which is a place of about five or six acres, surrounded by a high wall, containing many thousand ship, wall and field-pieces, which entirely cover the whole ground. They are ranged in long lines according to their size, in the most exact order. The brass pieces in particular were most beautiful. Cannon balls and bombshells, piled up among the cannons like small mountains, convicts chained to the wheel-barrow, prison ships, sheer hulks and tenders in the river, made the poor Canadian think himself out of his country. I saw the Artillery and Marine Barracks. The artillery brass field-pieces were mounted on several hundred fine carriages.

I glanced next at the docks. All seemed in confusion, but the noble ships upon the stocks showed, by their strength, beauty and workmanship, that there was order and regularity in this tumult. One one-hundred-and-twenty-gun ship, two eighty-four and three frigates were grand proofs of industry and art. The one-hundred-and-twenty-gun ship is called the *Nelson*. Mrs. Pilkington says Mr. D. W. Smith is married to her sister. He is in bad health, chiefly caused by grief for the death of his son David, who was killed in a boat sent to cut out a merchant ship somewhere on the coast of France, in May last. He went against the will of the captain, to accompany his friend, the lieutenant who commanded the boat. David was killed by the only shot that struck them. It passed through his body, and took the lieutenant's arm off.

The Quebec fleet is now on the coast of England, the *Everetta* in Torbay, and some at Portsmouth. I hear that the Governor has arrived, but I know not where to find him, and I am all anxiety to hear. Surely, my dear father, you have written by him, for the longer I am from home, the sweeter and more welcome is news from that dear spot. I shall see Henry Boulton to-morrow, who is entered at Gray's Inn, and inquire something about his father, where Mr. Firth is, and what Henry knows of occurrences at York.   I fear that his father cannot be cleared, and think more and more every day how safe you arrived in our snug and sheltered corner of the globe.   The French privateers now dash by dozens into every fleet, and make prizes in sight of the farmers in England. The other day a company of twenty actors who sailed for Barbadoes, were taken off Scilly, and carried into France, which afforded a laugh here.   This afternoon, as I passed the Mansion House, a great mob was collected.   My curiosity led me among them.   They were reading two bills posted up, giving an account of the capture of the *Batavia* and *Java*, with the number of French killed and prisoners.

The Colonel Pilkington of this letter is another familiar name in the early annals of Upper Canada. In the Duke de Rochefoucauld's diary, he is mentioned as a young officer of the Engineers, stationed then (1795) at Fort Niagara.   The Duke writes, "We dined in the Fort at Major Seward's, an officer of elegant, polite and amiable manners.   He and Mr. Pilkington, an officer of the corps of Engineers, are the military gentlemen we have most frequently seen during our residence in this place, and whom the Governor most distinguishes from the rest."

CHAPTER VI.

AMUSEMENTS IN LONDON——NEWS FROM YORK, 1811-1812.

From Thomas G. Ridout to his Brother in York :—

LONDON, 18*th December*, 1811.

YESTERDAY I received yours of the 19th October. I called this morning upon Henry Boulton, in Lincoln's Inn, where he is entered with Foster, Cooke & Frere, three solicitors of great practice. I found him busy at work. He had not yet heard from home, and everything I told him was new. He complains of the hard work. The office hours are from half-past nine till four and from seven to nine in the evening. For five years yet he will have to continue in this manner. Altered times for poor Henry! He looks very well, and is quite a blood.

I am very glad that you have Mr. Strachan at York. I almost forgot to say that Henry and I went to the Canada Hotel, in the Strand, to see Alex. McDonell. He is very well, and was glad to see me, telling us many things about York, which he left on 1st September. He told us that the North-West Company have determined to carry their trade through Yonge Street, of their grant of land, etc. The Attorney-General, Mr. Firth, is in England, though Henry has not yet seen him. In what a foolish manner did he leave you when his enemy, the Governor, whom he wished to avoid, cleared out about the same time. I fear from what Henry says, that his father will not be liberated. The difficulty is so great. They receive regular letters from him. He is allowed six miles on either side of Arras, goes into company, writes in good spirits, and pays thirty per cent. discount for English bills. James McDonell has come to London to get a commission in the army. He lodges at some place in Bishopsgate Street, and wishes to see me. Governor Gore is, of course, arrived in town, as the frigate reached Portsmouth last Friday; but I have not yet got my letters which father sent by Halton.

Last Saturday, Mr. Edmundson and I went for the first time to Covent Garden, to see the tragedy of "Pizarro" acted, Kemble and Mrs. Siddons performing the chief characters. On account of seeing the grand saloons in the upper part of the house, we took a box in the second tier. It is a most curious building. The pit was crowded. The boxes were filled with my lords and ladies. They are in five tiers, one above the other, to the gallery, where the gods and goddesses sport. They run entirely round the house, being supported by slender iron pillars, fluted and gilt. The boxes are also highly ornamented, as well as the ceiling; a gallery runs at the back of each tier, from which doors connect with every box, which are cushioned and lined with baize. From these galleries you go into saloons, whose walls are marble, and ceilings paintings. There are also many statues of great men, made of beautiful white marble, standing in niches—Shakespeare, Garrick, etc. Refreshments are sold in these rooms. Mrs. Siddons, the Queen of the Stage, who is now near seventy years old, made her appearance amid the clapping of hands. Her voice is so powerful, at the same time very grand. You hear it fairly shout in the theatre. When Pizarro says, " Call the guards, and take that woman into custody," she said, "Aye, call the guards, I say, call the guards." Putting on a look of the utmost defiance and contempt. Her manner of speaking and look sometimes is very much like mother's. I'm in earnest.

I must give you an account of the Lord Mayor's show, on the 9th of November, which day was ushered in by the ringing of every bell in the city, and bars were placed across the great streets to hinder the coaches from passing. By eleven o'clock the crowd had completely filled up King Street, Cheapside, St. Paul's Churchyard, Ludgate Hill, Fleet Street and Blackfriars. It was with the greatest difficulty I squeezed myself as far as the New York Coffee House, back of the Royal Exchange, to put my last letters in the *Orient's* bag. In returning, the mob was rushing down Cheapside, and I perceived the procession turning round the corner of King Street and bearing away for Blackfriars. The rich golden banners of the city waving over the multitude, preceded and followed by the different companies of London. Then came a string of coaches, reaching from King Street to Ludgate Hill. At ten o'clock they took the water at Blackfriar's Bridge. Mr. E. and I then went to Somerset House, and I obtained the key of the terrace from Mr. Pearson. Presently we saw the twelve stately barges, glittering with gold, having five or six flags made of cloth of gold, most curiously worked, move past us, followed by hundreds of small boats. There was a covering over each boat, supported by gilt Corinthian pillars, on top of which were several bands of music. The company sat beneath. They were rowed by twenty-four men dressed in white, and so they passed on by the sound of the trumpet, fire of small cannon, and martial music, to Westminster Bridge.

At three o'clock they returned in grand procession to dine at Guildhall, and wishing to see the last of this parade, Mr. E. got a place in the second story window of a gentleman's house in St. Paul's Churchyard. The streets were by this time covered with people, so that a person might have walked on their heads. In a little while we saw the vanguard, consisting of the West London Regiment, coming round Ludgate Hill, having a very fine band of music.

6

Then came the company of Merchant Tailors, of which the Lord Mayor is a member, dressed in gowns trimmed with fur, and six men bearing their colours; followed by the Apothecaries, Clothiers, Stationers, Goldsmiths, Grocers, and other companies of London, with their colours and two bands of music. Then came the band of the German Legion, mounted on black horses, next the city colours, and a knight equipped in Edward the Black Prince's armour, mounted on a black horse, his two esquires on each side, in half-armour, bearing his ancient shield, sword and lance; a band of music, another knight in shining brass armour on a white horse, esquires as before; immediately after the Lord Mayor, in his coach burnished with gold, very large, drawn by six horses, and covered with carvings of the city arms in a most magnificent manner, having out-riders. The coachman was dressed in green and gold. Two footmen rode behind, and six others walked after the coach, dressed in gold-laced cocked hats, green coats, with gold lace four inches broad, scarlet velvet breeches and white silk stockings. Next came another knight in steel armour, as the first, then my lady Mayoress in coach and six, with a band of music; next came the ex-Lord Mayor in coach and six, and his wife in coach and four. Next a very fine band of music, followed by all the aldermen and common council, in their separate coaches. The judges, nobility, ministry, and foreign ambassadors, gentlemen's carriages, a long list of Hackney coaches, and a London mob, with night coming on, closed this Lord Mayor's show, which was the most splendid that had been for many years.

The Strand bridge forms another great sight in London. It is a curious thing to see the foundations of such a work. In the beginning, they drive an oval circle of piles into the river; about three feet outside of them, they drive another close together, filling up the space with brick and earth, and throw some earth on the inside. They then erect a steam engine, and place two great cast-iron pumps of a foot in diameter into the enclosed pond, and by that means draw all the water out. After which, the bed of the river is levelled, and a frame of oak timber is laid on the bottom for a foundation, upon which the great stones are placed by machinery, and so they work dry beneath the level of the river, and the arch rises rapidly. Outside of the first pile, the next arch is begun at the distance of thirty feet, and to every arch they require a new engine house. About six hundred men are now employed, and they increase according to the number of enclosures, of which they have made four.

Drury Lane is also rebuilding, the walls of which have made their appearance four feet out of ground. The West India docks are drawing this great city down to them. Though they are three miles from the Royal Exchange, yet there are houses and streets all the way down excepting about quarter of a mile; so that from seven or eight miles beyond Hyde Park corner, to the West India docks, which is sixteen miles, and eight miles from north to south, is the true extent of this over-grown place. New squares, and hundreds of new houses are continually building. I am to write this night another letter, as the ship *Jane*, Captain Selkirk, sails to-morrow.

From Surveyor-General Ridout to his son Thomas in England :—

YORK, UPPER CANADA, 18th *December*, 1811.

I wrote to you about a month ago, acknowledging the receipt of your letters of the 22nd and 23rd August from London. A severe battle has been lately fought on the Wabash, between the Americans and the Indians, chiefly Shawanese, in which the former lost four hundred men and latter about sixty—the particulars are not yet made public. I heard of it three or four days ago at President Brock's, who had just received a letter respecting it from Detroit. I send you herewith a copy of a letter which I received last post from Mr. Adams, the Colonial Agent, and I send also a copy of my answer. General Brock has required from me plans of all the townships in the Province, with the locations, which will be very heavy work. We learn that the Solicitor-General is prisoner at Verdun, France. George has gone this evening to spend it with D'Arcy. Mr. Strachan has declined coming hither to replace Mr. Stuart, as he could not get himself to be the Bishop's commissioner. I therefore do not know how our school matters will be settled. 'Tis said a nephew of Bishop Mountain's will be our rector.

The President informed me that the Prince Regent, upon an application from the Society for the Propagation of the Gospel, has declared that any gentleman coming to this Province as a clergyman, and who shall remain in it ten years, upon his return to England, if so inclined, and producing a certificate of his good conduct whilst here, shall be entitled to receive one hundred pounds sterling per annum for life. I shall write my good friend Mr. Prince, on the subject, and I think it would be worthy the attention of a young gentleman, who had just taken orders, to come hither. Were he here now, the parish and school would be his in all probability. I shall write to the Governor on the subject and send Mr. Prince a letter of introduction, if he will have the goodness to permit it. A writing master has lately come hither who, by a new method, teaches to write a good hand in fifteen lessons. McDonell, Horace's master, has paid this teacher £25 to be instructed, and having obtained it, has broken up his own school, and has gone to Yonge Street to teach his newly-acquired art.

General Brock intends making this head-quarters, and to bring the Navy, Engineers, and all the departments here in the spring. He told me a day or two ago that he will build an arsenal between the park and the beach on the lake ; the Government buildings, or rather the public offices, in front of Mr. Elmsley's house ; a regular garrison where the Government House now is, and a Government House contiguous to the public buildings.   These intentions seem to show that he thinks of remaining with us, for a certain time at least, but you will not, of course, mention them.   I own I do not think that Governor Gore will return hither—his going home will, I dare say, as Mr. Watson wrote me on the 22nd August, obtain many advantages for this Province.   But if this is not to be a permanent military Government, his return hither, I should think, depends upon himself.   I should not be surprised if he be shortly created a baronet ; I own I do not like changes in administration.   You will, I presume, see His Excellency, he was much pleased with your letters from Quebec.   When you write, send me the British Imperial Calendar, price 4s. 6d., published by Messrs. Winchester & Son, 61 Strand.   If my name be not already inserted in it, let it be done.   I have as yet seen but little of our new Judge, Mr. Campbell ; he has rented Mr. Firth's house.

A Diary Letter from Thomas G. Ridout to his Brother in York:—

BRISTOL, 11*th February*, 1812.

I begin this letter by saying that I intend giving you a journal of my country excursion.

I left our friends in London by the Taunton coach, on the 26th December, at six in the evening, a cold frosty night, and in the morning we reached Basingstoke, thirty-five miles, and at eleven, we arrived at Salisbury, distant eighty-four miles, and Wincaston ; when I left the coach at half-past four, and found waiting at the tavern old John Collis, who nursed father when a child, with two of Mr. Ward's horses. Old John lashed my trunk on his horse, and I mounted a beautiful mare, and bore away for Bruton, distance five miles. At six I got in, having run one hundred and nine miles since the last evening. The Wards were dining out that day, but John came home and took me to Dr. Goldsboro's, where there was a large party. Aunt Ward received me with every mark of kindness. She is one of the finest old ladies I ever saw; though now seventy-three, she is as full of humour and jokes as a young girl, without any foolishness. Next morning Mr. Ward presented me with his beautiful mare for my use while in the country.

Sunday, December 29th.—We went to church. In this church-yard of Bruton lie the bones of the celebrated Robinson Crusoe, or Alexander Selkirk, round whose tomb I walked. He was a native of Bruton. This is a snug little town, containing one thousand five hundred inhabitants, and is pleasantly situated at the foot of a number of hills, and has the Brew running through. On the south side, at the distance of six miles, is a ridge of hills or high land, the estate of Sir Richard Hoare, on a point of which is erected a tower to the memory of Alfred the Great, who on this spot defeated the Danes in his first great battle. In the evening, we drank tea with Mrs. Burgess, where I met Mr. Stephens, one of the Proctors of Oxford, who was Mr. Jackson's secretary at the court of Berlin, and is now soon to be married to Miss Burgess. Mr. Ward's silk mills are very extensive, and of the most curious machinery. He is considered the greatest silk throwster in the west of England. In his different manufactures he now employs one thousand people, and as he is putting up new mills at Stowey, he will have one thousand four hundred people at work. On the 31st, J. Ward, his son Dan and I rode to Ditchell, about five miles from Bruton, where Mr. Ward has an establishment of two hundred reeling silk, and from thence to a place called Evercreech, another silk point.

January 1st.—I walked with Mr. Ward to see the East Somersetshire Volunteers reviewed, in which he is a captain. They went through their marching and manœuvring very well, but as to firing, the Yorkers can beat them.

January 2nd.—We mounted our horses and rode to Maiden Bradley, thence to the village at Hornisham, both in Mr. Ward's employ. Adjoining is the seat of the Duke of Somerset. Thence we rode to Longleat, in the county of Wilts, the estate of the Marquis of Bath. This seat is considered the most noble of any in England. Our ride from Bradley to Longleat was on a ridge. To the left was a very rich and beautiful country, studded with towns, villages and seats. Our view extended to Bath, Wells and Glastonbury. On the right was Beckford's Priory. We galloped on till we came to Longleat, which we entered by a grand gateway. Before us, at a distance of half a mile, was the mansion, having a grand avenue of trees leading to it. To the left was the pleasure garden, and on the right a sloping hill covered with wood, at the bottom of which runs the river Froome. The building is four hundred feet square, and four stories high, with a pond and a boat on the roof. In the park were about nine hundred deer quietly feeding; some of them milk-white. The estate is eight miles long and five wide. We came to a small lake of ninety acres, dug out, and well stocked with wild ducks, and a beautiful little sloop upon it. Last year a nobleman was drowned in it. The house was built three hundred years ago, of white Bath stone, the top ornamented with three domes and several towers. The road wound through several clumps of trees to the foot of the hill, which we ascended by a winding way to the top, when we came upon a down, whence we saw the whole country and Beckford Tower.

This Mr. Beckford is a man of £90,000 a year, and employed Mr. Wyatt to build him a house in the form of an ancient abbey. From the centre rises a Gothic tower three hundred feet high. The grand entrance is by the west, at a great mahogany door forty feet high, the hinges of which are made of brass and cost £300. His library consists of twenty thousand books. He has one thousand acres in wood, surrounding his dwelling, so that only the top can be seen, and the whole estate is surrounded by a fence of trees, planted so close that a child cannot enter. There is not a gentleman in England who will visit this man on account of his crimes, although he is one of the cleverest and most learned men in the country. Neither will he allow a stranger to see his abbey, and he amuses himself by driving a coach and six over his grounds. So much for Mr. Beckford. We returned, and dined at Bradley with John, and galloped to Bruton, eight miles, in three-quarters of an hour.

Friday, January 3rd.—Was an idle day. Spent the evening at Mr. Burgess's and won at speculation 12s.

Saturday.—Went out hunting the hare with Dan Ward, a pack of forty hounds, and about a dozen gentlemen. Came home at two, and rode to the top of Creechill.

Sunday, 5th.—Went to church, drank tea with Aunt Ward at Mr. Sampson's, from thence to a Methodist meeting.

Monday, January 6th.—Being invited by Mr. Moore, wholesale dealer at Shepton Mallet, I set out for that town with him, which we reached at twelve, eight miles from Bruton. Shepton Mallet is a large clothing town, and contains about 7,000 inhabitants. It lies at the foot of the Mendip Hills.

Tuesday, January 7th.—This morning, after breakfast, Mr. Moore took me to the chief cloth manufactory in the place. First the wool is well washed, next cleaned and picked of all particles of dirt. It is then mixed, and goes through a large carding machine, then through another, out of which it comes in long rolls. These rolls are fastened upon thirty spindles, and a large frame runs them out to the thickness of a cord. Then, by a similar machine, it is spun still finer; and again by another spun and twisted to its proper size, and given to the weavers. One person can weave about two yards in a day, for which they get ten pence a yard. The works are turned by a steam engine, having an iron wheel of twenty-eight feet diameter. After the cloth is woven it is beaten in soap and water for six hours, to cleanse it from the oil; from that it goes to the dyers; then it is thrown over a " horse," and carded with fine cards, to give it a grain, or right and wrong side; then to the shearers, who shear off all the fuz. It is now at last finished by the pressers and packers. Each fold is pressed between smooth glazed paper, which gives it a gloss. Thus are the famous woollens of England brought to such perfection.

At eleven we left Shepton for the city of Wells, six miles distant. This city lies most beautifully upon the slope of a hill. At the east end, on a rising ground, stands the ancient cathedral. It is considered as next to York Minster for the lightness and beauty of its aisles. The building was founded in 1150, and was two hundred years finishing; length, four hundred and fifteen feet, breadth at the cross, one hundred and twenty-one feet; having two western towers one hundred and twenty feet high, and a middle tower one hundred and eighty-two feet, supported by four grand arches. The western part has two large painted windows. The outside front is ornamented by statues of kings, bishops, abbots, etc. On entering, you see three grand ranges of arches of a yellow colour, and made of stone. The middle one is eighty-three feet high. In the cross aisle is a clock, made four hundred years ago by a monk of Glastonbury, called Lightfoot. In the library are five thousand old books, among the rest, one on vellum, written in 588, by a monk.

At one I left. Rode on alone to Glastonbury, distant five miles, and went to the White Hart Inn. An old blind man took me to the ruins of the abbey. We first went to St. Joseph's Chapel, which joins the abbey, and is dedicated to St. Joseph of Arimathea, who, in walking up to Glastonbury Tor, in rear of the abbey, stuck his staff into the ground, which there grew and became a thorn bush, and blossomed every year on Christmas eve. The old thorn is now destroyed, but a tree from it grows in the ruins, and was then (on the 8th January) in full bloom. The roof of the chapel has fallen in, leaving nothing but the walls, on which are carved the sun, moon and stars, kings, abbots, etc. There is another chapel beneath this. The arches of the windows are not pointed, but round, and curiously ornamented. This is called Saxon, and is more ancient than the Gothic. The ruins of this great abbey are some side walls and four tottering arches, which seem to wait with impatience for old Time to level them. They are covered with ivy, built of freestone, and appear as if bending with the weight of years. The abbot's kitchen is the most entire, being the same now as when first made. It stands about two hundred feet from the abbey, inside of a great gateway, at which formerly entered pilgrims from the Holy Land, and out of which issued daily provisions for five hundred people. This kitchen is an octagon of forty feet in diameter, with perpendicular walls twenty-two feet high, then finishing in a cone at the height of seventy feet. The walls are nine feet in thickness. No wonder the abbot said to the king, " that he would build a kitchen which all the wood in the king's forests could not burn down." In the inside are four fire-places and a large oven.

I dined at Glaston, and returned through Wells to Shepton. On the road I passed five hundred French prisoners, under an escort of horse and foot, marching to Stapleton prison, near Bristol. They were mostly young men, and very much like the Canadians. As I rode through them they spoke French to me, and said I had a good horse. Some Poles and Italians were the finest men of the whole.

Next day Mr. Ward and I went to Sherbourne, twelve miles. We passed through Pilcombe and Castle Carey, when we parted company, I taking the road for Cadbury Camp, a Roman station. The little village of North Cadbury lies at the foot of a hill. There I left my horse and walked by the old fosse or road. This camp was formed upon a large circular hill with a flat surface of five hundred yards in diameter, and rises in the midst of a great plain country. It looks like the Tower of Babel, from having four to six tiers of breast-works surrounding it. On the top is a wall of stone and earth, with four gateways, leading by winding and entrenched roads to the fort. The ground is very much turned up for curiosities. I stayed an hour on this Roman ground, and then continued my journey to Sherbourne, where I arrived at two. Passed the " Antelope," then went down Cheap Street, and round the Market Place to the " King's Arms," where I left my horse, and went on to Mr. Willmott's, of Westbury, at whose house we stayed.

Monday, January 13th, 1812.—Returned to Bruton. Next day rode to Stourton, the seat of Sir Richard Hoare, six miles off, and the Pen Pitts. We passed through a low, poor country, to the foot of the highlands ; then turned to the right for three miles, and came to the Pen Pitts, a large piece of ground of four hundred acres, lying on both sides of a vale, dug up into great and small pits, ten or fifteen feet now in depth, and so close together that a man can just walk between them. They are twenty thousand in number, and for what, by whom, and in what time they were made, neither history, tradition, nor conjecture can give any true or reasonable account. Some say it was a city built underground by the Britons in which to hide from the Romans. However, in the adjoining fields, have been fought some of the greatest battles in England, by the Romans, Saxons and Danes, and it was on this spot that the Saxons gave the Britons their last and most bloody overthrow, which drove the latter out of England.

We then rode into the park, and through beautiful rows of trees, along a terrace two miles in length, among hundreds of deer, till we came to Alfred's tower—triangular, built of brick and fine stone, erected in the year 1760, by Sir Richard Hoare, to the memory of Alfred the Great, who, on this summit, in 878, planted his standard, and three days after, in the same spot, fought and gained his first great battle over the Danes. Then we went to the pleasure grounds—a large garden or shubbery, having several temples in romantic situations. First, the temple of the muses ; next, the grotto, in a cave of which sleeps a nymph on a couch, out of which issues a stream of water. In another cave sat the water god, with an urn and a paddle in his hand. Thence to the Pantheon, a round temple, with niches inside, in which were statues. Amongst the rest, one of Hercules, worth two thousand guineas, and one of Lira Augustus, dug up at Herculaneum, and valued at three thousand guineas.

Next day rode to Stowey, thirty-five miles.

Friday.—Rode to Enmore Castle, six miles from Stowey, a large square castle, built of red stone, surrounded by a broad, deep moat, with drawbridge. The ground all around the castle is upon arches, under which are stables for three hundred horses.

Saturday, January 25th, 1812.—This morning was appointed for my seeing Taunton, the county town of that part of Somerset, distant twelve miles.

At twelve we arrived, and put our horses up at the "Castle Inn," in the middle of the town, opposite the market, so called from its being built on the site of an ancient castle. Two noble gateways and part of the walls still remain. This being market-day, we saw the town quite in a bustle. It contains about ten thousand inhabitants, carries on a great inland trade, and is the most flourishing inland town in the kingdom. The people are remarked for their foppery and dress. It lies on the Panet, which comes from Sherbourne, passes through this town and Bridgewater, and empties itself into the sea eight miles below the last town. In its course through this last place it sets fifty manufactories of silk, cloth, etc., to work. Crossing the street, I met Lieutenant O'Keefe, of the 41st. He seemed glad to see me, asked many questions about the girls at York; is here recruiting, and goes to Portugal in the spring. He says that Wyatt is in London.

Monday, 27th.—Left Stowey and returned to Bruton, where I arrived at five o'clock.

Tuesday, 28th.—Rode to Dr. Mitchell's, where I spent the day. He showed me his threshing machine, which does the work of twelve men; his mustard mills, where he makes two thousand bushels of mustard in a year; oil mills, annato mills, cider press, and grist mills, all going by one overshot water wheel, of twenty-five feet diameter. Having but a small stream of water, he built a windmill, which works a great pump placed in the basin below the mill and pumps all the water which feeds it back into the mill race. Mustard is worth from fourteen to twenty-four shillings per bushel. Mr. Ward, C. and E. came to dinner. After drinking six bottles of wine and some tea, the company broke up, and we rode back to Bruton. On our return, found a party of young ladies, and the children made me fulfil my promise of dancing Indian. So I got down my red

and black paints, and painted Mr. Ward like an old
chief, then Dan, Bet, Susan, Kate and myself like
Ottawas. Then we had an Indian dance, which
mightily pleased the whole company.

Saturday, February 1st, 1812.—Dan and I left
Bruton in a post chaise for Bristol, and drove up to
Bellevue, in Clifton, the residence of Mr. Burgess,
who is married to my cousin.

Sunday, 2nd.—Went to St. James' Church twice.
Called upon Charles Ridout at the fort.

Monday, 3rd.—Went to the Guildhall, Bristol,
where there was a very tumultuous meeting assembled,
to consider who should be their representative in
Parliament. I squeezed myself in. At twelve Mr.
Elden opened the meeting, and said that in consequence
of the death of their late member they were this day
called upon to consider who should represent them.
Mr. Protheroe then, amid acclamation, made a fine
speech, and offered himself; which was answered by
one Mills, a printer, jumping upon the table and
speaking, but the noise was so great that not one
word in fifty could be heard. A gentleman then read
an address from Sir Samuel Romilly, soliciting their
support. A lawyer of the name of Coats, a Jacobin,
seconded him, and began a long invective against
Protheroe, who wished to pass for a Whig, but was a
real Tory at heart; and began praising Mr. Fox, when
by a manœuvre of the Protherites, just at the time of
his highest pitch, a cry of "The gallery is falling,"
was set up, and in a moment the crowd rushed
forward and overturned everything, me along with
the rest, when I found myself alongside Mr. Protheroe.
So the meeting broke up in confusion. I dined at
the fort with Ridout.

BRISTOL, *Wednesday, 5th February,* 1812.

This being the day appointed for a general fast, we
got up and ate a hearty breakfast; then went to St.

James', where Mr. Biddulph preached. Mr. Burgess then took me to the Commercial Coffee Room, opposite the Exchange and Post Office. It is a large room, about sixty feet in length and forty broad, having a beautiful dome supported by twelve female figures. The room is lighted with five elegant lustres. There are four fire-places, with three tables round each. At one end of the room is a clock ; at the other, an instrument telling the wind, a barometer and a thermometer. This building was built, and is frequented by most of the commercial characters in Bristol,—it forms a kind of second Exchange. On the tables are newspapers from Ireland, London and Scotland, with different magazines and reviews.

Sunday, 9th.—Went to St. Mary's, Redcliffe, considered to be the first parish church in the kingdom. It was built in the year 1276, in the true Gothic style; length, two hundred and twenty feet ; height of middle arch, thirty-four feet ; has eighty windows ; the whole church stands upon arches. The chancel is paved with white marble. Above the Communion table are three famous paintings by Hogarth, illustrating the Resurrection. The paintings cost, with frames and putting up, £750. Admiral Penn is buried in this church. He has a very handsome monument erected to him, over which is placed his armour and some of the colours of the Dutch ships which he captured during the famous Dutch war. We were also shown the rib of the Hun cow, an enormous ribbone about eight feet long. Some stone coffins were shown, and the musical pillars, which sound like metal on being struck with the hand.

On my visit to Sherbourne, I went to see my old grandfather's house. I found it in ruins, the hedges are out of repair, and the avenue of trees leading to the house have their tops cut off. I also went to see the grammar school, which now consists of twenty boys, kept by Rev. J. Cutler. It was Christmas holidays. A girl came out and civilly unlocked the door. I walked up and down the room, saw the oaken benches, desks and wainscoting cut up and carved with 3,000 names; saw John Gibbs Ridout carved upon one. I went to Sherbourne church on Sunday, sat just below the fine old organ, and had a full view of the grandeur of this Gothic pile, which has stood unmoved in war and peace, through the storms and tempests of 700 years, its clustered pillars forming a lofty, deep arch. The massy walls seem to defy time, and I think that seven centuries may again roll away, and this building will remain in a perfect state. After church, James Ridout showed me grandfather's seat, near the pulpit, which I entered—the place beyond Lord Digby's. There, on that spot, fifty years ago, sat my father, in the other corner, grandfather. Here in this church, for generations, had the family been christened and buried; but I found myself more a stranger in Sherbourne than any other town I had been in. James Ridout, being churchwarden, showed me the parish books from 1540. In 1630 I saw the name of John Ridout in the vestry.

In after years, Mr. Ridout gave to a street in Toronto the name of Sherbourne, in remembrance of the old English town, the home of his ancestors.

CHAPTER VII.

A CANADIAN IN OXFORD, 1812.

From Thomas G. Ridout to his father in York:—

BRISTOL, 10*th February*, 1812.

I WENT to Jacobs' glass manufactory, supposed to be the first in the world. We were conducted into a large dark place, in the middle of which was a circular furnace containing five ovens of glass metal like melted barley sugar. They put in a long hollow piece of iron, then take it out and blow and turn it, giving, at the same time, the shape with the hand, and the size, by a pair of compasses; adding, now, for a wine glass, first the shank and then the bottom.

At five we went to the play. The theatre is built in King Street, and is a very beautiful building within. It was crowded beyond anything on account of being Braham's benefit night, and we got our places by mere chance in the side boxes. He is the finest singer in the kingdom. His principal songs that night were, "Though Time has from your Lordship's Face," "The Bewildered Maid," "Said a Smile to a Tear," "All's Well," and "The Death of Abercrombie." You would have been astonished to hear such singing. His benefit amounted to £200. The farce was "High Life Below Stairs," and was conducted with the greatest humour. The manager then came forward and announced that Mr. Betty, the young Roscius, had been prevailed upon by friends to embrace the stage again and act two nights in Bristol. Braham belongs to Covent Garden.

7

Wednesday, 12th February.—I went to see King's Staffordshire ware manufactory. There are fifty people employed, and every piece goes through the hands of twenty-three people. Most of the ware is made by turning, excepting plates, dishes, etc., which are made by moulds. After turning, it is smoothed and cut into shape by chisels, then baked in earthen boxes for fifty hours, and then taken to the dyers, who stamp the pattern upon a paper. This is then washed off, leaving a brown print, and the ware is a second time baked, to bake out the oil and bake in the color. From that it is brought to the glazer, who dips the cup into a tub of glazing stuff of a bluish color. It is then for the third and last time baked. The glazing turns white and transparent, through which is seen the blue print. Cups of different colors are painted with a pencil. Every stage is a different trade, to which is an apprenticeship of seven years.

I called upon Dr. Small, in Portland Square. He said his brother did very wrong in signing an acknowledgment of Governor Gore's just government of the Province. He said Gore will never return, and Mr. D. W. Smith will never go out again. Dr. Small is much like his brother, speaks almost with the same voice. He says there is no likelihood of getting John out of France. He and Boulton are at Verdun. John can't live for less than £100 a year, learns French, sees a good deal of company, and writes his uncle doleful letters.

14th February, 1812.—I am just returned from Bath, to which place I went on Friday last, on Mr. Ridout's horse. I rode up to the "Castle and Ball," put my horse there, and then took a letter of introduction which Mr. R. gave me to Matterson, a gentleman living under the Piazza to the right of the Pumproom, who very politely took me to all parts of the city, through crowds of ladies and gentlemen, who were lounging through the streets. Some were invalids, rolled upon little waggons; some flying in sedan chairs, up and down, to and fro. The gentlemen dressed in breeches, stockings and cocked hats; the ladies in the most superb manner—pelisses laced with gold cords and Hussar's hats, having three circles of gold cord round them, with two great tassels of gold upon the left side. What is called a reticule, which contains their pocket handkerchief and work, is hanging by a gold chain to the arm, and is fringed with gold. I went to the Pump-room, which is very large and grand. On one side is the pump, where a woman stands and distributes old King Bladud's waters to old and young, sick and well. An old duchess of eighty and a child of four were both drinking the waters while I was there. I had a glass; it is very hot and tastes very mineral. At one end of the room is an orchestra, where bands of music are continually playing. The company at the same time walking up and down in crowds, not minding the music, but buzzing like merchants on 'change. At the end of each tune they clap their hands and kick up a riot, for what they don't know.

From Thomas G. Ridout to his Brother in York:—

LONDON, *12th March*, 1812.

I wrote to you from Bristol a long letter by the *Medford*, for New York, which sailed 20th February. I remained eighteen days altogether there, amusing myself riding about the country, going with the girls to the play, hearing young Betty and the famous Braham perform to crowded houses, seeing the amazing manufactories, etc. I was at Dr. Small's two days, and saw his church, gardens, etc. When I left Bristol he gave me a letter of introduction to the Vice-Chancellor of Oxford, which I took advantage of; and another to John Lewis Esq., of St. James' Palace. I am quite ashamed of not answering your letter in particular, and you may think I have entirely forgotten Toronto. An American war was much looked for in England, and I was quite distracted about you all, but the Yankees seem to have thought better of it. I have seen Alex. McDonell, who says that York is much improved, and that the North-West Company trade will pass through Yonge Street. He spoke of the general prosperity of the Province.

Flour will at all times sell well in England, though the merchants here limit their correspondents at Quebec to give only 6s. 6d. per bushel, allowing the current exchange. Staves sell low. Potash is flat, and American oak out of repute, by mere prejudice of these English, who think their " heart of oak " superior to any in the world. Yellow pine, thirty feet by fourteen inches square is high. England is destitute of timber, therefore must always get supplies for her immense consumption from Canada or the Baltic, which I am glad to hear is shut, so our timber will, of course, rise in proportion to the Northern restrictions. In all probability, one thousand sail of prime merchantmen will enter the port of Quebec this summer, as the merchants here know not where to send their shipping. Freight out, which very few but regular traders can get, is from forty-five shillings to £3 per ton ; home at the rate of £60 per one thousand staves, which are calculated to take up ten tons of ship room, which just agrees with what *Kendrick* carries. The reason of potash being so low is the great decrease in the manufactures of this country in some branches, for which pot or pearl ashes were much used. The markets of Quebec and Montreal will be again overstocked, and British goods nearly as cheap there as in London.

Trade has revived very much within these two months, though not to compare with former times. The taxes are enormous, and land rents at about £5 per acre, and sells for £100 per acre and upwards. John Ward gave £100 per acre for some land in Glastonbury Vale, it is rented at £7 an acre.

I must commence this second sheet with my journey from Bristol to Oxford. Accordingly, on Tuesday, the 26th of February, I left Bristol, having, the preceding day sent my trunk by the stage to Oxford, to be left at Cox & Richardson's, in High Street. It was a fine day, and the girls got up at six, and made me take a hearty breakfast, and at parting each gave me a present—Susan, an elegant silk purse; Betsy, a watch ribbon, and Jane a fine gold ring. I took a place on the outside for Newport, distant eighteen miles, for four shillings and sixpence, which place we reached at eleven, and drove to the "Black Lion." The road led through a delightful country. On the right, we were bounded by a range of fertile hills, and to the left, at the distance of two miles, lay the Bristol Channel, which is here but three miles wide and runs through a very rich country. On the opposite side is the county of Monmouth. There are two ferries here over into Wales—one nine, and the other twelve miles above Bristol, and you can go over for sixpence. At Newport I left the stage, and took the left-hand road, which I followed for two miles, till I came to the village of Berkeley, famous for its ancient castle, which is now the most entire remains of ancient baronial power and grandeur in the kingdom. It is now the residence of Colonel Berkeley, Mr. Small's friend.* The castle is surrounded by a great moat. The walls are of immense thickness of stone, and look black and venerable with age. On going to the castle I passed through Dr. Jenner's yard. He lives in this village, where he has a very elegant house, and a great eagle hopping about before the door. Berkeley Castle was built in the year 1100, and is famous for the death of Edward II., who was so cruelly murdered here. The hall was fitted up in the ancient style, with armour, etc., around it, with a great oaken table and handsome

* Berkeley Street, Toronto, is named after this place.

seats on the sides; the floor paved with chequered marble, and the banner of Cromwell's wars waving over the chimney; the roof supported by elegant Gothic rafters like those in Westminster Hall. Altogether it reminded me of—

"The feast was o'er in Branksome Hall."

I was shown the dungeon, in the form of a D, wherein King Edward was confined, and the old iron bed on which he slept. In this gloomy place was a trap-door, which let down into the dungeon of death, twenty-six feet in depth, surrounded by thick walls and three feet deep in water; a horrid place, where the light of day has never entered in for these 700 years, and whence the groans of the condemned wretch were never heard. In an adjoining room, which was only different from the dungeon by having a small window, that poor unfortunate king was put to a cruel death. The instrument by which he suffered is yet there, and looks only fit for such acts. From these dismal chambers I went to the gay apartments, which are fitted up in princely style; tables and chairs' covered with gold, paintings by great men, and a lot of fine things. I must not forget the royal bed-stead of Richard II., who stayed some time at this castle. It was put up in 1332, but is now an old crazy thing, and only kept as a curiosity. I saw Queen Elizabeth's dressing-room, gold table and look-ing-glass, and her state bed, and a curious cabinet made of ebony, ivory and gold, 600 years old. The rooms of James I., hung with Gobelin tapestry on cloth of gold, Vandyke's paintings, etc. The Prince of Wales' rooms, gold candlesticks, plate, ink-stands, etc.; all the tables are covered with gold-leaf. I also saw the bedstead which Sir Francis Drake took with him round the world, made of ebony and ivory, with his four cabin chairs. The walls of the castle form the dwelling part, and a stone building divides it

into two courts, one of which formed the grand parade
and the other raised about twenty feet above it, and
surrounded by a high wall, was the keep where the
prisoners who were confined in the adjoining dun-
geons had the liberty of walking. The roof of the
castle is covered with lead. In the centre rises a fine
look-out tower, where the warlike flag once waved,
and from whence they could spy their enemies at a
distance.

At one, I left Berkeley, returned to the main road,
and dined at a little country inn. As no coach would
pass till seven, I determined, therefore, on walking to
Gloucester, distant eighteen miles, and accordingly,
left the "King's Head" at three, and reached Gloucester at nine. After taking a glance at three or four
taverns, I suited myself at last at a very good one,
where I slept soundly until seven next morning;
breakfasted, and went to see the cathedral, which is
very old, and first built by Osric, King of Northumberland, in 650, afterwards partly rebuilt in the year
900, and the west end and south side in 1400, so that
it contains three orders of architecture. It is 444 feet
in length, 100 wide, and the height of the middle
aisle, eighty-six feet. The painted window at the
east end is the largest in England, being eighty-three
feet in height and thirty-six wide. The pillars are
what is called Saxon, twenty-one feet in circumfer-
ance. Here lies interred, under a most magnificent
chapel, the body of Edward II.; Robert, Duke of
Normandy; and Osric, King of Northumberland.
The cloisters were built by Henry VII., and are esteemed the finest of the kind, forming a quadrangle
of trees with the branches, all of stone. The great
tower was built by Cardinal Wolsey, and is 230 feet
high.

Gloucester contains about 7,000 inhabitants and is
an ill-built city, having only one good street in it. I
paid my bill at the " White Lion," took a place in the

"Prince Regent," for Oxford, distant forty-eight
miles, for thirteen shillings, and taking my seat alongside the coachman, at ten a.m. we drove out of Gloucester.   Outside was my honour, an Irish captain in
the 11th Dragoons, of the name of McMahon; a
Welshman, from Caermarthenshire, called Owen
Jones; a lieutenant in the navy; an Oxford tailor,
and a London cheesemonger; a Sherbourne man for
a guard, and a jolly Hampshire coachman.

We passed at two through Cheltenham, a large
town of 5,000 inhabitants, and famous for its mineral
springs.   It is a second Bath with regard to its
waters, but not in buildings, which are of brick.   It
was full of quality, though, and is one of the fashionable rendezvous.   A mile from the west end we passed
the house of General Le Fevre, Bonaparte's favourite,
and presently after met the man himself.   He is a
tall, handsome, active and well-made fellow, about
thirty; he has the countenance of a veteran, a quick
and piercing eye, and walks as if he now commanded
armies.   He burns to return to France, and feels his
situation very galling to his ambition.

We changed horses at Frog Mills, eighteen miles
from Gloucester, and again at Long Neat, eighteen
miles farther.   At nine in the evening, passed the
Burford, seven miles from Oxford, when the mail
coach passed us in fine style, though it left Gloucester
two hours after us, and was to be in London at seven
next morning.

It was a beautiful moonlight night.   Three miles
from Oxford we walked up a hill a mile long, and presently after rattled down into the low grounds, which
were covered with water. I could see as we approached
the towers and turrrets of an ancient city, and the
effect was indescribable.   In the course of a mile we
passed over seven stone bridges—over the Isis, Tamar,
and several other streams.   Oxford is situated in the
midst of a great meadow or flat, three miles in

breadth. At eleven, we drove under the ruins of the old castle, now the county gaol, on our right, and Magdalen College on the left, through Broad Street into High Street, then turned to the right a hundred yards, and brought to at the "New Inn," opposite the Town Hall, where I left my companions. The dragoon and lieutenant continued on their journey—one for Portugal and the other for the Adriatic station. I slept till seven next morning, when I got my trunk from Cox's, dressed myself gay, and inquired the way to Wadham College, where lived my friend, Robert Stevens. I went up High Street, turned to the left, passed All Souls' College on one side, and St. Mary's Church and schools on the other, and continued straight on to Wadham. I went through a gateway into the quadrangle—for there are no doors on the outside of the Colleges—and found Mr. Stevens in his room giving a Greek lecture. He received me with the utmost politeness, and asked me to wait until he had finished his lecture. The rooms in this college are very commodious, consisting of a good sized parlour, furnished in good style, well painted and papered, a sofa, glasses and a bedroom, dressing-room and study, for which all but fellows pay £10 a year rent, finding their own furniture. Mr. Stevens then put on his robe of office, which is a silk gown with rich velvet sleeves, and a cap the same as students wear. He has always two men with maces walking before him. The first thing we did was to see Wadham College, which is the most uniform building in Oxford, as it has never been altered since it was built in 1613, by Nicholas Wadham, whose statue, with Dorothy, his wife, stand in niches over the hall portico. The chapel is very handsome, having seven large windows of painted glass. The hall is one of the largest in Oxford, about one hundred feet in length, and very high and wide, wainscoted and ceiled with oak, carved in a most curious manner, and the walls hung with paintings. On either side is a long range of oaken tables, and oak benches where three hundred people can dine.

We then went to Christ College, the largest in the city, and built after the vast plan of Cardinal Wolsey. It consists of four courts or squares. The stately west front of the great quadrangle is a magnificent Gothic building, 382 feet in length, terminating at each end with two corresponding turrets. The great gate is in the middle of this front, and over it an ancient tower, in which hangs the great bell, called "Tom," which weighs eight and a half tons, on the sound of which the scholars of the university are to retire to their respective colleges. The great quadrangle is 264 by 261 feet. On the south side of the quadrangle is the hall, to which you ascend by an elegant staircase of stone. This hall is by far the handsomest in Oxford, being 150 feet in length, and of great height. The roof is framed of timber, curiously wrought, and the cornice has 300 coats of arms carved and painted in their proper colours. At the upper end is an ascent of three steps which runs the whole breadth, where the noblemen dine, above the masters, who dine at a double row of tables on each side. They were then laid, as the college dines at two. All the plates and dishes were of pewter, with silver tankards. The chapel was built for a cathedral before the year 1200.

We then went to the theatre, where all public speeches and debates are said. On the ceiling the Arts and Sciences are painted. We then crossed the court to the Radcliff library, which is a fine building surrounded by pillars, and has a dome 180 feet high. From the top I had a complete view of Oxford. The library contains 40,000 volumes; it was built by a private gentleman and cuts a very great appearance in Oxford among the ancient towers and turrets. Thence we went to University College. This library contains 450,000 volumes—ancient, modern, and in all languages. Among the Arabic and Oriental manuscripts, in which they are very rich, Mr. Stevens showed me the Alkoran of Tippoo Sahib, presented by the East India Company, with gold cover and clasps, very much ornamented. The paper is vellum, of the finest kind, every character written in gold, illustrated with the same. This college stands on the south side of High Street, opposite the Queen's, and is 260 feet in front, three stories, and has two noble towers in front and another over the chapel. We visited in this, and the course of the two following days, Baliol College, All Souls', Brazen-nose (so-called from having a brazen nose over the gate, it is opposite All Souls'), Magdalen College (called Maudlin), the richest in the University, which supports 120 commoners and fellows. It lies upon the Charwell, at the east end of the city, and has the finest groves of trees in England. I knew one of the Fellows of this college, Dr. Goldsboro.

New College, which lies east of the schools and theatre, was built in 1379, and is a building 200 feet square. The chapel is remarkable for its beautiful painted windows, which are as old as the college. The garden is laid out in an elegant manner. They have a bowling green here. The gardens are partly enclosed by the ancient city wall, which, with its battlements and bastions, may be traced along the north and south sides. Oriel College contains 140 students, and is a building 280 feet square. It is near St. Mary's Church, in High Street. On the north side of High Street, opposite University College, is Queen's. It is an oblong square, 300 feet by 220 feet, divided into two courts by the hall and chapel, the latter 100 feet long and 30 feet wide. It maintains 200 students, masters, etc., who are all called to dinner by the sound of a trumpet. I have said a great deal about High Street, and I must tell you it is the grandest street I have seen in England. It winds from east to west like a river through the city, every wind

of which opens to the view some grand and state y
college. Magdalen College Hall, University and
Queen's, St. Mary's Church and Hall, New College,
the schools and Brazen-nose, all stretch along this
street.

I must now tell you how I passed my time there.
Dressed myself smart in breeches, shoes and stockings
—for boots are not allowed to be worn—and as the
clock struck four, Mr. Stevens took me into the great
hall to dinner. On each side was a long oak table, with
benches, pewter plates, silver forks and spoons, and a
silver tankard of ale to each plate. We were, by right,
the first to enter, and accordingly marched up to the
farther end near the fire-place, to the master's table,
which runs across, and is raised two steps higher than
the common hall. Dr. Swaine sat at the head, I upon
the right hand, Dean Gardiner upon his left; Mr.
Stevens next to me, and eight others, of whom I knew
Drs. Wyndham and Templar. Our dinner consisted
of soup, served in a silver tureen, roast veal, pudding
and pies, cheese, etc., and a silver tankard of ale.
This College is very rich in plate. Our table was
further distinguished from the long ones by having
whole joints. The students have what is called commons. I was surprised to see the upper end of each
table occupied first, and so on by degrees to the foot;
all the students having on gowns, shoes and stockings,
for boots are not allowed. I was going to tell you
what they call commons. To each college is a large
kitchen, with cooks in abundance, who, upon their
own account, find the mess; and each student, according to his degree, goes first into the kitchen, immediately before dinner, and looks at the bill of fare, and
orders a plateful of beef or mutton, etc., and, if he
likes, a slice of pudding, for which he is charged by
the clerk, who sits at a desk in one corner, and a
waiter follows him into the hall with it. That is the
reason I saw the heads of the tables filled first,

because the elder fellows had the prime run of the kitchen, across which a bar is put to prevent the young chaps from disturbing cookey. We were waited on by the butler and steward. As we were eating cheese, a man came round the table with a slate, asking every person how many pieces of bread they had taken. For each piece he charges one halfpenny. As soon as we had dined, Dr. Gardiner gave a sign, and every person in the hall rose and stood outside their seats, and an undergraduate came up to our table, made a bow, and repeated a long thanksgiving in Latin, and a prayer for the prosperity of the King, kingdom and college, and a prayer for and thanks to old Nic. and Dorothy Wadham, which Dr. Gardiner answered in a few Latin words. Then we took our hats and left the hall, all standing until we were out.

We then went into a handsome wainscoted-room, with a good fire and plenty of wine-glasses and arm-chairs. This is called the Common Room. Presently old Mrs. Ford, who has served the college for the last forty years, came limping her ancient form into the room with oranges, apples, cakes, and nuts; each man drank a pint of wine, for which they paid the butler on the spot, at the rate of 4s. 6d. per bottle. Every week he pays that money into Dr. Wyndham's hands. At seven we broke up, and Mr. Stevens took me to a lady's house in Oxford, where there was a large party. At nine Mr. Stevens left to go his nightly rounds as proctor, with two men as attendants. His business is to clear the streets of vagabonds, to see that every student is snug within the colleges. After that hour his authority is supreme over Oxford, and its environs to the distance of two miles, and he can imprison any person he chooses. At half-past ten he called for me, and we went home to Wadham, where he had provided a good bed for me. Next morning, 29th February, at eight o'clock, I went to St. Mary's Church, next the schools and Brazen-nose, where

Latin service was performed. The Vice-Chancellor entered in state, followed by the two proctors, doctors, deans, etc, These prayers, every student who intends taking degrees in the ensuing term, is obliged to attend. Their names were called over. There were about 500 there. We breakfasted in Dr. Swain's rooms—for in Oxford it is a rule that several breakfast together at each other's rooms in turn; and the Oxonians are famous for good breakfasts. They vie with one another in that respect. Mr. Stevens had the Greek lectures to attend to, so he committed me to the care and guidance of Dean Gardiner, who promised to show me the remainder of the lions. Accordingly, we went to the schools to see the ceremony of a master taking his degree, before the Vice-Chancellor, who sat in state, with the proctors below him, and doctors and masters on either side. The ceremony was long and curious. Everything that was said was in Latin.

We then went to the rest of the colleges I had not seen, and to the museum, where I saw the skull of Oliver Cromwell, Guy Fawkes' lanthorn, and the sword the Pope gave Henry VIII., when Defender of the Faith; a loadstone that attracted 145 pounds of iron; Roman and Carthaginian swords and curiosities. We then went to hear Sir Christopher Pegg deliver an anatomical lecture. Then dressed for dinner, at which I did my duty, and drank wine till seven. The conversation was first on books and the manuscripts found in Herculaneum. Then very politely turned, to please me, on America. I was in my element, and we all seemed well entertained. Three of the students were invited to tea, and we played whist. A barrel of London oysters was brought in at ten, and we made a glorious supper.

Sunday I was invited to breakfast by Mr. Hall, a young blood of Oxford, where I made a most sumptuous meal. We went to St. Mary's Church, and heard a Bampton lecture, which is a sermon against the Mahometan religion. I had the honour of sitting with Mr. Wyndham, in the Masters' seat. The sermon was said first, and the prayers after. Mr. Stevens and I took a walk to a certain oak on the top of a hill, whence we had a delightful view of Oxford, which is unlike any other city. Dined as usual. One of the students, Colonel Lethridge's son, appeared in hall in boots, and was ordered out.

Monday, I bade good-bye to my good friends, left Oxford in the "Alfred" coach at eight, and reached Tyburn, in Oxford Street, at three, having gone at the rate of eight miles an hour. The day was beautiful, and we passed through many fine and populous towns. London was in a cloud of smoke.

CHAPTER VIII.

LONDON AND WOOLWICH.

From Thos. G. Ridout to his father in York :—

LONDON, 17th March, 1812.

ON Monday, the first of March, I arrived in Paternoster Row from Oxford, where I had been for three days, living at Wadham College. By the kind attention of Mr. Stevens, I was enabled to see more of that famous place than most strangers. I was at preachings, prayings, lectures and dinners, convocations and suppers, and saw all the lions and whelps of the town. On Tuesday, the third, I went about visiting my friends, and took a letter up to Montague Square, to Miss Stevens, Mr. S.'s sister, who lives with General Stevens in that most gay and fashionable spot.

The Quebec convoy sails from Portsmouth on the twentieth, by which these letters go. I saw the *Everetta* the other day down by the tower. There are now about 5,000 sail of merchantmen in the river, which form a most interesting sight. I was sent the other day down to the London Docks, about two miles below the bridge. They are building a beautiful seventy-four and two more ships in Blackwall Docks, near the East India Docks. At Deptford, another seventy-four, with three frigates, are on the stocks; and at Woolwich, a most magnificent ship, of 120 guns, will be launched this summer. You will think it very singular that I have not yet seen Governor Gore, who has been upwards of two months in England. I missed him by going into the country. Yesterday he attended the Prince Regent's levee.

The French and Russians are going to war again, therefore, the Baltic will be open this summer to the British, which will take off great quantities of the manufactures of England, and lower the price of bread, which at present is very high.

It is now thought the Americans have given up all thoughts of war. How foolishly I fly from one subject to another, but I must tell you everything. Mr. Pearson, Secretary to the Lottery Office, in Somerset House, very coolly, last January, took a pistol and shot himself through the heart. The cause of it was that he had embezzled the public money to the amount of £16,000. Government immediately seized everything. George Ridout is down at Bristol, where he is to be ordained by the Bishop of Gloucester. His father has purchased him a living near Bruton for £3,000.

On Friday last, went to Covent Garden with John. The play was the "Virgin of the Sun," a most superb thing. On Sunday, went with uncle in the carriage to Hampstead and dined at Mr. Watt's, a great stockbroker. On Monday, I am going to the annual dinner given by the Governor and Stewards of Bartholomew's Hospital, to have a sight of one of these great English feasts. When at Bristol, uncle sent me a letter saying that he had just received a note from Mr. Hamilton, who wishes me to come to town, as this was their busy season, and I might, by being in his counting house, get well acquainted with the trade of Canada, and thus fitted for a good situation in Mr. Coltman's house, whose business is of the most extensive kind. The firm was Ridsdale, Hamilton & Coltmans; but finding the business too much scattered, by a branch being in America, another in Leeds, and a third in London, they determined on dissolving, giving the Quebec business entirely to the Coltmans. Mr. Coltman is accordingly expected every day. I shall sail soon in one of his ships. If by industry and assiduity in learning to measure timber, keep books

8

and fit out ships I can qualify myself to super-
intend their works at Portneuf, he will obtain
that situation for me. We are busy in fitting
out three ships, one for New Brunswick, another for
Newfoundland and a third for Jamacia. They have
cut out work enough for the Newfoundland ship, as
she goes there with goods, then loads with fish for
Jamaica, and gets a cargo of rum there for Quebec, and
returns thence to England, laden with timber. Yesterday I went to the Paymaster-General's office for £4,200,
and have just returned from the Bank of England, where
I discounted £9,000 more. My business is chiefly
making invoices and settling insurances. Mr. Hamilton
and I are good friends. I am acquiring knowledge in
business and quickness, which I never had before.
This London is a curious place. We are now shipping
for New Brunswick £30,000 worth of goods by our own
ship *The True Briton*. I must now make haste and
run to the " New York Coffee House," and put this
into the *Ocean's* bags.

From Thomas G. Ridout to his father in York :—

London, *17th April*, 1812.

The outside of the letter is thus marked :—Ship
Akeroyde, received 28th August, 1812, through the
United States, opened.

I met Alexander McDonell in Fleet Street, on the
12th inst., and went to call upon Major Halton, in
Beaumont Street. Very fortunately I met Governor
Gore in Portland Square. He turned round at the same
instant I did, and seemed glad to see me. He asked
me which way was I going. I told him to call on Major
Halton, to get his address, which he immediately gave
me, and told me to call on him. Accordingly, on the
14th, I went to his house, No. 25 Upper Grosvenor

Street, a corner house looking into Hyde Park. I was shown into the library, and in a few minutes the Governor came in and received me most cordially. He told me he had seen you a day or two before he left York. We had a long confab of an hour and upwards, in which time the Governor told me everything concerning Upper Canada. That Mr. Firth was completely dismissed from all employment under Government—entirely from his own representation of the Governor's conduct, in which he called the Governor villain, tyrant, rascal, hound, etc.—without the Governor interfering in the least.

He told me he was pleased at my intention of returning to Canada, which he said was now the best country in the world to advance in, and that he would not give up the governorship of that Province for anything the Government here could give him, and that he was going out again this summer.

He said, "I prefer it far to any other appointment, though there are so many scoundrels out there; yet they cannot injure the country or lower it in my opinion." He went on to say, "This voyage to England has been of great service to me. Don't you think I am much thinner than when in Canada?" buttoning his coat at the same time.

He asked me how I liked England, was I happy? I answered I was as happy as a person away from his native country could be.

"I know," he said, "how you feel—surely the frosts and snows of Canada are far preferable to the fogs and mists of this country." Then continued, "The town of Penetanguishene is coming on rapidly, that is, the North-West Company intend carrying the trade through it, and in a few years it will be of some consequence."

I told him of my being pressed at Plymouth, and only escaping by having his letters, at which he laughed heartily. He said he was going down to Devonshire shortly, where he had spent many happy years.

I went in the afternoon to see Tom Prince, at the Duke of Brunswick's, and was gratified by a sight of the Duke's sons, Princes Charles and William. They are two very fine little German fellows, and have a great resemblance to the royal family. The house is a little beyond Vauxhall, upon the river.

Before this reaches York, you will have heard of the riots in England. Nottingham, Manchester, Leeds, Birmingham and Sheffield have been scenes of the utmost confusion within these few weeks past. In consequence of the scarcity of provisions and an almost total failure in the manufactories and flatness of trade, the workmen are thrown out of employ, and fill the poor-houses. Some say it is an artificial scarcity, and that speculators have bought up all the grain, so as to compel the people to pay them their extortionate prices. Government has posted troops in every large town to keep the people down. By the machinery, now generally used in the manufactories, nine-tenths of the people are thrown out of employment.

London continues in a quiet state. Its markets are well supplied, though at a high rate; and as long as there is any trade in the kingdom this city will always have the preference. In France, and over most parts of Europe, there is the like scarcity, and even worse, but you do not hear of their rising in this manner. From the Baltic and America they look for great supplies, which I hope they will receive before things get much worse. The loss of the American trade is considered a very severe stroke; a renewal of the commerce is anxiously looked for. The army in Portugal draw all their provisions from Ireland and England, which must be an expense and drain never before known. Thank God, I have not felt yet anything like starvation, and therefore should not be a croaker; but the present state of things deserves to be mentioned. There are 1,200 ship carpenters in London out of employment, and you see many common people in the streets with bills in their hats, "I want work, and can have a good character." Written in chalk on the houses I see, "More Taxes" and "Rebellion." How happy ought all Canadians to be to live contented in their own country, where they enjoy plenty and peace.

Mrs. Woolam has invited me to St. Alban's, where I intend going shortly. Next week I shall go and see "Macbeth" performed at Covent Garden. On Monday night I go with the Princes to Astley's Theatre.

The other day I called in to see Polito's wild beasts at Exeter 'Change; saw a lion and lioness, tiger and tigress, a hyena, two panthers, two leopards, two sloths, a wild cat, a camel and a Canada bear. In the second room was an elephant and rhinoceros. In the third room was an ostrich from Nubia, ten feet high; two ostriches from New Holland, a pelican, a dodo, storks, parrots, Brazil birds, kangaroos, opossums, casimir goats, monkeys, baboons and many other animals.

Monday 20th.—Dined at G. Ward's at half-past five. We went in two coaches to the play, which was one of Shakespeare's, "Julius Cæsar," in which are those speeches we used to say at school. What a sight Covent Garden is of a full night! It contains four thousand five hundred people. The pit looks like a black swarm of bees all in motion; and when the curtain is down a buzz, like the Royal Exchange at four o'clock, fills the house. Kemble has got his plays up with the most magnificent scenery. The Roman Senate House with Cæsar, Brutus, Cassius, Marc Antony, Casca, was very fine. The meeting of the conspirators while it thundered and lightened, seemed like reality. Kemble's helmet and shield are of silver, burnished with gold. Standard-bearers, with the Roman eagle, attended Cæsar wherever he went. The afterpiece was "Timour the Tartar," of which I cannot now give you a description. Golden chariots, troops of cavalry, fierce engagements, bloodless battles, castles on fire, thunder and lightning, a tempestuous sea and a stormy night, form this much-famed piece.

At half-past twelve it broke up. Then for confusion, men and boys running about with torches, crying for coaches—"Lady Gamble," "Lord Yarmouth," "Lord Radnor," "No 984," etc, etc.

Saturday 25th.—Philip Prince and I went to Astley's Theatre. He went above to see Mr. Astley, while I stayed in the hall. Down came Mrs. Astley and invited me up, and I drank a glass of wine with them. It was odd to see Mrs. Astley come on the stage, just after I had been speaking to her.

Monday, 27th.—Admiral Taylor and his nephew breakfasted with us on their way with George to Oxford. John and I promised to accompany them to High Wycombe, twenty five miles, so we got on board the "Black Lion," Water Lane, at half-past eight, and drove off. When we reached Uxbridge—a large town, fifteen miles from Tyburn and eighteen from St. Paul's—it came on to rain, so we left poor G., and walked to town, though twenty stages, seventy waggons and carts, forty gentlemen's carriages and thirty-five horsemen passed us in two and a half hours.

London, *29th April*, 1812.

This day being Easter Monday, the Lord Mayor gave a grand dinner and ball, at which all the foreign ambassadors, princes and noblemen, etc., were present. In the course of the day John procured a ticket for me to go to the ball, No. 2850. You may suppose I was not a little pleased with it. Mr. Hamilton had obtained a ticket for two of his sons, so we made an agreement to go together at half-past ten. Already was Cheapside, the Poultry and Cornhill filled with carriages, lighted torches, and confusion. We walked and got in very well through the crowd. Some of the carriages were three or four hours getting through Cheapside. The first room we entered was the Egyptian Hall, lighted by great glass chandeliers and festoons of lamps. A row of pillars on each side of the room, which supported the roof, were entwined with beautiful lamps made of cut-glass. At one end was a military band playing "God save the King." The other end had great folding doors, opening into the dining-room, laid out in four rows of tables extending the whole length. The dinner, itself, was the only thing moved, every ornament remained. Down the middle of each table there was a row of the most curious ornaments in frame work, about three or four feet high, made of wood and gilded—men, horses, castles, abbeys and battles. The room was lighted with cut-glass chandeliers, suspended from the roof, with fifty or sixty lights in each; figures of men and women holding lustres in their hands. The pillars here were fluted, and down every second groove was a string of lamps. These two lower rooms were crowded with gentlemen and ladies. We then went up stairs into the ball-room. At the east end, under a canopy of gold, seated on a throne of the same, sat the Lady Mayoress. On her right hand was seated the Duke of Cambridge, next to him the Duke of Brunswick, and the Spanish Ambassador; on her left, some lords. Immediately behind her were twelve young ladies in waiting, dressed in state like old Queen Bess's picture, with white feathers and diamonds. The Lady Mayoress, a pretty woman about twenty-eight, was dressed in a gown spangled with gold, I suppose, with great hoops. Her belt was studded with precious stones, and clasped by the same. Her hair sparkled with diamonds; she wore a gold comb set with jewels. The Duke of Cambridge was dressed like a general, with a great star upon his left breast—of diamonds I suppose—and two diamond rings on his fingers, and a red sash over his shoulder. The other noblemen had blue sashes. There were some Spanish and Portuguese

officers there. At twelve, the Duke of Cambridge left
the ball. There was very little dancing. John and
Frank H. danced, and as Frank was going down
merrily, his foot slipped on some wax that had dropped
down, and he fell on his face, to the great amusement
of the company. I got some ice cream and cakes with
great difficulty. Frank came down to get a drink, but
to no purpose. He mistook an Alderman, in his scarlet robes, for one of the servants, and said to him,
" Go, like a good fellow, and get me a drink, I'll give
you sixpence to go, and bring me a pot of porter. The
Alderman, turning round, fiercely said, " Do you know
who you are speaking to?" Very unexpectedly I
met Henry Boulton there, walking with some ladies,
and we had a great chat, and we thought what would
Joel, Jim Campbell or McDonell say to us strut-
ting about a Lord Mayor's ball-room with our opera
hats under our arms, among 5,000 gay Londoners.
At half-past three I left the Mansion House, well
pleased at my night's amusement.

From Thomas G. Ridout to his Brother at York:—

LONDON, *6th May,* 1812.

Yesterday I received with heartfelt satisfaction
your letters of the 15th and 20th January. Though I
am in the midst of pleasurss, of which I freely partake, yet would I exchange all and every scene of this
wonderful metropolis, for old Ontario's northern shore.
I almost envy you your deep snows and frozen lakes
during the last winter, and am glad to hear that balls and
regular assemblies were again the order of the day at
York, which must have proved a great addition to the
confined pleasures of our poor sisters. How willingly
would I give up going to hear Catalini at the Opera
to-morrow evening, or Mrs. Siddons, in " The Game-
ster," on Saturday, that mother and sisters might take
my place.

Should our country be visited by an American war (which I fear is too probable), what a dreadful situation will you all be in! Do you think, if that is the case, I could bear to remain quiet in England? No, never! Though I don't boast of my untried courage, or of being a son of Mars, yet would it be my greatest pleasure to share the fate of my family. So that the little ones were secure, we would keep our rifles cocked and primed, mount guard together, share every fatigue, and play Brother Jonathan a few Canadian tricks. Now, I hear you say, " Oh, dear ; how brave Tom speaks, what a warlike humour he is in, since he is four thousand miles away." Well, never mind. Time brings about all things, and we shall yet " live upon the maskinonge and fatten on the musquash." I am very glad that General Brock has a notion of making York head-quarters for the grand army.

Yesterday morning I roused Henry Boulton out of bed, and breakfasted with him on rolls and radishes; he never drinks tea. You know he is a second time articled, and will not be out of his time until he is twenty-seven years of age. Think how old he will be when he commences business. Here he has to do more work in one day then he did in three at home. I dare say he will be a good chancery lawyer, a thing of little consequence in Canada until a court of that kind is established. The other day he paid £112 fees for being entered at Westminster and Lincoln's Inn. Mr. Firth is now practising in his native town o Norwich. The mayor and corporation must have been delighted at the return of so amiable a man. Mr. Boulton is still a prisoner at Verdun with poor John Small. They live together. Henry has seen a lady who met sometime ago his father, who was very well ; but Small fretted much, and looked wan and thin. I pity the poor fellow. The number of English gentlemen at Verdun has caused the living there to be very expensive. They have balls, feasts, horse-racing and hunting within their limits, building villas and laying out gardens, to the admiration of the French, who respect John Bull, above all other prisoners. Boulton is their English lawyer—gives advice and transacts business. I shall write again by the *Indian Queen.*

From Thomas G. Ridout to his Father in York :—

LONDON, *May 23rd*, 1812.

After seeing Mr. Adams, I called upon the Governor, who received me in his usual friendly manner. He had just received three letters from York, up to the 16th March—from Mr. Selby, Colonel Claus and Mr. Stanton—wherein they mention all were well, of course, including you ; that Parliament had been dissolved after a very disorderly meeting, in which the Opposition had carried everything before them, imprisoned Nicoll and memorialized the Prince Regent against the Chief. A few days before, the Governor had given me the York paper of the 12th February, containing General Brock's very warlike speech, and the answers of both Houses; in consequence whereof, and the threatening posture of the Americans, they had granted £5,000 towards training the militia of the Province. The Governor remarked they did not play the deuce so when he was with them. I also learn that the Indians are all on our side. He hinted that if there were war, George and I should have commissions—in the militia, I suppose. How dreadful, my dear Father, would your situation be, if our peaceful and delightful country should be visited by war, rendered more cruel by the Indians engaged on both sides. If you, mother and the children were at Quebec, I should not mind the Yankees.

Never has the British Government been in the situation it now is. Mr. Perceval dead, and all public offices in confusion, and the great men caballing one against the other. If they repeal the Orders in Council, the American trade will flourish beyond all former periods. They will then have the whole commerce of the continent in their hands, and the British, though blockading with powerful armaments the hostile ports of Europe, will behold fleets of American merchantmen enter in safety the harbours of the enemy, and carry on a brisk and lucrative trade, whilst the English, who command the ocean, and are sole masters of the deep, must quietly suffer two-thirds of their shipping to be dismantled and to lie snug and useless in little rivers or alongside huge, but empty warehouses. Their sailors, in order to earn a little salt junk and flinty biscuit, must spread themselves like vagabonds over the face of the earth, and enter the service of any nation. If, on the contrary, they continue to enforce their orders—trade will still remain in its present deplorable state. An American war will follow, and poor Canada will be obliged to bear the whole brunt of American vengeance. The Governor says that if that time should come, England will not forsake us. The veterans who fought at Talavera, Barossa and Badajos, will show the sons of Kentucky, the long-shanks of Connecticut and Genesee pumpkin-eaters, that it would be better for them to stay at home and eat mush and milk, than meet British troops of the present day.

I begin to think all this noise is nothing but a squall from the westward. If the present embargo continues any length of time, it will be of great benefit to Canada; not only by causing a large carrying and smuggling trade in the Provinces, and an outlet for the heavy stock of British manufacturers, which the Canadian merchants have on hand, but by raising to a very considerable price the produce of Canada in England and the West Indies.

The sales of potash, pearlash, timber, and peltry are now rather flat; but a brisk sale and great advance is shortly expected. Tobacco is upon the rise, there not being above 40,000 hogsheads now in London market. Flour sells almost at the price of life in England. Manchester, Birmingham, Nottingham, Sheffield, and several other places, have the appearance of garrisoned towns. When I was at St. Alban's, I saw two regiments of horse pass through that town on their way to quell the insurrections. The rioters are almost as daring as the Whiteboys of Ireland were. I do not wonder at the manufacturers becoming so desperate; most of them having been out of employment for the last six months. The introduction of machinery into the manufactories have caused many hands to be dismissed; against this they wreak their vengeance.

The Governor asked me to walk with him down to the Haymarket and conversed all the way. Among other things he said: "What do you think? That blackguard Joe Willcocks dined with General Brock and turned Government man for awhile, and then joined his own party again."

On Saturday morning, the 7th May, I set out for St. Alban's, accompanied by George as far as Highgate, where we saw the famous tunnel through the hill that had fallen in when the work was nearly completed.

The sun was hot, the roads very dusty, and what added to my discomfort were the trotters of many thousand sheep that I met coming from the north for the London market. On Monday, at seven, passed through Barnet and over Barnet Heath, where the great battle was fought between the houses of York and Lancaster, in which the Earl of Warwick lost his life.

I met with a most hearty welcome at St. Alban's; after breakfast we walked upon the Roman ramparts of ancient Verulam.

On Sunday, went to the Abbey church. How grand and venerable does that building appear.

Went on Monday, with Betsy, to Miss Kindar's house, and to see the beautiful Mrs. Storey. She took me like a show to the different families in St. Alban's, and introduced me to the old Countess Dowager Spencer, granddaughter of the great Duke of Marlborough, and mother to Lord Spencer, formerly First Lord of the Admiralty. The old lady spoke to me very politely of America, and asked if I knew Captain Vigareaux, of the engineers.*

I returned to London on Thursday.

No doubt Mr. Perceval's death will make some noise in America. I saw the assassin, Bellingham, executed at Newgate, on the morning of the 18th inst., and his body afterwards at the dissecting room, Bartholomew's Hospital. I am going with my uncle and G. to a grand rout this evening, at G. Ward's, known and described as Ann Ward's fashionable drum.

I am still at Hamilton's, getting brushed up in London business. I don't doubt but we shall have 1,000 sail at Quebec this year.

The cotton, woollen and iron trade never were so flat and dull as at present. Sugar rather brisk— Martinique, Guadaloupe and Trinidad sugars have lately been included and rated as British plantation, which, instead of paying thirty per cent. port duty, amounting to a prohibition, now pay twenty per cent. Nothing has been exported to the United States for this year past. Flour now would bring fifteen dollars per barrel, which could be sent from Lake Ontario to London for eleven dollars.

I am invited to Sir John Seabright's grand ball, to be given at St. Alban's. He is a member for Hereford.

* Afterwards distinguished in the war of 1812.

From T. G. Ridout to his Brother in York:—

LONDON, 1st *June*, 1812.

DIARY LETTER.

It is now the sixth month since you wrote me last by the *William* and *Indian Queen.* I hope you received the letters I wrote by them in April or May.

Trade has received a dreadful shock here from Bonaparte's edicts and the Non-Importation Act. However, the merchants have in part recovered, and begin again to look about them. The crash of ruin among the first traders in January, 1811, is passed by, and the great probability of a free trade in the Baltic this summer with Russia and Sweden, has occasioned some speculation in Colonial produce, and a briskness in the East India sales, with a slight rise of the stocks which are at present low.

I think we shall have a comfortable voyage out. As for being taken, there is little danger, so that we clear the chops of the channel, which now and then in foggy weather, is much infested by French privateers.

Monday, 18th May, 1812,—This morning Bellingham was executed at the debtor's door, Newgate.* From the leads of St. Sepulchre's, H. and I saw the execution much better than if we had been in the mob. He was a great, tall, raw-boned fellow, and dressed like a gentleman. He walked with a quick and firm step upon the platform. On his appearance, the immense mob, which extended from Fleet Street into Smithfield and the streets leading thereto, took their hats off and gave a great shout, crying out, "God bless you." Every precaution had been taken against a rescue. A circle of constables, six deep, was formed around the platform, within which the City Marshal and other officers rode. Two troops of horse were

* Spencer Perceval, Prime Minister of England, was assassinated on the 11th May, 1812. The people evidently attributed the distress in England to his administration, and therefore looked upon his assassin, Bellingham, as somewhat of a martyr.

stationed beyond Blackfriar's, and a squadron in Smithfield, so as to be in readiness in case of a disturbance. He (Bellingham) looked quickly round him, when two men pulled a muslin cap over his face, and tied his eyes round with his neckcloth. He prayed about a minute, and as St. Sepulchre's tolled eight, he sank down in the midst of the shouts of thousands and tens of thousands, who cried, "God bless you." Every man had his hat off. E. and I saw his body the next day in the dissecting room, Bartholomew's Hospital, stretched on a slab. We viewed him an instant with horror, then turned away.

Thursday, 21st.—The day of Ann Ward's rout. Everything was in the most fashionable and elegant style. At these routs one can walk, sit or stand, as he pleases; play cards or look on. There were ices, iced lemon and cream, and delicacies in abundance, handed about upon large silver salvers. The whole finished with a supper and some dances.

I am tired of these fashionable entertainments. I had rather be out spearing and hunting than partaking of Cockney amusements.

Sunday, 24th May.—Henry Boulton dined with us, and we all walked in Kensington Gardens till five. I can tell you Henry is quite a buck.

You are now preparing I suppose, for the 4th of June, which day is hardly thought of in London. How beautiful must the woods begin to be with you! As for these English trees, I hardly look on them as wood. They are so small and stunted, but the hedges and smooth fields make the country look very fine at this season.

Last night I went to the Lyceum theatre in the Strand. The play was "The Duenna," lecture upon heads by Palmer, and the "Honest Thieves," with which we were much entertained.

On Sunday last we went in a coach to Kensington Gardens. The day was fine, and the whole face of the gardens was covered with people, dressed in the most elegant manner. I never saw anything to equal it. They walked in crowds through the numerous lawns and avenues. I had old Mrs. Ward under my arm, and would not have exchanged her for any on the turf. People must have thought I was grappled with a Duchess. Her remarks on the different people were capital. It was what may be called a genteel mob, which extended for some miles round the park and gardens. The fineness of the day had induced London to send out all her gay sons and daughters to the promenade. I had the good luck to see the Princess Charlotte driving on the Royal course in an open chariot with one old lady. She is not handsome, nor tall, but looks a good deal like her father, and the old King. Her mother, the Princess of Wales, drove past a little while after in a coach and four. She is a great fat Dutchwoman.

From Thomas G. Ridout to his Brother in York :—

London, *6th June*, 1812.

I take this opportunity of answering your letter of the 9th March, which I received this morning. I am sure you will be glad at my return to America. If you are involved in a war with the Yankees (of which I now fear there are too many sad prospects), my reasons for returning will be tenfold increased. I think, at any rate, we shall have commissions in the Canadian corps now raising in the country. The preparations for war on both sides of the lakes must be very interesting to you, as well from the novelty of the thing, as from the active part we shall take in the contest. In what ruin and distress will our dear country be involved! In England they consider Canada as one of their finest colonies, and will defend it to the last. There will be plentiful supplies of troops and money sent out, and having the Indians as our allies, they think the Americans will not be able to hold the country. Two packets of letters, which I sent by the way of New York, I am afraid will never reach you. Governor Hull being at Detroit with eight thousand men ready to fall on our devoted country, alarms me, and we hear that thirteen thousand have been drafted from the militia, and ten thousand ordered to the back frontiers; that magazines are forming at Albany and up the Hudson. This forebodes war upon Canada. People here think the Americans are bent upon it, and that their demands will be so extravagant that the English would rather fight it out. I suppose our militia are by this time well trained, and Allan's* company one of the best in the Province.

To give you some idea of the great scale on which the English prepare for war, I wish you had been with me yesterday at Woolwich. On Saturday I received a note from Colonel Pilkington inviting me down, and offering to convey these letters and any packages to Upper Canada by a friend of his now going out to that Province.

Yesterday I went down in the stage, and was received in the most polite manner by the Colonel and his lady. He himself took me to the brass foundry, and there I saw the brass cannon run in clay moulds solid, then bored by boring machines. The outside turned and ornamented by chisels and finely polished. The trunnions are also done in a very curious manner, and lastly the King's arms and the year are engraved, when the piece is proved. If bad, it is melted down again. They save all the shavings.

The Warren, as this place is called, is enclosed by a wall a mile and a half in circuit, and is on what formerly was a marsh, now filled up and levelled with gravel, extending along the bank of the river. There are great storehouses and workshops dispersed along the wall, and the whole intermediate space between

*Hon. Wm. Allan.

9

that and the river (except where they are building a large square of storehouses) is one immense field of cannon, placed close to the ground, without their carriages, upon iron railways, and arranged in long rows side by side in the most beautiful order and exactness. There, at one view, you behold sixteen thousand pieces of iron ordnance. Some are of the most heavy metal, besides an immense number of brass pieces, which are kept separate, and are so bright you can see your face in them.

At the west end there are several hundred brass guns captured from enemies. Amongst them some beautiful Turkish ones, having the crescent marked upon them. They are very highly ornamented. Some are octagon on the outside; of seventeen or eighteen feet in length.

I saw the boys making cartridges—done in an instant. There is a machine by which they plane blocks of wood for the gun carriages of ships by means of a large horizontal wheel. Another place they turn iron axle-trees, like wood, making iron shavings.

There is also an immense number of howitzers and mortars, with their iron beds, to the left of the cannon, and four great pyramids of shells as large as iron pots. Dispersed among the guns are a great many pyramids of cannon ball, of different weight. They were loading some ships with guns, ammunition and ball. A cargo of copper had just arrived from Malta. Three hundred and fifty convicts were at work getting gravel out of the bed of the Thames, by a steam engine, and wheeling it about to fill up the marsh, and in building a beautiful stone quay the whole length of the arsenal upon the river. They were all chained by the leg and dressed in gray clothes. The buildings are of fine yellow brick and look very handsome. At twelve o'clock I saw several thousand workmen march out of the gate to dinner. At one they returned all in a body.

Colonel Pilkington wishes to go out to Canada. He says it is the finest country he ever saw.

At three the Colonel and I went to the grand artillery barracks, fronting a large common, at the upper part of which is the Royal Academy of Woolwich, situate under a rising ground. It is built in the form of a castle, with piazzas or cloisters between the wings and centre. The artillery barracks are 2,500 feet in length. Behind are three large squares, enclosed by the horse barracks and stables. There are 2,000 horses here. In front of the barracks is a double range of mounted brass guns; before the grand entrance, two beautiful pieces taken at Copenhagen. To the west was a great park, full of brass guns and ammunition and waggons, ready for service. In our walk we made the whole circuit of Woolwich and returned to dinner, after which we rode in a coach to Blackheath, and returned to the artillery parade, between the barracks and academy. Here I saw the finest set of men in England, consisting of 5,000 artillerymen and two bands of music. I saw the church at Blackheath where Mr. Perceval is buried, and the house of the Princess of Wales, in Greenwich Park.

. . . .

I rejoice to hear that, in York, you keep up to old times in price of living and that flour is so cheap. Here, wheat is 18 shillings a bushel. I dare say no more supplies will be sent out of Canada, as Government will buy all it can to form magazines in case of a war. On Monday, the 15th, I suppose the election takes place, we have here drank success to Squire Ridout.

From Thomas G. Ridout to his Father in York :—

LONDON, 10*th June*, 1812.

Your letters quite surprise us at the rapidity of their journey. That of the 24th March, containing your address, was received on the 6th inst. On Sunday, I was in Kensington Gardens from two till seven, and was amused beyond anything at the immense crowds. I saw the Princess Charlotte again. The Duchess of Sussex and Kent live at Kensington Palace. On the evening of the 4th June, the public offices, places of amusement, and the houses of the King's tradesmen, were illuminated with glass lamps.

The stocks are low. Insurance to Quebec, 8 guineas out, 10 home; if there is war will rise to 20 guineas. Freight out, from £2 10s. to £3 per ton; home, £7 to £8. Not one ship in seven can get any freight, so that they run in ballast. Potash and timber begin to rise. Canada white oak staves are considered better than American or Baltic, upon which last there is an enormous duty laid in favor of Canada. The smuggling between Heligoland and the continent is put an end to.

People are afraid that Canada will fall to the Americans. I am not quite of that opinion. The Prince Regent is considered half a fool. The great men of England are divided into many parties, and after Perceval's death, everything was in confusion, and the country was left without a government for a month.

York is yet, I hope, to be my place of residence. In the course of a few years it will be nearly as large as Montreal. I am glad that General Brock and you are such good friends. Governor Gore says it is a piece of folly to fortify the garrison, as it is no place of defence.

CHAPTER IX.

FIRST NOTES OF THE WAR, 1812.

AMONG the causes assigned by the American Government for declaring war against Great Britain were the " Orders in Council," and the " Right of Search." While the European war was raging, England's arch-enemy, Napoleon, had declared in his Berlin decree of 1806, all vessels liable to seizure that had touched at a British port. The English " Orders in Council," 1807, retaliated by declaring that only ships, which had touched at a British port should be permitted to enter a French port. Napoleon then declared the British Islands in a state of blockade, and interdicted all neutrals from trading with them. Great Britain retaliated by placing the French Empire in a state of blockade, and cut off from it the commerce of neutral nations.

This state of affairs pressed heavily on American commerce, as American merchantmen had, during the war in Europe, almost monopolized the carrying trade of the world. The orders were unpopular in England, as much distress had been caused by them. They were rescinded on the 23rd June, 1812, but their repeal had not the slightest effect in restoring tranquility. The Americans maintained that they had been repealed, not to render justice to the United States, but to rescue a large portion of the British population from starvation.

As to the other grievance, the "right of search," claimed and practised by Great Britain upon American vessels navigating the high seas, it was stated that England had impressed no less than 6,000 mariners who claimed to be citizens of the United States, and that 1,000 American vessels had been seized and confiscated.

England had experienced great difficulty in manning her immense navy, and claimed that these men were British subjects and deserters.

Whatever may have been the ostensible reasons of the Americans for declaring war, there is no doubt "a deadly hatred to England and a deadly love to France" was a potent one.

The Prince Regent in his address to Parliament, said that the real origin of the contest was the avowed sympathy of the Americans with the aggressive tyranny of France.

So war was declared against England by Congress, on the 18th June, 1812, by a vote of seventy-nine to forty-nine. Canada became the battle-field.

The population of Lower Canada was at that time 225,000; of Upper Canada, 75,000. The population of the United States was about 8,000,000.

Yet, with a frontier of more than a thousand miles to

defend, a gallant little band of regulars and militia held the enemy at bay for nearly three years.

At the opening of the war in July, 1812, the regular force in the Canadas consisted of seven regiments of infantry, one of veterans and invalids, and a detachment of artillery, amounting in all to about 4,500 men.

The enemy relied on the impossibility of Canada receiving aid from England, also on the supposed disaffection of the inhabitants.

How erroneous this latter supposition was, time soon proved.

A veteran soldier, Sir George Prevost, was now Governor-General of British North America, and Commander-in-Chief.

In Upper Canada, General Brock was acting Lieutenant-Governor, or President of the Council, during the absence in England of Mr. Francis Gore.

What he was to Canada at this crisis history has written in letters of gold. He believed in his Canadian citizen soldiers, and they did not show themselves unworthy of his trust.

In Upper Canada, the Militia Act provided that all from the age of eighteen to forty-five should turn out six days in each month for drill. It also provided that two flank companies should be formed from every battalion, which companies should be the first employed in actual service, and might be marched to any part of the Province, where the President of the Council thought their services would be most required.

In Lower Canada, it was enacted that every man between sixteen and fifty years of age was to be a militiaman, also the Government was authorized to call out "by ballot, or command, 2,000 bachelors between the ages of eighteen and thirty, and them to keep during ninety days under the command of such officers as they should appoint, and to march, train, and otherwise exercise them."

In case of war in the Province, they were to be kept in service during two years.

The embodied militia, as well as the volunteers, were to have the same pay and allowances as His Majesty's regular troops. No substitutes were allowed.

In a quaintly translated extract from the papers of that date, we read of the formation of the corps known as "The Voltigeurs," so celebrated during the war.

This corps, now under the command of Major de Salaberry, is completing with despatch worthy of the ancient warlike spirit of the country.

Captain Perrault's company was filled up in forty-eight hours, and the companies of Captains Duchesney, Panet and Ecuyer, have very near their complement.

The young men moved in solid columns towards the enlisting officers, with an expression of countenance not to be mistaken.

The Canadians are awakening from the repose of an age, secured to them by good government and virtuous habits.

Their anger is fresh, the object of their preparation simple and distinct.

They are to defend their king, known to them only by acts of kindness, and a native country long since made sacred by the exploits of their forefathers.

As to uniform, a letter from Æneas Shaw, Adjutant-General of Militia, dated York, 29th April, 1812, says :—

As it is not ascertained whether Government will provide clothing for the militia, His Honour the President (General Brock) recommends in the event of any portion of them being in the meantime called out into the field, that for their own convenience, as well as the benefit the service, each man, as far as his circumstances and situation allow, will provide himself with a short coat of some dark-colored cloth, made to button well round the body, and pantaloons suited to the season, with the addition of a round hat. It is also recommended to the officers, on every occasion when in the field, to dress in conformity to the men, in order to avoid the bad consequences of a conspicuous dress.

On the eve of the war this letter is written :—

From George Ridout to his brother Thomas in England :—

YORK, 25*th June*, 1812.

The pleasant news of your appointment, together with your entertaining account of your journey to Oxford, has made our house joyful; however, mixed with some alloy, when we consider the hazardous and immense voyage you have before you, and the risk you run of being made a prisoner by the French. The papers here are filled with accounts of daily captures.

As to the Americans disturbing us, we understand that the question for war has passed the Congress by a majority of sixteen. Preparations are making here to receive them. The flank companies are paraded every week, a fort is building here, preparations are made at Niagara, and some new vessels are on the lakes. All this will avail little unless we are supported by a regular force of ten thousand men, which number I am afraid it is impossible for the English to spare. I have the honor to be an ensign in a battalion company, viz.: the Town one. Colonel Chewett has given me to understand that in a short time I am to be promoted to a lieutenancy in the Grenadier company, which company is nearly of a size, tolerably well disciplined. Duncan Cameron is the captain.

There was an express sent to General Brock informing him that a body consisting of four thousand Indians are ready at a moment's warning to offer their services to the British.

The Americans have twelve hundred Kentucky men now at Detroit; a body of six hundred at Niagara; and indeed, both lakes on the south side are lined with them.

I know not whether father has told you that John is a midshipman on board the *Royal George*, on this lake.

Little John Radenhurst is here with a large detachment of the Newfoundland regiment, who are distributed on board the several vessels on the lakes as marines.

Among other news, I must not omit letting you know, that father is a Member of Parliament for the West Riding of the County of York and Simcoe. He was returned by a majority of a hundred and forty-two, against Sheppard, the only candidate who opposed him; as Hamilton, the morning of the election, resigned his interest in favor of Sheppard. His heart failed him when he saw father's friends to the number of one hundred and fifty turning Leach's corner, huzzaing, with flags flying. Only six of the old members are returned, consequently the remainder of the twenty-six are new. They will compose a very respectable House. John McDonell is one of them. He was returned for Glengarry. Our election here lasted three days. General Brock is much pleased with father's success. We had a famous electioneering dinner after the polls closed, consisting of most of the gentlemen in York.

The two last packets we have received from you appear to have been opened. I expect it has excited the curiosity of the American postmaster to see such large packets constantly passing in the same hand and addressed to one person.

June 27th, 1812.—Since I wrote, an express has come here announcing that war is declared. Every one is in motion. General Brock went off to Niagara last night, with despatches to the Indians, who are all in readiness. I do not know what we will do with our large family. The militia are ordered out. I must now go. Adieu!

The John McDonell mentioned in this letter, as the member returned for Glengarry, is the McDonell, General Brock's *aide-de-camp*, who so soon after this date was off to the war, and who met a hero's death on the Heights of Queenston.

The news of the declaration of war came to General Brock, we are told, by special express from New York, sent by John Jacob Astor to Thomas Clark, of Niagara Falls.

CHAPTER X.

OPENING OF FIRST CAMPAIGN, 1812—DETROIT.

THE American plan of attack was to invade Canada with three armies. The army of the West on the Detroit frontier, the army of the Centre on the Niagara, and the army of the North on Lake Champlain. The latter was under the immediate command of General Dearborn, Commander-in-Chief of the American forces.

At that time, as we have seen, Sir George Prevost was Commander-in-Chief of the British forces in Canada, with head-quarters at Montreal; and Major-General Brock was in command of the Upper Province, head-quarters at York, now Toronto.

The British Generals found themselves on the declaration of war, with but a few battalions of regular troops (less than five thousand men) at their command, with which to occupy and defend all the posts from Quebec to St. Joseph on Lake Huron. A part of a company was stationed at the latter place; two companies of the 41st regiment were at Fort Malden, near Amherstburg, and a battalion was divided between Fort Erie, Fort George and Burlington Heights—just sufficient to guard these places in times of peace.

When the storm of war broke on Canada, it was in

KINGSTON

INE

THE O

OS

NEW

ORDS.)

Upper Canada that the shock was first felt, and on General Brock was laid the responsibility of conducting the opening operations of the campaign. His first orders (26th June, 1812), were sent to Captain Roberts, then commanding the small detachment of regulars at St. Joseph, a military post, or rather block-house, on an island of that name in Lake Huron, forty miles north-east of Mackinaw. These orders were, to gather what men he could for the attack of Michillimackinac* an important island outpost of the Americans, commanding the entrance to Lake Michigan. This post, also known as Mackinaw, was then the centre of the fur trade with the Indians, and was guarded by a force of seventy-five men under Lieutenant Hancks, U. S. artillery. Captain Roberts enlisted in his service about one hundred and fifty voyageurs, armed with muskets and fowling pieces, and set out with these volunteers and his own small detachment of forty-six men, for the capture of the fort. They embarked on the 16th July in batteaux and canoes, and, under cover of the night silently approached the white cliffs of Mackinaw. The Americans were completely taken by surprise, and the officer in charge, not having received any instructions from head-quarters, thought his wisest course was to surrender. This event took place on the 17th July, 1812, and apparently unimportant as was the achievement, it had the effect of establishing confidence

* Old Fort Michillimackinac, so celebrated in Pontiac's wars as the scenes of dreadful massacres, was on the mainland near by.

throughout Canada, and of confirming the Indian tribes of the North-West in their allegiance to Great Britain.

Very shortly afterwards, two American vessels laden with furs, came into the harbour, ignorant of the capture of the fort, and were taken possession of, though subsequently restored to their owners by Major-General de Rottenberg.

There is no doubt that the alliance with the Indians was an important factor in the struggle with the Americans. They fought in this war of 1812, not for love of King George, but because they hoped to receive from his hands the justice they had sought in vain from the Americans. It was the last throb of national life in their now degenerate race.

One leader they had, Tecumseh, who recalled to their memories their famous chief of fifty years before, Pontiac, whose name had been a terror in the West. Tecumseh was, at this time, forty-three years of age. He was considered by the Indians, as was also his twin brother—the Prophet—to be of supernatural birth. His influence was enormous, not only among his own people, the Shawanese, but throughout the tribes of the West. His mission was to bring into a confederation or league, all the tribes of North America, in order to regain, if possible, their old boundaries, and to resist the further encroachments of the white race.

The personal appearance of Tecumseh is thus described :—

His height was about five feet nine inches, his face oval, his nose handsome and straight, his mouth beautifully formed, like that of Napoleon I. His eyes clear, transparent hazel, with a mild, pleasant expression when in repose, but when excited, they appeared like balls of fire. His complexion more of a light brown or tan, than red ; (his whole tribe, as well as their kindred, the Ottaways, had light complexions). His limbs were straight, he always stood very erect, and walked with a brisk, elastic, vigorous step. He invariably dressed in Indian tanned buckskin. A perfectly well-fitting hunting frock, descending to the knee, was over underclothes of the same material ; the usual cape and finish of leather fringe about the neck, edges of the front and bottom of the frock ; a belt of the same material, in which were his side-arms (a silver mounted tomahawk and a knife in a strong leather case), short pantaloons, connected with neatly fitting leggings and moccasins, with a mantle also of buckskin, thrown over his left shoulder, used as a blanket in camp and a protection in storms. Such was his dress when I last saw him on the 17th August, 1812, in Detroit. (See Colonel Hatch's Chapter of the War.)

It is stated that, though Tecumseh could speak English sufficiently well to hold conversation on ordinary topics, he never spoke any language but his own at any council, nor when in presence of any officer or agent of a government. He always avoided speaking to any official, except through an interpreter, as his ideas of the honour of his people and race precluded official intercourse in any but the Shawanese tongue. This, then, was the powerful ally destined to take such an important part in the coming war with the Americans.

On the 12th July, 1812, General Hull crossed to Canada from Detroit, and issued his boastful proclamation to the people of Canada, offering the alternative of peace, liberty and security; or war, slavery and destruction. From Fort George, General Brock issued a counter-proclamation, and despatched Colonel Proctor, of the 41st regiment, with a small body of troops to reinforce Fort Malden, near Amhertsberg. Here Proctor was joined by Tecumseh and his Indians. General Hull made his head-quarters at Sandwich, eighteen miles from Amhertsberg, in an unfinished house belonging to Colonel Baby, and remained there with his army for about four weeks. Predatory excursions were made by his troops in the neighbouring country; but in spite of his proclamation, the people did not show the slightest desire to be annexed. Numerous skirmishes took place with Proctor's forces at the river Canard, and with the Indians under Tecumseh. On the 5th August, the latter, with a few regulars, crossed the Detroit River, and succeeded in capturing a convoy of provisions from Ohio, also a detatchment on their way from Detroit with General Hull's despatches.

At the time of the war of 1812, only the Eastern and Southern parts of Ohio were settled. With the exception of a few old French posts, it was an unbroken wilderness, an untouched forest, occupied by powerful Indian tribes.

A succession of reverses seemed to have disheartened General Hull, who had a wholesome dread of Indian warfare, and he decided to recross the river to Detroit. This he did on the 8th of August, and once more took up his abode in the citadel. This citadel was an enclosure of about two acres, surrounded by sixteen-foot pickets of squared cedar, within which were the officers' quarters, public stores, and other buildings.

The intelligence of the capture of Fort Michillimackinac was the means of largely augmenting Tecumseh's forces, for, as soon as he heard of its downfall, he despatched runners to all his associate tribes, bidding them assemble at Malden immediately, and telling them that the Americans, by not marching on Malden, and by the easy discomfiture of several detachments, had shown they would not fight; that the braves should come forward with all speed, so as to participate in the capture of the army and share in the plunder, which would be great.

His appeal was promptly responded to, and by the 15th August, 700 warriors had joined him.

While these events were happening on the western frontier, an extra session of the Legislature had been called at York on the 29th July, by General Brock, whose speech rang out in these clear and earnest words :—

10

GENTLEMEN OF THE HOUSE OF ASSEMBLY, — We are engaged in an awful and eventful contest. By unanimity and despatch in our councils, and vigour in our operations, we may teach the enemy this lesson, that a country defended by freemen enthusiastically devoted to the cause of their King and constitution, can never be conquered.

The answer by the Legislature, signed Thos. Scott, Speaker, 29th July, 1812, was as follows :—

When invaded by an enemy whose avowed object is the entire conquest of this Province, we, laying aside all inferior considerations, do most willingly obey your Honour's commands, by appearing in our Legislative capacity, for the purpose of using our utmost efforts for the protection and defence of everything that is dear to us as subjects and as men.

The Assembly was prorogued as soon as it had passed the necessary Supply Bill, and most of the members took the field for active service.

General Brock now determined to strike a decisive blow, and formed the daring plan of proceeding at once, with what troops he could raise, to the western frontier.

He knew that the Fort of Detroit was a most important position from which to control Upper Canada, and determined to wrest it, if possible, from the Americans. He had about forty men of the 41st regiment with him, detached from the little garrison at Fort George, and 250 militia. Among these were many of the young men of York, who had volunteered for the expedition.

One of General Brock's *aides-de-camp* was John McDonell, the newly-elected member for Glengarry, and Acting Attorney-General for the Province. He was then in his twenty-fifth year. The other *aide* was Major Glegg, of the 41st regiment.

Among the volunteers is found a name well known afterwards in Canada—John Beverley Robinson, then a student in McDonell's office.

It was a hazardous enterprise which this little army undertook; but Brock was a leader whom they were all willing to follow, and the courage and confidence with which he inspired his men, lived long after his brave spirit had passed away.

On the 5th of August, 1812, the expedition set out by way of Lake Ontario to Burlington. They then marched by cross-roads to Long Point, where they arrived on the 8th, and then continued their journey in open boats along the rough and dangerous coast of Lake Erie. After four days' and nights' hard rowing, they reached their destination at Amherstburg, on the 12th August, 1812. Here Brock and Tecumseh, the most picturesque figures of the war, met; and a halo of romance still lingers over the meeting of these two men, whose names were destined to be handed down in song and story. (In some respects, the soldier and the savage were kindred spirits. Both were bold in purpose, ready in resource, trusted by their followers. Over each hung the shadow of an early heroic death.

Brock now found himself at the head of an army of

one thousand four hundred men, half of whom were Indians. After a brief consultation with Tecumseh, who, we are told, sketched a plan of Detroit on a piece of birch bark for his guidance, he determined, in spite of the disparity of numbers between his forces and those of the Americans, to demand a surrender. He had by this time, 15th August, established himself at Sandwich, opposite Detroit, in the quarters at the Baby mansion, so lately vacated by General Hull.

From there he wrote his demand for surrender, and sent this missive to General Hull by Major Glegg, and Lieutenant-Colonel McDonell.

HEAD-QUARTERS, SANDWICH,
August 15th, 1812.

SIR,—The forces at my disposal authorize me to require of you the immediate surrender of Fort Detroit. It is far from my inclination to join in a war of extermination; but you must be aware that the numerous body of Indians, who have attached themselves to my troops, will be beyond my control the moment the contest commences.

ISAAC BROCK,
Major-General.

His Excellency Brig.-Gen. Hull.
Commanding at Fort Detroit.

General Hull's answer was :—

I have no other reply to make, than to inform you that I am prepared to meet any force which may be at your disposal, and any consequences which may result from any exertion of it you may think proper to make.

General Brock, on receiving this reply, determined to attempt the capture of the fort by assault. His force consisted of thirty Royal Artillery, two hundred and fifty of the 41st regiment, fifty Royal Newfoundland, four hundred militia, and about seven hundred Indians. For artillery, he had three six-pounders and two three-pounders. Two English gunboats were on the Detroit river. One, the *Queen Charlotte*, Captain Finnis, a sloop of war, armed with eighteen twenty-four-pounders; the other, the brig *Hunter*.

On the Canadian side of the river was a battery, under the command of Captain Dixon. This opened fire on the evening of the 15th August, and continued the cannonade on the morning of the 16th, when one of the balls struck and killed Lieutenant Hancks, who had been in command at Mackinac, and was then a prisoner of war on parole in Fort Detroit. The same ball passed on and mortally wounded Surgeon Reynolds, of the Ohio Volunteers.

Early on the morning of the 16th August, General Brock crossed the River Detroit, at Sandwich, where it is about three-quarters of a mile wide, and landed at Spring Wells, about two miles below the fort; formed in column, and marched up to within a mile of the fort and halted. His Indian allies, led by Tecumseh, had landed two miles below on the previous evening, and moved up to the edge of the woods, keeping a mile and a half distant, to the west of the main body.

With his small force and only five guns, it certainly looked a very daring deed for Brock to attack a strong fort defended by twenty-six pieces of ordnance of large calibre, with one thousand nine hundred and forty men posted in and around the fort, and three hundred and sixty men of another detachment, who had left a day or two previous on a short expedition, and were now on their way back.

The following description of Fort Detroit, in 1812, is given by Colonel Hatch, American Quarter-master at the time of its capture :

It is a parallelogram, with strong bastions at each angle, surrounded by a moat or ditch twelve feet wide at the surface, eight feet deep; a palisade or abattis of hardwood stakes, ten feet high out of the ground, sharpened at the top, and firmly set in the escarp at the base of the rampart, with an inclination of about forty-five degrees; the rampart rising perpendicularly twenty-two feet, pierced with embrasures for cannon; strong double entrance gate, with portcullis well ironed, on the east front, protected by a projecting frame-work of hewed logs extending over the moat, pierced for small arms, and a drawbridge; sally ports near the south-west and north-west bastions; a parapet, banquette and terreplein, around the entire of the inside, in the bastions as well as the body, on the latter of which are mounted twelve-pound and nine-pound guns, besides those of smaller calibre and also the howitzers, each bastion having guns raking the moat and counterscarp. Standing on the banquette near the flag-staff at the south-eastern angle of the body of the work, and looking southward, no house or building intervenes. All to the south for two miles, and all to the west for one to one and a half miles, is a level common.

The road from Spring Wells passes up across the ground between the fort and the river. A few village dwellings are on the river side of this road, and a few farm-houses on the west side. Fronting this road are posted the twenty-four-pound field guns, two twelve-pound iron, and two six-pound brass guns. In front of the southern curtain, fifty feet in advance of the counterscarp, is one six-pounder; at the south-west angle is one nine-pounder and one six-pounder; in front of the western or rear curtain is one six-pounder; at the north-west angle, one nine-pounder and one four-pounder, with arrangements to rapidly concentrate at any point at which the enemy might show itself. In May's orchard on the west is posted the 1st regiment Ohio Volunteers; next to them, extending to the centre of the west curtain, is the 2nd regiment; and then the 3rd regiment, which covers the north-west bastion and waggon train; while, in the fort, is the entire of the 4th United States regiment and a part of the artillery companies. All these guns were loaded with ball and grape. All these troops were well armed.

Scarcely had the assault begun by the firing of the battery on the Canadian side, when, to the surprise, as much, it is said, of the Americans, as of the Canadians, a flag of truce was displayed, and a messenger was seen approaching.

General Hull had decided to capitulate.

By the terms of capitulation, signed 16th August, 1812, the whole territory of Michigan was ceded to the British, two thousand five hundred American troops became prisoners of war; thirty-seven pieces of brass and iron ordnance, four hundred rounds of twenty-four-pound shot, one hundred thousand cartridges and two thousand five hundred stand of arms fell into General Brock's hands.—(Colonel Cass's report to the American Secretary of War.)

This was indeed a sorry ending for the army of the West, whose General, but a few weeks before, had boastfully declared his intention of annexing Canada to the United States.

On the morning of the 17th, the victory was celebrated by firing a salute from the Esplanade, in front of the fort, General Brock, with his suite, appearing in full dress to receive the spoils they had so bravely won.

The cannon used on this occasion was one of the brass six-pounders taken by the Americans at the battle of Saratoga on the 16th October, 1777, which fact was recorded on the cannon in raised letters of brass.

The salute was returned from the guns of the *Queen Charlotte.* *

Colonel Hatch, in his quaint little book, gives a description of Brock as he saw him that day:—

His personal appearance was commanding. He must have been six feet three in height, very massive and large-boned, and apparently of immense muscular

---

* The much-regretted brass field-piece came again under the folds of the stars and stripes at the battle of the Thames, and the *Queen Charlotte,* which looked like a thing of life as she sailed up the stream with her flags and streamers flaunting, fell from her high estate of that day of triumph, and ended her career of honour in that great struggle on Lake Erie, on the 10th September, 1813, when her flag descended upon a bloody wave. (Hatch.)

strength. His *aides*, McDonell and Glegg, were elegant young men, nearly, if not quite six feet in height, and in their splendid uniform, all three presented a brilliant appearance.

We can well believe the scene was an impressive one, as the victorious commander stood with his troops in the blaze of the August sunshine, while the conquered foes laid their arms down in sullen silence at his feet.*

Beside him stood Tecumseh with his swarthy band of braves, who probably were a little disappointed at the bloodless nature of the victory.

General Brock lost no time in making preparations to return. He dismissed the militia of Michigan to their homes, placed the volunteers on parole, and sent General Hull† with a thousand of his regular troops

* Copy of returns made by one of General Hull's *aides* and the British Quarter-master.

One thousand nine hundred muskets and accoutrements stacked by the effective men of the 4th United States regiment and the Ohio Volunteers upon the Esplanade, as they marched from their positions in and around the fort ; seven hundred muskets and accoutrements brought by the militia of Michigan, and stacked upon the Esplanade; four hundred and fifty muskets and accoutrements brought in by the detachment and the corps of teamsters, and stacked in front of the citadel.

† One cannot but have a feeling of pity for the conquered general, who was a veteran of the Revolutionary war. On his arrival at Montreal he was treated with great consideration by Sir George Prevost, and released at once on parole, only, however, to find a more cruel reception at the hands of his own countrymen. He was tried by court-martial, for the shameful capitulation, as it was called, found guilty, and sentenced to death. His reasons for surrender, he said in his defence, were, that he had not provsions enough to maintain the siege, the expected reinforcements of the enemy, and the savage ferocity of the Indians. His sentence of death was remitt d on account of past services, but his name was struck off the army list, and the Republican hero was left in his old age a disgraced and broken-hearted man.

in boats to Fort Erie, thence to Montreal, as prisoners of war.

Leaving Colonel Proctor in command at Detroit, General Brock set out on his homeward journey on the 18th August, and sailed down the lake to Fort Erie in the *Queen Charlotte.*

He arrived at York on the 22nd August, where, we read, he was received in triumph. Addresses of welcome were heaped upon him, to which he replied with characteristic simplicity. Quebec was illuminated in his honour.

He gave full credit to the conduct of his " homespun warriors," as the following answer to the address presented to him at Kingston shows :—

4th September, 1812.

Nothing but the confidence which the admirable conduct of the York and Lincoln regiments of militia excited, could have induced me to undertake an expedition such as lately terminated so much to the advantage of the country.

I have reason, from the reports made to me by the officers stationed at Kingston, to rely with equal confidence on the discipline and gallantry of the militia in this district. It is with the highest satisfaction I understand that, in the midst of unavoidable privations and fatigue, they bear in mind that the cause in which they are engaged involves their dearest interests, and the happiness of their families.

Fêtes and congratulations were not, however, suited to Brock's vigorous spirit, and he chafed under the delay occasioned by the unfortunate armistice, con-

OPENING OF FIRST CAMPAIGN, 1812—DETROIT. 147

cluded by General Prevost, on the 4th August, whereby hostilities were stopped for a time on the Niagara and Champlain frontiers. The effect of this armistice was to give the Americans time to reinforce their armies, and to strengthen themselves on the lakes.

A naval success on the Atlantic on the 19th August, when H.M.S. *Guerriere* was taken by the *Constitution*, had gone far to console the Americans for their discomfiture at Detroit, and they were now hopefully preparing for another invasion on the Niagara frontier, where Major-General Van Rensselaer had assembled an army of about six thousand men, and had established a camp at Lewiston.

On the 30th August, General Dearborn's *aide-de-camp* arrived at Montreal, with despatches to Sir George Prevost, announcing that the President of the United States had not thought proper to authorize a continuance of the provisional measure entered into by His Excellency and General Dearborn through the Adjutant-General, Colonel Baynes; consequently the armistice was to cease in four days from the time of the communication reaching Montreal, and the ports of Kingston and Fort George.

The following significant paragraph appears in an extract from a Kingston paper :—

This morning (5th September, 1812), at one o'clock, His Honour the President (Brock) left town, it is supposed for Niagara, in consequence of hostilities being renewed.

CHAPTER XI.

QUEENSTON HEIGHTS, 1812.

ONE disastrous effect of the armistice that had just ended, was, that while it lasted the Americans had secured the unrestricted navigation of Lake Ontario; and this was of the utmost importance to them, as the supplies for their army, ordnance, etc., collected at Oswego, could only be taken to Niagara by water, the roads being in such a wretched condition.

On the 26th September, General Dearborn wrote to General Van Rensselaer, "At all events we must calculate on possessing Upper Canada before the winter sets in."

General Brock had only at his disposal for the defence of the Niagara frontier a force of about fifteen hundred men, of which a large proportion were militia and Indians.

The Indians were under John Brant, a son of the celebrated chief Thayendanegea. Small garrisons held Forts Erie and Chippewa, composed of some of the 41st, and the flank companies of the 2nd Lincoln militia. A considerable number of militia were at Queenston, and posted along the line of the river to watch the movements of the enemy.

From Fort George, the head-quarters of General
Brock, to Queenston, at every mile batteries were
thrown up, the principal ones being a redan battery on
Queenston Heights, and a strongly mounted battery
on Vrooman's Point, which commanded the Lewiston
and Queenston landings.

Among the militia posted in and near Fort George,
were the flank companies of the 1st regiment of Lincoln militia, under Captains Crooks and McEwen;
the flank companies of the 4th Lincoln militia, under
Captains Nelles and W. Crooks; Captains Hall's, Dur-
and's and Applegarth's companies of the 5th Lincoln
militia; Major Merritt's yeomanry corps, and a body
of Swayzes' militia artillery, under Captains Powell
and Cameron.

One corps of York militia was specially favoured by
General Brock. It was composed of young men,
sons of the earliest residents of York; and the names
on its honour roll are still familiar in many a household of the good city of Toronto. The right flank
Grenadier company was officered by Captain Duncan
Cameron; senior lieutenant, William Jarvis; junior
lieutenant, Archie McLean; third lieutenant, George
Ridout. The light company was commanded by Captain Stephen Heward. His three lieutenants were
John Beverley Robinson, S. P. Jarvis, Robert Stanton. Most of them were school-fellows, brought up
under the rule of Dr. Strachan at Cornwall.

It was early in the morning of the 13th October,

1812, that the American Army began crossing the river below the Queenston Heights. The story of that eventful day is told so well by one who took part in the fight, that his letter is given in full. One more glimpse we have in it of the heroic Brock, as he rides to his death on that gray October morning, waving his hand in passing by to his gallant lads from York, and bidding them press on.

Letter from one of the York militia present at the battle of Queenston, giving an account of the day:—

BROWN'S POINT, *October 14th*, 1812.

About half an hour before daylight yesterday morning, Tuesday, the 13th October, being stationed at one of the batteries between Fort George and Queenston, I heard a heavy cannonading from Fort Grey, situate on the height of the Mountain, on the American side, and commanding the town of Queenston.

The lines had been watched with all the care and attention which the extent of our force rendered possible, and such was the fatigue which our men underwent from want of rest and exposure to the inclement weather which had just preceded, that they welcomed with joy the prospect of a field which they thought would be decisive. Their spirits were high, and their confidence in the General unbounded.

From our battery at Brown's Point, about two miles from Queenston, we had the whole scene most completely in our view.

Day was just glimmering.

The cannon from both sides of the river roared incessantly.

Queenston was illuminated by the continual discharge of small arms.

This last circumstance convinced us that some of

the enemy had landed, and in a few moments, as the day advanced and objects became more visible, we saw a number of Americans in boats attempting to land upon our shore, amidst a tremendous shower of shot of all description, which was skilfully and incessantly levelled at them.

No orders had been given to Captain Cameron, who commanded our detachment of York Militia, what conduct to pursue in case of an attack at Queenston; and as it had been suggested to him that in the event of a landing being attempted there, the enemy would probably endeavour, by various attacks, to distract our force, he hesitated at first as to the propriety of withdrawing his men from the station assigned them to defend.

He soon saw, however, that every exertion was required in aid of the troops engaged above us, and without further delay, marched us to the scene of action. On our road, General Brock passed us. He had galloped from Niagara, unaccompanied by his *aide-de-camp*, or a single attendant.

He waved his hand to us, desired us to follow with expedition, and proceeded with all speed to the Mountain. Lieutenant-Colonel McDonell and Captain Glegg passed immediately after. At the time the enemy began to cross, there were but two companies of the 49th regiment, the Grenadiers and the Light Company, and I believe three small companies of militia, to oppose them.

Their reception was such as did honour to the courage and management of our troops.

The grape shot and musket balls poured upon them at close quarters, as they approached the shore, and made incredible havoc.

A single discharge of grape from a brass six-pounder, directed by Captain Dennis, of the 49th Grenadiers, destroyed fifteen in a boat.

Three of the bateaux landed at the hollow below

Mr. Hamilton's garden, in Queenston, and were met by a party of militia and a few regulars, who slaughtered almost the whole of them, taking the rest prisoners.

Several other boats were so shattered and disabled that the men in them threw down their arms and came on shore, merely to deliver themselves up prisoners of war.

Thus far things had proceeded successfully, and the General on his approach to the Mountain was greeted with the intelligence that all our villainous aggressors were destroyed or taken.

As we advanced with our company we met troops of Americans on their way to Fort George, under guard, and the road was lined with miserable wretches suffering under wounds of all descriptions, and crawling to our houses for protection and comfort. The spectacle struck us, who were unused to such scenes, with horror; but we hurried to the Mountain, impressed with the idea that the enemy's attempt was already frustrated, and the business of the day nearly completed.

Another brigade of four boats was just then crossing, and the 49th Light Company, who had been stationed on the Mountain, were ordered down to assist in preventing their landing. No sooner had they descended than the enemy appeared in force above them. They had probably landed before the rest, while it was yet dark, and remained concealed by the rough crags of the Mountain.

They possessed themselves of our battery on the height.

General Brock rushed up the Mountain on foot, with some troops, to dislodge them, but they were so advantageously posted and kept up so tremendous a fire that the small number ascending were driven back.

The General then rallied, and was proceeding up the right of the Mountain to attack them in flank, when he received a ball in his breast. Several of the 49th assembled round him.   One poor fellow was severely wounded by a cannon ball and fell across the General.

They succeeded, however, in conveying his body to Queenston.

We were halted a few moments in Mr. Hamilton's garden, where we were exposed to the shot from the American battery at Fort Grey, and from several field-pieces directly opposite to us, besides an incessant and disorderly fire of musketry from the sides of the Mountain.

In a few minutes, we were ordered to advance on the Mountain. The nature of the ground and the galling fire prevented any kind of order in ascending. We soon scrambled to the top, at the right of the battery, which they had gained, and were in some measure covered by the woods. There we stood and gathered the men as they advanced, and formed them in a line.

The fire was too hot to admit of delay. Scarcely more than fifty collected, about thirty of whom were of our company, headed by Captain Cameron, and the remainder of the 49th Light Company, commanded by Captain Williams.

Lieutenant-Colonel McDonell was there mounted, and animating the men to charge. He was seconded with great spirit and valour by Captain Williams, who exclaimed, " Feel firmly to the right, my lads, advance steadily, charge them home, and they cannot stand you."

But the attempt was unsuccessful.

The enemy were just in front covered by bushes and logs. They were in no kind of order, and were three or four hundred in number. They perceived us forming, and, at about thirty yards distance, fired. Lieutenant-Colonel McDonell who was on the left of our party, most heroically calling upon us to advance, received a shot in his body and fell. His horse was at the same instant killed.

11

Captain Williams, who was at the other extremity of our little band, fell the next moment apparently dead.

The remainder of our men advanced a few paces, discharged their pieces, and retired down the Mountain.

Lieutenant McLean was wounded in the thigh, and Captain Cameron, in his attempt to save Colonel McDonell, exposed himself to a shower of musketry, which he most miraculously escaped.

He succeeded in bearing off his friend, and Captain Williams recovered from the momentary effect of the wound in his head, in time to escape down the mountain. This happened, I think, about 10 a.m.

Our forces rallied about a mile below.

General Sheaffe, with the 41st from Fort George, nearly three hundred in number, came up soon after with the field-pieces of the Car Brigade.*

All the force that could be collected was now mustered, and marched through the fields back of Queenston, ascended the Mountain on the right, and remained in the woods in rear of the enemy till intelligence was gained of their position. During this time, the Americans were landing fresh troops unmolested, and carrying back their dead and wounded in their return boats.

About three o'clock p.m. General Sheaffe advanced through the woods, towards the battery on the Mountain, with the main body, composed of the 41st and the Niagara militia flank companies (with field-pieces) on the right. The Mohawk Indians, under Captain Norton, and a Niagara company of Blacks, proceeded along the brow of the mountain on the left, and the Light company of the 49th, with our company of

---

* The "Car Brigade" referred to was a volunteer company of farmers' sons, who had offered their services to Brock, together with their draught horses, free of expense, on the eve of the war. He had accepted their patriotic proposal, and, by 3rd July, 1812, this brigade was completed, and fully equipped, under Captain Holcroft, of the Royal Artillery.

militia broke through the centre. In this manner we rushed through the woods to the encamping ground on the Mountain which the enemy then occupied, and which had been the scene of their morning's success. The Indians were first in advance. As soon as they perceived the enemy they uttered their terrific war-whoop, and rushing rapidly upon them, commenced a most destructive fire. Our troops instantly sprung forward from all quarters, joining in the shout. The Americans gave a volley, then retreated tumultuously, and fled by hundreds down the Mountain. At that moment Captain Bullock and one hundred and fifty of the 41st, and two flank companies of militia appeared advancing on the road from Chippewa. The consternation of the enemy was complete. Though double in number, they stopped not to withstand their pursuers, but fled with the utmost precipitation. Never were men more miserably situated. They had no place to retreat to, and were driven by a furious and avenging enemy, from whom they had little mercy to expect, to the brink of the Mountain which overhangs the river. They fell in numbers—the river presented a shocking spectacle, filled with poor wretches, who plunged into the stream from the impulse of fear, with scarcely the prospect of being saved. Many leaped down the side of the Mountain to avoid the horrors which pressed on them, and were dashed to pieces by the fall. The fire from the American batteries ceased.

Two officers were now seen coming up the hill with a white flag, and with some difficulty the slaughter was suspended. They were conducted up the Mountain to General Sheaffe. A cessation of hostilities for three days was asked for, and assented to. Thus, about four p.m., ended the business of this day, so important to the inhabitants of this Province. The invasion of our peaceful shores by its unprincipled neighbours, has terminated in the entire loss of their army, with everything brought over, not excepting their standards, with the very modest device of the Eagle perched upon the globe.

We have taken over nine hundred prisoners, with sixty of their officers. Except the wounded men, who were carried over in their boats, while they retained possession of the Mountain, scarcely a man has straggled back to relate to his country the disastrous event of an expedition planned by their unrighteous government.

The view of dead bodies which strewed the ground, and the mangled carcases of poor suffering mortals, who filled every room in the village, filled us with compassion.

Still have we much to sorrow for, we have a loss to deplore which the most brilliant success cannot atone for. That general, who led our army to victory, whose soul was wrapped up in our prosperity, is now shrouded in death.

Lieutenant-Colonel McDonell, too! . This heroic young man, the constant attendant of the General, after his fall, strove to support to the last a cause never to be despaired of, because it involved the very salvation of his country.

But he was not destined to witness its triumph. His career was short but honourable; his end was premature, but full of glory.

He will be buried at the same time with the General.

It was, indeed, a baptism of blood for our young soldiers, though all too soon they became accustomed to the horrors of war.

Archie McLean, who was wounded in this battle, and to whom McDonell's last pathetic cry of "Archie, help me!" had been addressed, was afterwards taken prisoner at Lundy's Lane, but lived to become Chief Justice of Upper Canada.

Among the officers of the militia mentioned in General Sheaffe's report as having signalized themselves for the gallant and steady manner in which they led the troops under their command, were Lieutenant-Colonels Butler and Clark; Captains Hatt, Durand, Rowe, Applegarth, James Crooks, Cooper, R. Hamilton, McEwen and Duncan Cameron; Lieutenant Butler, Lincoln militia, and Lieutenant Richardson, York militia.

While the action at Queenston was going on, the guns at Fort George had been bombarding Niagara, and had silenced that Fort. The firing was ably directed by Colonel Claus and Brigade-Major Evans, and the guns were under the immediate direction of Captains Powell and Cameron, of the Militia Artillery.

It is difficult to understand how the Americans dare to claim even a partial victory at Queenston, in the face of the following despatch sent from Major-General Van Rensselaer to Major-General Dearborn, the American Commander-in-Chief:

"14th October, 1812.

"Wadsworth surrendered with all his forces, nine hundred men."

General Sheaffe's prisoners amounted to more than his army, not counting the Indians engaged.

The following letter gives a short account of what followed the battle, and of the burial of General Brock.

From Lieutenant G. Ridout to his Brother in York:—

BROWN'S POINT, 21*st October,* 1812.

As I have already given father a short account of the transactions of the 13th inst., I think it unnecessary to repeat it, as you have, of course, been made acquainted with the contents of my letter of that date. Were it not for the death of General Brock and McDonell, our victory would have been glorious, and really a matter of triumph ; but losing in one man, not only the President of the Province, but our ablest general, is an irreparable loss under the existing circumstances at a time when his moderation and impartiality had united all parties in pronouncing him the only man worthy of being at the head of affairs. One field-piece, one stand of colours, one ammunition waggon, 1,200 stand of arms, besides those seized by the Indians and militia, amounting to at least 400 more, together with 1,000 prisoners, were the fruits of that day's success.

As Congress meets in November, no doubt that Van Rensselaer, the American general, had been urged to make an attack by Madison, so that the latter might make a favourable report of the game at Washington. General Smyth, the Democrat, has now the chief command. He asserts that he is determined to conquer Canada, even if he loses a hundred thousand men. Such gasconading is not to frighten us, as it is well known that the American Government is not able to feed, clothe and equip so great a force. About an hour since, two men marched down to Niagara, under a guard. They crossed the river above Fort Erie. So they say. They state that the American force is about 12,000, that the greater part of that army is stationed at Lewiston, a village opposite Queenston, that the Americans intend making three attacks at different places, that they are determined to have the command of the lakes, and for that purpose have nearly

400 men on the two lakes, constructing gun-boats, and refitting merchant vessels.   All this may be a trick of the Yankees to engage our attention to the fortifying of Queenston, while in reality they may be concerting measures for crossing at Chippewa, or above that place. The latter, I think, is the case, as large bodies of the enemy have been seen moving up from Niagara in that direction.

I do not think the time is far distant when another attack is to be made.   With another regiment, I have no doubt that the country would be perfectly safe from all attempts they might make to subdue us. General Brock and McDonell were buried on the 17th, in one of the batteries of the garrison, called the York battery, as our men were employed in constructing it. It was his desire to be buried in it, showing even to the last a preference to everything belonging to the name of York.

The burial was the grandest and most solemn I ever witnessed, or that has been seen in Upper Canada.   I was one of poor McDonell's pall bearers.   The coffins were preceded first by a company of regulars, then a band of music, then the corpses, followed by another body of regulars and militia.   The whole distance between the Government House and Garrison, where they were interred, was lined by a double row of militia and Indians, resting on their arms reversed. Minute guns fired during the whole procession.*   Mr. Addison read the service in a very impressive manner.

The American prisoners, officers and men, are the most savage looking fellows I ever saw.   To strike a greater terror in their enemies they had allowed their beards on their upper lips to grow.   This, however, had no other effect upon us than to raise sensations of disgust.   I was over yesterday with a flag to the

* Minute guns were also fired by the Americans at Fort Niagara and at Lewiston, as a mark of respect to a brave enemy, by command of Major-General Van Rensselaer. (Lossing).

American garrison, and witnessed the destruction made by our cannon. Every building is completely riddled, but owing to the want of furnaces on our side, we were unable to fire their garrison.

This is a letter of military occurrences.

That the day is not far distant when peace may be restored, and the roar of cannon and whizzing of balls may be no longer heard, is the sincere wish of your affectionate brother.

CHAPTER XII.

END OF FIRST CAMPAIGN, 1812.

AFTER the battle of Queenston, an armistice was agreed upon by General Sheaffe. This armistice, which was not approved of by Sir George Prevost, was confined to the frontier between Erie and Ontario, to be terminated at forty-eight hours' notice. It is not likely the fiery Brock would have consented to this delay, which was of no advantage to the Canadians, and only afforded the Americans time to reorganize their demoralized forces, and prepare for a second descent on the Niagara frontier. General Smythe had succeeded Van Rensselaer in the command of the army of the Centre, and had assembled at Buffalo about 5,000 men, to whom he boastfully promised that in a few days he would plant the American standard in Canada. Their watchword was to be "The cannons lost at Detroit or death." So confident was he of conquest, that he told the commandant at Fort Niagara to save the buildings of Fort George and Newark, for winter quarters for his army.

No reinforcements had arrived for General Sheaffe. The militia, who, after Queenston, had returned to their homes to gather in the remains of the harvest, now came back to their posts, determined to defend every inch of the ground. By the American account, the force collected at Black Rock, near Buffalo, was 4,500 men. On the morning of the 28th November, they were to embark from the Navy-yard, near Buffalo, for the conquest of Canada. There were seventy boats, calculated to hold forty men each, lying ready for the expedition, also five scows to hold 100 men each, and ten scows for the artillery.

Before daylight on the 28th November, part of this force, about 450 men, under Major Boerstler and Captain King, crossed the river, and landed about two miles below Fort Erie. At this point there was a battery, and a detachment of the 49th regiment, under Lieutenants Bartley and Lamont. This detachment made a gallant defence, but was almost cut to pieces. Lamont was wounded severely; Bartley retreated to the edge of the woods, and joined Captain Whelan of the Newfoundland Fencibles, and three companies of the Lincoln militia, who were coming to the relief of the battery. The enemy had taken the works, but the Canadians charged and re-took them at the point of the bayonet.

Captain King, General Smythe's *aide-de-camp*, and forty men were taken prisoners. Colonel Cecil Bishopp, then at Chippewa, heard the firing, and ordered Lieutenant-Colonel Clark of the Lincoln militia, and Major Hatt with a detachment of the 49th regiment, to the scene of action. The guns, which had been displaced by the enemy, were remounted by Captain Kirby of the militia and Bombardier Jackson, and brought to bear on the retreating boats. The American account of this affair says, that the main body of the Americans was so tardy in embarking, that their small force on the Canadian side under Boerstler and King were taken prisoners, and about five hundred British were drawn up in line on the shore, sounding their trumpets and bugles, prepared to receive the others. General Smythe, although 2,000 men were embarked, ready to proceed, ordered a postponement of the expedition. Sunday, 29th of November, another order for embarkation, and another postponement came. Then General Smythe, bethinking himself no doubt, of General Brock's method at Detroit, sent a flag of truce, and a summons to Colonel Bishopp, commandant of Fort Erie, to surrender the fort, and so avoid further bloodshed. Colonel Bishopp sarcastically replied, " Let your general come and take it." This, however, the doughty American did not consider prudent to attempt, but thought it his duty, as he says in his despatch, " to follow the cautious counsels of experience, and not precipitation."

On the 1st December, his troops were embarked, only waiting the word of command to proceed, when he gave orders instead, to disembark, as the invasion of Canada was abandoned for the season. It is but justice to the Americans to say that they were disgusted with their cowardly commander. General

Porter's account (American) says, 4,000 men disbanded, firing their muskets in every direction. General Smythe's excuse for his conduct was, that he had not enough men, and could not depend on those he had. He also accused General Porter, the contracting agent for the army, of interested motives in wishing the army to be in Canada, as he would not then be obliged to supply it; as his present contract was a losing one. However, that might be, the fates were not propitious to the army of the Centre in the year 1812.

Nor was the Grand Army of the North much more fortunate. General Dearborn had 10,000 men under his command on the Lower Canadian frontier. He, however, attempted nothing but a few unimportant and unsuccessful skirmishes. Late in November, he determined on a more ambitious enterprise. Major de Salaberry commanding the Canadian Voltigeurs, who were guarding the advanced posts on the line, received intelligence that the Americans, 10,000 strong, were advancing upon Odelltown. There was no time to be lost, and Major de Salaberry set about strengthening his position. The French-Canadians rallied on all sides, to repulse the invaders; the roads were barricaded with felled trees, and every post was guarded. On the 20th November, at three in the morning, the enemy, about 1,400 strong, were noticed fording the River Lacolle, near Rouse's Point. Here there was a log guard-house, which was set on fire by the Canadian guard, who, keeping up a brisk firing, withdrew. The Americans became confused in the darkness, and fired on each other, maintaining their suicidal contest for half an hour, when, the moon rising, their mistake was revealed to them, and they retired in confusion to Champlain. The whole Montreal district was now roused. Sir George Prevost called out all the militia for active service, and so bold a front was displayed that General Dearborn, despairing of a successful attack on Montreal, retired with the Grand Army of the North, to safe winter quarters at Plattsburg.

Thus closed the campaign of 1812.

The discomfiture of Generals Hull, Wadsworth, Van Rensselaer and Smythe, had been complete.

Dearborn had remained inactive. Not a foot of Canadian territory had been lost. The invaders had not only been repulsed in every quarter, but had lost, for the time, a considerable portion of their own territory. Colonel Proctor still held Fort Detroit and the State of Michigan, and the guns of Fort Niagara were silenced.

On December 29th, the Parliament of Lower Canada met, and the Governor-General in the opening Speech expressed his satisfaction at the termination of the first campaign, "in the complete discomfiture of the plans of the enemy for the conquest of Upper Canada, by the capture of Michillimackinac and Detroit, and the surrender of the invading army with its general; the brilliant achievement at Queenston, and other recent advantages gained over the enemy, both in Lower and Upper Canada." In England, on the last day of November, 1812, the Prince Regent, in his Address to Parliament, congratulated the country on the brave stand made in Canada.

The following letter gives an interesting description of affairs in Upper Canada at the close of the year 1812. It is dated Toronto, not York, showing that even then there was a clinging to the old name, which was destined to be the permanent one.

The letter gives an account of the affair at Black Rock, on the 28th November, and also tells of the preparations for the coming campaign that were being made at York and elsewhere.

Volunteering was going on with vigour and patriotic zeal.

To show the alacrity with which the youth of the country flew to arms, it may be mentioned that three of the Ridout boys had enlisted, the eldest only twenty-one years old; what was done in this household was done in many a home throughout Canada.

Letter from Lieutenant Thomas G. Ridout, afterwards Deputy Assistant-Commissary-General, during the War, to his Cousin in England:—

TORONTO, UPPER CANADA, *January 5th,* 1813.

MY DEAR BETSEY,—Five tedious months have passed away since I bid you and all my young English friends a long farewell. Our Canadian winter has set in very severe, and here I am on the north shore of Lake Ontario, whose great surface is frozen as far as the eye can reach, and appears like an immense desert of snow. On the land side we are surrounded by a forest of pines, 180 or 190 feet in height. The Five Nation Indians, who have come down to the war, are encamped on the skirts of the woods back of the town. They keep us alive with their war dances, and make the dark cedar woods echo with savage yells.

The excellent musket your father presented me with has not seen any actual service further than an affair between the *Royal George* and American fleet, in which I happened to be present, by going on board to see my brother John, who is a midshipman, and behaved himself very well on that day. I continued in her, cruising on the lake, ten days, when we returned to port, and I was obliged to finish my journey by a march of 238 miles, along the banks of the lake, with a knapsack and musket on my shoulder, and a young Mississauga Indian for a companion.

My brother George and myself have the honour to be Lieutenants in the Toronto volunteers, and we have just returned from Niagara (where I joined them about a month ago) to this place, where we spend our winter. "Wide awake" is the word for the spring. Great preparations are making on both sides for an active campaign next summer. The Americans, in order to secure the command of our great inland seas, have upon this lake a naval force of two frigates of thirty-six guns, a brig of war and corvette, of eighteen guns each, and sixteen heavy armed schooners, besides two frigates on Lake Erie and another on Lake Huron, which will all begin to act upon us about the 1st of May next, when the winter breaks and navigation opens. On our part, we have two large frigates on the stocks in this town, at which 400 workmen are employed. They will be rigged and finished, notwithstanding the cold weather, in twelve weeks, and are to be manned by 500 officers and seamen from Halifax, who are now on their way through the woods to this country. At Kingston, the eastern end of Ontario, we have two corvettes of twenty guns each and are building a third. Upon Lake Erie we have another frigate on the stocks.

The Americans have 2,000 seaman upon the lakes of Canada, one-third of whom are British. The transportation of heavy guns, rigging, anchors and other naval stores for these new ships, is very expensive to Government, as they are drawn by horses over the snow from Quebec, a distance of 700 or 800 miles, a greater part of which is through the woods. Messages and deputies have been sent to all the Indian tribes within 1,000 miles, to come down to the war by the month of April next.

In a proclamation, which General Smythe lately made to his Yankee army at Niagara, he offers forty dollars reward for every Indian scalp, and orders death to every Canadian found fighting beside a savage warrior; but his threats are laughed at, and will only be retaliated on his own men. On the 28th November last he sent 400 men across the river, about thirty-two miles above Niagara, (Newark), who surprised and killed all our soldiers at two batteries and spiked the guns. This was three hours before daylight, when Captain McAntire formed some men of the 49th and a few militia, and immediately charged through them when they broke and fled to the river and were made prisoners. At daylight, 1,000 more in thirteen large boats came over. Not a shot was fired until they came within one hundred yards, when our men opened six field-pieces and a stream of musketry upon them, which sunk three boats in a minute. The remaining ten, terribly cut up, rowed within forty feet of our shore, and cried for quarter which was refused; and they were forced to return under a severe fire, that killed and wounded upwards of five hundred of their number and struck such a panic in the great General Smythe, that he disembarked 6,000 troops, out of

113 large boats and scows, who in a few minutes were about to follow their forlorn hope. The reason he gave was, that the militia could not be trusted, which was no sooner known than 3,000 men marched off by companies to their respective homes, firing every round in the air, and threatening to put their general to death for the insult offered their courage. Since that time his camp is broken up, and the regulars gone into winter quarters. The American Government pay their private soldiers ten dollars per month, besides allowances. As an inducement for men to enlist, they each receive a grant of two hundred acres of land in Upper Canada, and the whole country is to be given up for plunder or booty, as they term it. The British troops receive but three and one quarter dollars per month, with which they are more comfortable. Last night a poor sentinel froze to death at his post in three quarters of an hour.

One of our frigates is laid on the keel of a fifty-gun ship.

P.S.—We have just heard that General Dearborn, with 18,000 men, is within two days march of our Niagara frontier, we all expect to be ordered to-morrow from this side of the lake to Niagara, when our whole force will amount to 7,000 men, the greater part militia. The Yankee general, Harrison, who invaded the Indian country with 6,000 men, has been defeated by the Indians of the Wabash, and his whole army destroyed.

The affair of the *Royal George*, mentioned in the letter, took place on the 9th November, 1812, off Kingston harbour. Commodore Chauncey, commanding the *Oneida*, with a fleet of seven vessels, lay in wait off the "Ducks," on the 8th November, for the *Royal George*, Captain Popham, of twenty-six guns, the *Duke of Gloucester*, ten guns, and the *Prince*

12

Regent, fourteen guns, who were returning from Fort George.

These vessels got safely into the Bay of Quinte, and during the night, proceeded towards Kingston harbour, whither the Commodore followed them on the morning of the 9th November. A fierce engagement of two hours took place, but the fire from the *Royal George* and the Kingston batteries, proving too hot, the American vessels sailed back to Sackett's Harbour. On the way, the *Oneida* fell in with the *Earl of Moira* escorting a sloop, containing General Brock's private effects, silver, etc. These were taken, but were honourably restored to his cousin and secretary, Captain Brock. Commodore Isaac Chauncey, whose name will appear very frequently in these chronicles, was, at the time of the breaking out of the war, in charge of the navy-yard at Brooklyn, New York.

The skrimish with the *Royal George* on the 9th November, 1812, was his first appearance as the commander of a squadron.

John Ridout, who bore himself so well on that exciting day, was then but fourteen years old. He served as midshipman for a year, but was made prisoner at the taking of York, in April, 1813. He was then, with other militia prisoners, placed on parole.

He escaped the perils of the three years' war, to meet a tragic death, in 1817, in a duel, almost the last fought in Upper Canada. The duel was occasioned by a quarrel with a former friend, ten years his senior.

The fatal encounter took place in a field on the west side of Yonge Street, in what is, at the present day, the centre of Toronto.

In the old churchyard of St. James' Cathedral, whose quiet is now invaded by the busy hum of a great city, the young midshipman sleeps, beside his old father. The stone that marks his resting-place, blackened by time, and half covered with the mould of three-quarters of a century, bears this inscription:—

In memory of

JOHN RIDOUT,

Son of Thos. Ridout, Surveyor-General.

His filial affection, engaging manners and nobleness of mind gave early promise of future excellence. This promise he gallantly fulfilled by his brave, active and enterprising conduct, which gained the praise of his superiors while serving as midshipman in the Provincial Navy during the late war. At the return of peace he commenced with ardour the study of the law and with the fairest prospects, but a blight came, and he was consigned to an early grave, on the 12th day of July, 1817, aged 18, deeply lamented by all who knew him.

CHAPTER XIII.

SECOND CAMPAIGN, 1813—FRENCHTOWN, OGDENSBURG, YORK.

THE information contained in the letter of the 5th
January, that General Harrison's army had been
destroyed by the Indians on the western frontier, was
not correct.   Probably an exaggerated report of some
American reverses had reached York.

General Harrison, afterwards President of the
United States, and grandfather of the present President, was the most formidable of the generals then
charged with the invasion of Canada.   General Dearborn now, at the opening of the campaign of 1813,
commanded in person the army of the Centre, from
Buffalo, Lake Erie, to Sackett's Harbour, at the lower
end of Lake Ontario.   The army of the North, on
Lake Champlain, was commanded by General Hampton, while Generals Harrison and Winchester shared
the command of the army of the west, from Buffalo
westward as far as the British frontier extended.
These generals were to attempt the recapture of
Michigan, still held by the British troops under
Proctor, in alliance with the Indians under Tecumseh.
For this purpose, General Winchester, with about

1,000 men, advanced from the Miami river, and proceeded to take possession of Frenchtown, on the River Raisin, about twenty miles south of Detroit. The capture of the place was easily effected, as it was only occupied by a small body of Canadian (Essex) militia, and some Indians. As soon as Colonel Proctor, then at Malden, heard of the capture of Frenchtown, he collected his troops, consisting of about 600 regulars and militia, and 200 Indians, and marched with haste to dislodge the Americans. At daylight, on the 22nd January, 1813, the attack began. Such was its impetuosity that in half an hour the left wing of the American force was driven from its position, and its retreat cut off by the Indians. General Winchester was taken prisoner by a Wyandot Chief (Roundhead), and sent to Colonel Proctor.

The left wing of the Americans was then attacked, and after a stubborn resistance, capitulated. The prisoners of war were upwards of 600.

Charges were made by the Americans that the prisoners at Frenchtown, or Riviere aux Raisins, were inhumanly massacred. No doubt atrocities were committed by the Indians in spite of the efforts of their chiefs, who are said to have behaved well. A paper of 2nd February (*Chilicothe Journal*) says, "Those who had surrendered on the field were taken prisoners, those who attempted escape were tomahawked."

Major Richardson, of the 41st, gives the following

description of the appearance of the Indians as they marched beside their white allies :—

No other sound than the measured step of the troops interrupted the solitude of the scene, rendered more imposing by the appearance of the warriors, whose bodies, stained and painted in the most frightful manner for the occasion, glided by us with almost noiseless velocity; some painted white, some black, others half black and half red, half black and half white; all with their hair plastered in such a way as to resemble the bristling quills of the porcupine, with no other covering than a cloth around their loins, yet armed to the teeth with rifles, tomahawks, war clubs, spears, bows and arrows, and scalping knives. Uttering no sound, and intent on reaching the enemy unperceived, they might have passed for the spectres of those wilds—the ruthless demons which war had unchained for the punishment and oppression of men.

Colonel Proctor says, in his despatch to Sir G. Prevost :—

After suffering, for our numbers, a considerable loss, the enemy's force posted in houses and enclosures, which from dread of falling into the hands of the Indians, they most obstinately defended, at length surrendered at discretion; the other part of their force in attempting to retreat by the way they came, were, I believe, all, or with very few exceptions, killed by the Indians.

The next affair of importance was Colonel Mc-Donell's brilliant and successful attack on Ogdensburg.

During the winter skirmishing parties from the garrison at Ogdensburg had crossed the frozen St.

Lawrence, there only about a mile in width, and had committed numerous depredations, even carrying off, it is said, on one occasion fifty inhabitants of the neighbourhood of Prescott as prisoners.

About seven o'clock on the morning of the 22nd February, 1813, Colonel McDonell crossed the ice with a force consisting of 480 regulars and militia, advanced under a heavy fire from the American fort, and drove the enemy's infantry to the woods.

The gallant colonel of the Glengarries tells the story of the fight as follows :—

My force consisted of about 480 regulars and militia, and was divided into two columns; the right commanded by Captain Jenkins, of the Glengarry Light Infantry Fencibles, was composed of his own flank company, and about seventy militia; and from the state of the ice, and enemy's position in the old French fort, was directed to check his left, and interrupt his retreat, while I moved on with the left column, consisting of 120 of the King's regiment, forty of the Royal Newfoundland, and about 200 militia, towards his position in the town, where he had posted his heavy field artillery.

The depth of the snow retarded, in some degree, the advance of both columns, and exposed them, particularly the right, to a heavy cross-fire from the batteries of the enemy, for a longer period than I had expected ; but pushing on rapidly after the batteries began to open up on us, the left column soon gained the right bank of the river, under the direct fire of the enemy's artillery and line of musketry posted on an eminence near the shore.   Moving on rapidly my advance, consisting of the detachment of the Royal Newfoundland and some select militia, I turned his right with the detachment of the King's regiment, and after a few discharges from his artillery took them with the bayonet, and drove his infantry through the town, some escaping across the Black river into the fort.

The majority fled to the woods, or sought refuge in the houses, from whence they kept up such a galling fire, that it was necessary to dislodge them with our field-pieces, which now came up from the bank of the river, where they had stuck on landing in the deep snow.

Having gained the high ground on the brink of the Black river opposite the fort, I prepared to carry it by storm, but the men being quite exhausted, I procured time for them to recover breath, by sending in a summons requiring an unconditional surrender.*

During these transactions, Captain Jenkins had gallantly led on his column, and had been exposed to a heavy fire of seven guns, which he bravely attempted to take with the bayonet, though covered with 200 of the enemy's best troops.

Advancing as rapidly as the deep snow and the exhausted state (in consequence) of his men would admit, he ordered a charge, and had not proceeded many paces when his left arm was broken to pieces by a grape shot; but still undauntedly running on with his men, he almost immediately after was deprived of the use of his right arm by a discharge of case shot; still heroically disregarding all personal considerations, he nobly advanced cheering his men to the assault till exhausted by pain and loss of blood he became unable to move.

His company gallantly continued the charge under Lieutenant Macaulay; but the reserve not being able to keep up with them they were compelled by the great superiority of the enemy to give way,

* The message sent was : "If you surrender, it shall be well ; if not, every man shall be put to the bayonet." Forsythe's answer was : "Tell Colonel McDonell there must be more fighting done first." (Lossing).

leaving a few on a commanding position, and a few of the most advanced in the enemy's possession, nearly about the time that I gained the height above mentioned.

The enemy hesitating to surrender, I instantly carried his eastern battery, and by it silenced another which opened again, and ordering on the advance the detachment of the King's and the Highland company of militia, under Captain Eustace, of the King's regiment, he gallantly rushed into the fort; but the enemy retreating by the opposite entrance escaped into the woods, which I should effectually have prevented if my Indian warriors had returned sooner from a detached service on which they had that morning been employed.

The spoils taken in this affair were eleven pieces of cannon, all the ordnance, marine, commissariat, and quarter-master-general's stores, four officers and seventy rank and file prisoners, also two armed schooners and two large gun-boats which were burnt. The loss was : One sergeant, seven rank and file killed ; one field officer, two captains, five subalterns, four sergeants, forty rank and file wounded.

Many are the names mentioned in the despatch as conspicuous for gallant conduct on that day. Among others Lieutenant Macaulay, afterwards Sir J. B. Macaulay, Chief Justice of Upper Canada. He served throughout the war, and also distinguished himself at Oswego, Lundy's Lane and Fort Erie.

His regiment, the Glengarries, was a Highland Catholic regiment composed of men, who, under the leadership of Alexander McDonell, priest of the clan of Glengarry, had emigrated from Scotland to Canada in 1803. They settled in the Eastern district, where they obtained, through the influence of their devoted friend and leader, a grant of 160,000 acres of land.

When Canada was threatened with invasion, in 1812, Alexander McDonell with his kinsman, George McDonell, the hero of Ogdensburg, formed a regiment called the Glengarry Light Infantry Fencibles, whose soldiers fought for their adopted land as their forefathers of old had fought for bonny Scotland. Lieutenant-Colonel George McDonell, known also among the Highlanders as "Red George," who was in command at the taking of Ogdensburg, distinguished himself in many another fight, notably at Chateauguay.

The fighting chaplain, Alexander McDonell, always accompanied his regiment into the field, and where "'Maighster Alastair' led, there never foot went back." He became afterwards the first Catholic diocesan Bishop of Kingston, and lived to a good old age.

John McDonell, *aide-de-camp* and military secretary to General Brock, who met his death on the heights of Queenston, was another kinsman of the Bishop's.

Parliament met at York, on the 25th February, 1813—and now, instead of the lamented Brock, it was General Roger Hall Sheaffe, who opened it as President.

His speech reads :—

It affords me satisfaction that the first time I am called upon to address you in this place, I have to offer you my cordial congratulations on the uniform success which has crowned His Majesty's arms in this Province. The enemy has been foiled in repeated attempts to invade it. Three of his armies have been surrendered or completely defeated, and two important fortresses wrested from him. In this glorious campaign the valour and discipline of His Majesty's regular troops have been nobly supported by the zeal and bravery of our loyal militia.

In April, 1813, the ice broke up at Sackett's Harbour, where the American squadron, under Commodore Chauncey, had wintered.

A plan was organized by General Dearborn, in which he proposed, in co-operation with the fleet, to take possession of Little York, the capital of Upper Canada, and to proceed thence to the assault of Fort George, the bulwark of the Niagara peninsula.

At that time there were only a few Canadian vessels, on the lake, and these were badly manned, and ill-provided.

Sir James Yeo, with a reinforcement of English seamen, did not arrive until May, 1813. The fort at York was not strong enough to defend the town, and besides, the majority of the fighting force of Upper Canada were at Fort George, and scattered along the western frontier. About 200 militia, 300 regular troops and 100 Indians, were all that could be mustered for the defence of the place, whose only inhabitants were old men, women and children.

No doubt the lake was anxiously scanned each morning to see what vessels were in sight.

In Surveyor-General Ridout's diary for 1813, there are numerous jottings of passing events.   The first entry is : * —

YORK, *Monday, 26th April.*

At four p.m. the enemy's fleet was reported to be about twenty miles from hence, and apparently coming hither.

Tuesday, 27th April. — At seven this morning, enemy's fleet came to anchor off the garrison, and began firing and landing men.   There were fourteen vessels, had above 1,000 seamen and 2,000 troops on board, and carrying upwards of 100 guns.   We had to oppose them only five guns, 300 regulars and 208 militia.

The approach of the fleet being discovered from the garrison at York, Gen. Sheaffe, who was at that time in command there, hastily collected his whole force, consisting of less than 700 regulars and militia, and some Indians, and disposed them in the best way to resist the landing of the American force.   The Grenadier company of the 8th regiment was paraded on the shore of the Humber Bay, very near to what is now the entrance to High Park.   The Indians, under the command of Colonel Givins, were placed in groups, in and about

* This diary is written on the blank pages of an almanac, whose title-page bears this inscription : "The Quebec Almanac, for the year 1813, being the first after Leap Year.   Printed and sold by J. Neilson."

the woods. Strong field-works had also been thrown up towards the town. The Indians were intended to act as sharpshooters, and were to annoy the Americans at the point where the wind would allow them to land.

Commander Chauncey, of the American fleet, says in his letter to the Secretary of the Navy, of the 28th April, 1813 :—

U. S. SHIP MADISON, off York.

We arrived here yesterday morning and took a position about one mile to the south and westward of the enemy's principal fort, and as near the shore as we could with safety to our vessels. The place fixed upon by the Major-General and myself for landing the troops, was the site of the old French fort, Toronto. The debarkation commenced at eight o'clock in the morning, and was completed about ten. The wind blowing heavy from the eastward, the boats fell to the leeward of the position fixed upon, and were in consequence exposed to a galling fire from the enemy, who had taken a position in a thick wood near where the first troops landed.

Major Forsythe, with his riflemen in several large bateaux, were the first to land.

General Pike, who was watching the boats from the ship, saw his troops pause under the hot shower of bullets, and springing into the boat reserved for himself and staff, pushed off for the shore, closely followed by three companies of the 15th American regiment, under Major King. Before he reached it, Forsythe with his men had landed, and was already engaged with the principal part of the British troops and Indians under the immediate command of General Sheaffe. A hot contest followed, and the Canadians vainly endeavoured from the bank, to keep the invaders at bay. With the small number of troops at Sheaffe's command, resistance was almost useless. The Glengarry corps fought valiantly with Forsythe's brigade, contesting every inch of the way, while the Grenadier company of the 8th made a formidable charge on the American column. Another reinforcement now arrived from the ships, rendering the situation of the Canadian force more hopeless than before. They were compelled to retire towards the fort, fighting all the way. The Americans, having landed all their troops, were ordered to march on the retreating force, who were making their way to the garrison.

The invading column marched on, the artillery crossing with difficulty the little streams that intersected the road along the lake. The Canadians attempted, at their first battery, to check their advance, but without success. The enemy still moved on, and our men retreated to the second battery, at about 300 yards distant from the garrison. Here they spiked the guns.

Commander Chauncey's letter says :—

As soon as the troops were landed, I directed the schooners to take a position near the forts, in order that the attack upon them might be simultaneous. The schooners were obliged to beat up to their position, which they did in a very handsome order, under a very heavy fire from the enemy's batteries, and took a position within about 600 yards of their principal fort, and opened a heavy cannonade, which did great execution.

In the meantime General Pike had come up to the second battery, and halted there, while he sent forward a corps to discover what was going on in the garrison, as every appearance indicated its evacuation. This was, indeed, the case. General Sheaffe and the regulars were making their way towards the Don in rapid flight to Kingston. While the corps of observation were returning, there was a sudden explosion of a powder magazine, just outside the barrack yard, which brought dire destruction to both victors and vanquished. How it happened is still shrouded in mystery, and many are the conflicting reports. The Americans accused the British General of a deliberate plot to annihilate their whole force on their entrance to the deserted garrison. That this was not the case, seems borne out by the fact that about 100 of our men were killed and wounded by the explosion. The Americans lost by it about 250 men, among them General Pike. In consequence of his death, the command of the American troops devolved for a time upon Colonel Prince. At two in the afternoon, the American flag was substituted for the British, and at four General Dearborn (who had landed on hearing of General Pike's fall) was in quiet possession of the town.

Before evacuating the place, General Sheaffe had

ordered the destruction of the new ship, then on the stocks and nearly finished.

The only vessel taken, was the *Duke of Gloucester*, then lying in the harbour for repairs. The *Prince Regent* had fortunately left for Kingston on the 24th, and so escaped capture.

General Sheaffe in his official report says, that the contest was maintained nearly eight hours; showing that, though defeated, a stubborn resistance had been made.

General Sheaffe was blamed for his precipitate retreat, but it is difficult to say what other course lay before him. The Americans were three to one. He had no large guns. The fort was rendered untenable by the bombardment from the ships. If he had remained to surrender with the militia he would undoubtedly have been sent with his regular troops to some American prison, while he knew the custom was in the case of the militia, to merely place them on parole.

Among the names of those who were on this occasion made prisoners of war are:—Lieutenant-Colonel Chewett, Major Allan, Captains John Wilson, John Button, Peter Robinson, Reuben Richardson, John Arnold, James Fenwick, Duncan Cameron, David Thompson, John Robinson, Samuel Ridout, Thomas Hamilton, William Jarvis, Quarter-Master Charles Baynes; Lieutenants John H. Schultz, George Mustard, Robert Stanton, George Ridout, William

Jarvis, Ed. McMahon, John Wilson, Eli Playter; Ensigns Andrew Thompson, Andrew Mercer, James Chewett, Charles Denison, George Robinson, D'Arcy Boulton.

The following letter gives some further account of what happened after the capitulation :—

Letter from Thomas G. Ridout :—

KINGSTON, *May 5th*, 1813.

I left York on Sunday, the 2nd inst., at noon, at which time the American fleet, consisting of the *Madison, Oneida*, and ten schooners, with the *Gloucester*, were lying at anchor about two miles from the garrison, wind-bound by a south-east wind. All their troops were embarked the evening before, excepting a small party, who burnt the large blockhouse, government house and officers' quarters. At nine in the morning a naval officer came down to town and collected ten men out of the taverns where they had been all night.

The commissariat magazines were shipped the preceding days. The lower blockhouse and government buildings were burnt on Saturday. Major Givins' and Dr. Powell's houses were entirely plundered by the enemy, and some persons from the Humber. Jackson and his two sons, and Ludden, the butcher, had been riding through the country ordering the militia to come in and be put on their parole.

Duncan Cameron delivered all the money in the Receiver-General's hands (to the amount as I understand of £2,500) over to Captain Elliot of the American navy, the enemy having threatened to burn the town if it was not given up.

On Friday, the thirtieth, the Chief Justice, Judge Powell, my father (Thos. Ridout), Dr. Strachan and Duncan Cameron, called upon General Dearborn, re-

13

questing he would allow the magistrates to retain their authority over our own people. Accordingly, he issued a general order saying it was not his intention to deprive the magistracy of its civil functions, that they should be supported, and if any of the United States troops committed any depredation, a strict scrutiny into it should follow. The gaol was given up to the sheriff, but no prisoners. The public provincial papers were found out, but ordered to be protected, so that nothing was destroyed, excepting the books, papers, records and furniture of the upper and lower Houses of Assembly. It was said that they had destroyed our batteries and taken away the cannon. The barracks were not burnt. The American officers said their force on the 27th was 3,000 land force and 1,000 seamen and marines, and that their loss was 500 killed and wounded.

CHAPTER XIV.

1813.—FORT GEORGE, SACKETT'S HARBOUR, STONEY CREEK,

BEAVER DAMS.

ON the 2nd of May, 1813, the Americans evacuated York. Commodore Chauncey first conveyed General Dearborn and his land force to Fort Niagara, where a large body of American troops were then stationed, and then, with his fleet, returned to Sackett's Harbour, bearing with him the wounded from York, and the stores captured there. After a short time spent in refitting the fleet and obtaining reinforcements, the Commodore sailed back to assist in the assault of Fort George. The American land force at Niagara was then about 6,000, under Generals Dearborn, Lewis, Boyd, Winder and Chandler. Their fleet on Lake Ontario consisted of fifteen vessels with fifty-nine guns. To oppose them, General Vincent, in command at Fort George, had but a force of 1,400 men, composed of eight companies of the 49th and detachments from the 8th, the 41st Glengarries and Newfoundland corps, with 350 militia and some artillery. The right division was commanded by Lieutenant-Colonel Harvey, from Fort George to Brown's Point, near Queenston ;

the left, to Four Mile Creek, was commanded by Colonel Myers ; the centre division at the fort, by General Vincent. Five of the twenty-four pounders taken at Detroit had been brought to the Niagara frontier, four of which had been mounted at Fort George ; the fifth was on the shore, near what was afterwards Fort Mississauga. On each side of the river, between Fort George and Queenston, were batteries, scarcely a mile apart. On the evening of the 26th May, 1813, Commodore Chauncey began cannonading the fort, but owing to his scanty supply of powder, General Vincent did not return the fire. Early on the morning of the 27th, the bombardment began again, and under cover of a dense fog, which hid them until within fifty yards of the shore, the Americans approached, and effected a landing on the lake-side of the town.

A stubborn defence was made by the brave little garrison, but in vain. The heavy cannonade from Fort Niagara, and from the American fleet wrought sad havoc within Fort George. After three hours' hot fighting, when almost every gunner was disabled, and resistance was no longer possible, General Vincent spiked his guns, destroyed the magazine, and retired on Burlington Heights, by way of Queenston.

It would have been an easy matter for the Americans now, to have hemmed in and annihilated General Vincent's little army, reduced as it was, by the loss of 400 men, but General Dearborn let the opportunity slip by, and Vincent effected his retreat to Burlington Heights unharassed. Colonel Cecil Bisshopp, who was stationed at Fort Erie, and Major Ormsby at Chippewa, with their detachments, were ordered to join the retreating force. The whole Niagara frontier was now defenceless, and at the mercy of the Americans.

We are told that many were the scenes of sorrow and distress as the little army passed on, leaving behind them the unprotected women and children, who expected the Americans would take possession of the land, and drive them from their homes.

Referring to the defence of the Niagara frontier, Thomson says :—

Such was the spirited earnestness of both officers and men at the batteries, that when, in the most tremendous of the bombardment, they had fired away all their cartridges, they cut up their flannel waistcoats and shirts, and the soldiers their trousers, to supply their guns.

No wonder we read that, after the retreat from Fort George, the army were destitute of clothing, without shoes, and as an officer writes to the Commander-in-Chief, in rags.

On the day of the capture of Fort George, another disaster befell the British arms at the eastern end of Lake Ontario.

Sir James Yeo had just arrived at Kingston with 500 English seamen, and Sir George Prevost thought it would be a good time, in the absence of Commodore Chauncey at Niagara, to make a descent on Sackett's

Harbour and destroy the naval stores there. It was a well-planned design, but unfortunately was not well carried out. On the 27th May, the expedition, consisting of about 1,000 men, four frigates, some gun-boats and bateaux set out from Kingston, and succeeded in capturing some boats from Oswego, with troops on board.

Sir George Prevost's over caution delayed the attack until the following morning, by which time, General Brown, in command at Sackett's Harbour, was able to make preparations for defence. About 500 American militia were placed on Horse Island, guarding the entrance to the harbour.

The British troops succeeded, however, in landing on the morning of the 29th May, under cover of a heavy fire from their boats.

They advanced towards the fort, and were met by about 400 American regulars and some militia, under Colonel Backus. A sharp contest ensued. The American colonel was killed and part of his troops fled. Unfortunately, at this moment, Sir George Prevost imagined that he had fallen into a snare, and that the retreating Americans were really executing a masterly manœuvre, and were about to hem him in. He, therefore, much to the chagrin of his troops, ordered an immediate retreat to the boats, and the fleet returned ingloriously to Kingston. The only damage done was by the Americans themselves, for, thinking they were about to capitulate, they had set on fire the naval magazine (containing all the stores captured at York), the hospital, the barracks, and a frigate on the stocks.

The British loss in this disastrous expedition was one officer and forty-seven men killed, and about 200 wounded and missing.

In Mr. Ridout's diary is this entry :—

Saturday, May 29th, 1813.—Our attempt upon Sackett's Harbour failed.

To return now to the Niagara frontier. General Vincent reached Burlington Heights on the evening of the 29th May, and immediately picquets were placed, and reconnoitring parties sent out to watch for the expected advance of the Americans. They had not long to wait.

Generals Winder and Chandler were despatched in pursuit, with about 3,000 men, including cavalry and artillery. They halted first at the Twenty-Mile Creek (Jordan), where they received the incorrect information that Vincent was in a strong position at Burlington Heights,* and had received reinforcements from Kingston.

---

* Burlington Heights, where General Vincent found a safe retreat, form the extreme western end of Burlington Bay, a picturesque inlet at the western extremity of Lake Ontario, which is now the harbour of the city of Hamilton. General Vincent's entrenchments were partly in what is at the present day Hamilton cemetery, and partly in the grounds of Dundurn Castle, now the residence of Senator MacInnes. A curious eye may still trace the earthworks. The Heights then (1812) were neither excavated by a railway, nor pierced, as now, by the Des Jardins Canal. The only access to them was over an isthmus defended by field-works. On one side a stone could have been dropped sheer a hundred feet into Burlington Bay; on the other side into a deep marsh. ("Picturesque Canada.")

The Americans proceeded on their march, and arrived towards the evening of the 5th June, 1813, at Stoney Creek, about seven miles from General Vincent's lines, at Burlington.

Stoney Creek was scarcely a village, for there were only a few scattered houses, some taverns, and an old church on the hill side, one of the oldest in the Province.* "The clattering of cavalry hoofs, the clanking of swords, the heavy rattle of artillery, and the long, strange array of invading soldiers as they filed along the narrow road, struck the few inhabitants of the hamlet with wonder and astonishment. It was soon whispered that a battle was to be fought the next day."

And now the American soldiers lay down to take their much-needed rest. It had been a hot, sultry day, and the march had been long and fatiguing. Their camp was pitched on a plain surrounded by gentle slopes, and watered by a bright, clear stream.

The cannon were planted in a position to sweep the road towards Burlington Heights. On each side, near the road, the artillerymen slept beside their guns. Behind them were the cavalry. In advance of the rest, a party of fifty, took possession of the old church. The settlers in the vicinity were held as prisoners, lest they should carry any information to General Vincent. The weary and exhausted men lay with their arms in readiness beside them, and soon darkness closed over the sleeping camp.

* Demolished in 1871.

A few miles away, on the Heights, were Vincent's soldiers, and it seemed as if the morning light would bring to them annihilation or retreat.

York had been taken, a powerful fleet was on the lake to oppose them. There were no supplies to be had, and there were but ninety rounds of ammunition to each man. Under these circumstances, a night attack with the bayonet, was proposed by Colonel Harvey* and agreed to by General Vincent.

W. H. Merritt, who commanded a Canadian cavalry troop, and had been engaged in reconnoitring the position of the enemy, writes :—

All my hopes depended on this bold enterprise, for had we not attacked them they would have advanced the next morning, and in all probability we would have retired without risking an action, as our force was not one-third of theirs. Proctor and the whole upper country would then have fallen.

* John Harvey, afterwards Sir John, the hero of Stoney Creek, was born in 1778, entered the army as ensign in the 80th, in 1794. Served through the campaign in Holland, 1794 ; at the Cape of Good Hope, 1796 ; in Egypt, 1800 ; in India from 1803 to 1807 ; on active service all the time.

In June, 1812, he was appointed Deputy Adjutant-General to the army in Canada, and arrived in Halifax late in the year 1812.

The services of such an experienced veteran soldier were invaluable.

The advice he gave when asked by Sir George Prevost as to the best method of defence for Canada was brief, but decided :

" First, by the accurate intelligence of the designs and movements of the enemy, to be procured at any price ; and, secondly, by a series of bold, active, offensive operations, by which the enemy, however superior in numbers, would himself be thrown upon the defensive."

Many years after the war he was Governor of New Brunswick, afterwards Governor of Newfoundland, and finally, Governor of Nova Scotia, where he died, 1852.

About seven hundred men were detached for the dangerous enterprise, and to Colonel Harvey was given the conduct of the attack.

At about half-past ten at night this little band of heroic men started down the lonely road eastward. There was no moon, only at intervals heat lightning lit up the scene. Not a word was spoken, not a sound of any kind broke the stillness of the night. Even their guns were ordered to be unloaded, lest a stray shot should give the alarm.

They arrived in sight of the first American sentinel at nearly two o'clock on Sunday morning, the 6th June. To his challenge, the cold steel was the answer. Another challenge from the next on guard, and again the poor wretch was transfixed. His groans alarmed the third sentinel, who challenged, fired and fled. Not a moment was now to be lost. Colonel Harvey, whose plans had been perfectly organized, instantly ordered his men to deploy into line. He and Lieutenant Fitzgibbon took the road straight ahead, Major Plenderleath* of the 49th regiment, swept round to the left, and Colonel Ogilvy of the 8th regiment, with some of the 49th regiment, opened to the right. The sentry at the church door was approached under the shade of the trees, and killed, and the whole party in the church were made prisoners.

* Lieutenant-Colonel Plenderleath was an estimable and courageous officer of the 49th regiment. He served with conspicuous gallantry during the War of 1812, but suffered severely from wounds received during the struggle.

Now came a scene of wild confusion. The excitement of the attacking soldiers had been wrought up by their enforced silence, and with terrific yells they burst with fixed bayonets on the surprised Americans.

In a moment the flats and the hills were a scene of wildest commotion. The Americans had, by this time, recovered from their first confusion, and soon the dark hill-side for nearly half a mile was illuminated by a volley of their musketry.

Following the flash and crash came a silence, broken only by the clanking of arms, and the groans of the wounded and dying.

Then again came from the camp the roar of musketry and shock of artillery, and the trees and tents were lighted with the glare.

These two volleys did terrible execution among Harvey's troops, and goaded them to fury.

In the darkness they got confused, but Colonel Plenderleath soon rallied them, and as the order came for another charge with the bayonet, the men dashed forward on the guns. Five cannon with thirty men, and one of the American generals were taken in this fierce charge.

Colonel Ogilvy had just previously captured the other general as he was coming out of a house, where he had been rudely awakened from his slumbers.

Confusion now prevailed on all sides, and with the loss of their guns and generals, the Americans decided to retire from the field.

In the *melee* before the capture of the guns, about fifty of the 49th regiment were taken prisoners.

It was so near daylight that Colonel Harvey thought it prudent to retire also, as the day would disclose the insufficiency of his force, and so encourage the Americans to renew the conflict.

A large body of the enemy reappeared at seven in morning, and proceeded to destroy the provisions, carriages, spare arms, and blankets, which they could not take away with them in their flight. Their dead they left to be buried by the Canadians, so side by side on that field sleep friend and foe. Some were buried where they had bivouacked the night before, on a projecting point of the hill, east of the creek and north of the road. Others sleep in the graveyard, close to the spot where the old church stood. General Vincent's official report of the battle of Stoney Creek says :—

The action terminated before daylight, when three guns and one brass howitzer with three tumbrils, two Brigadier-Generals, Chandler and Winder, and upwards of 100 officers and privates remained in our hands. The British loss : killed, one lieutenant, three sergeants, nineteen rank and file ; wounded, two majors, five captains, two lieutenants, one ensign, one adjutant, one fort major, nine sergeants, two drummers and 113 rank and file ; three sergeants and fifty-two rank and file missing.

This was a large gulf in a force of 704 men, but they had accomplished their purpose; and the midnight attack at Stoney Creek saved the country for the time.

The Americans did not halt on their retreat until they reached Forty-Mile Creek (Grimsby), where they camped, but their misfortunes were not yet complete.

Sir James Yeo with his squadron had sailed from Kingston on the 3rd of June, and appeared at the mouth of the creek at daylight on the 7th, and commenced firing at the American camp, which had been reinforced by Generals Lewis and Boyd. The Americans got into a panic between the fire from the ships and the appearance of some Indians on a hill above the camp.

They decided to retire to Fort George, and left behind, in their hasty flight, 500 tents, 100 stand of arms, 140 barrels of flour, and about seventy wounded men. Seventeen bateaux, laden with supplies **for** the Americans, were also taken at the same time by Sir James Yeo.*

After the brilliant success of Stoney Creek, there was no further thought of retreat for Vincent's forces. In fact the beseigers became the beseiged, and General Dearborn's outposts and foraging parties were continually harassed by attacks from the various detachments of British troops that now hemmed the invaders in at Fort George. The defenders of Canada were few in number, but their hearts were fired with patriotic zeal,

---

* Entry in Mr. Ridout's diary:—*Sunday, 6th June*, Whitsunday. Defeated the Americans at Stoney Creek.

and they had leaders willing to do and dare everything. Such men as Vincent and Harvey, and Cecil Bisshopp, and Fitzgibbon, and Clark of the Lincoln militia, and Merritt of the light cavalry, and Brant and De Salaberry, led their troops with such vigour and skill, that it was impossible for the enemy, in spite of their immense superiority in numbers, to obtain a foothold in the country.

Another reverse came to the Americans soon after their defeat at Stoney Creek, and this time it was a woman's hand that brought them disaster. At a place called Beaver Dams, or the Beechwoods, (about twelve miles in a direct road from Queenston), where now is the town of Thorold, was a depôt of provisions for the Canadian troops, guarded by a detachment of thirty of the 49th regiment under Lieutenant Fitzgibbon,* with some Indians and militia, in all about 200 men.

In order to surprise and dislodge this outpost, an American force of 500 men, with fifty cavalry and two field-pieces, under Colonel Boerstler, set out from Fort George (Niagara) on the 23rd of June.

---

* Lieutenant Fitzgibbon, Adjutant of the 49th, enlisted as a private soldier in 1798, was soon promoted to be sergeant; served in Holland, was drafted as a marine on board Nelson's squadron, fought at the battle of Copenhagen, won his commission by merit. After the battle of Stoney Creek, he obtained permission to organize an independent company of picked men, to act as rangers or scouts in order to harass the enemy in advance of the army. Lieutenant Fitzgibbon distinguished himself at Fort George, Stoney Creek, Fort Erie, and especially at Beaver Dams. After the war he became the Colonel of the 1st regiment of Toronto militia, and Assistant Adjutant-General to the militia of Upper Canada. He ended his long career in England as a military Knight of Windsor.

A surprise was meditated, in retaliation, no doubt, for the affair of Stoney Creek. Laura Secord, wife of a Canadian farmer, who had been wounded in the battle of Queenston Heights, accidentally heard of the designs of the Americans, and determined to give the outpost timely warning. She set out alone before daybreak on the 23rd June from her house at Queenston, and arrived at Fitzgibbon's head-quarters, a stone house known as De Cew's, near the Beaver Dams, at sunset of the same day. On account of the American sentries and outposts, she had to avoid the high road and beaten paths, thus making her toilsome journey nearly twice as long. In spite of weakness and fatigue, this heroic woman went on her way through pathless woods, over hill and dale and unbridged streams, till she reached her destination.

Her warning came just in time. Lieutenant Fitzgibbon disposed of his little force to the best advantage possible, placing them in ambush on both sides of the road, taking every precaution to make it appear that he had a large force in reserve.

Between eight and nine of the morning of the 24th June, the advance guard of the American riflemen appeared. A volley from the woods received them and emptied their saddles. Soon firing came from all directions, and bugle calls, and Indian yells. The bewildered Americans imagined themselves in the presence of a much superior force. Finding his men were losing heavily from the fire of the unseen foe, and that they were suffering from fatigue, and the intense heat of the day, Colonel Boerstler directed a general retreat upon the artillery in the rear. The Indians raised an exultant yell, and the Americans fell back in confusion. At this moment Lieutenant Fitzgibbon appeared with a white flag, and demanded the surrender of the whole American force. Intimidated by the bold request and wishing to avoid, as he thought, the slaughter of his men, the American colonel, who was also severely wounded, consented to the terms offered. By the capitulation 542 men, two field-pieces, some ammunition waggons, and the colours of the 14th U. S. regiment were delivered over to the Canadians.

The timely arrival of Major du Haren * from Twelve Mile Creek, with a reinforcement for Fitzgibbon of 200 men, enabled the victors to guard their prisoners.

For this brilliant achievement Lieutenant Fitzgibbon received his company and captain's commission.

As to Laura Secord's reward, it has come to her in the fame that rests on her name whenever the story of 1812 is told.

The heroine lived until the year 1868, and sleeps now in that old cemetery at Drummondville, where lie so many of our brave soldiers. There is no " Decora-

---

* Shortly before the affair of Beaver Dams Major du Haren had arrived in Upper Canada with a reinforcement for General Vincent of two flank companies of the 104th or New Brunswick regiment, also a body of 340 Caughnawaga Indians from Lower Canada, commanded by Captain Ducharme and Lieutenant de Lorimier.

tion Day" in Canada, but if there were, surely this woman is entitled to the laurel wreath.

After the disastrous events of the month of June, General Dearborn resigned the command of the American army, and was succeeded by Generals Boyd and Lewis.

Emboldened by success, the Canadians took up the offensive, and numerous dashes were made into American territory; while Vincent, with only 1,800 men, beleaguered Fort George, where a force of about 4,000 men were idly shut up, fearing to venture beyond the range of their cannon.

Sickness had broken out among the American troops, and disease was doing its work in reducing their numbers.

On the 4th of July, 1813, a bold dash was made by Colonel Clark (2nd Lincoln), with a small force of Canadian militia from Chippewa, on Fort Schlosser. He was successful in capturing the guard, and a large quantity of provisions and ammunition. A week later another dash before daylight was made by Colonel Cecil Bisshopp and Colonel Clark, with about 250 men, on Black Rock, near Buffalo.

The Americans were completely taken by surprise, and before they could rally from the sudden attack, their barracks, naval arsenal, a block-house and large schooner, were destroyed. Quantities of provisions and ammunition, of which the Canadians were sorely in need, were carried off.

14

Though the expedition was quite successful, it cost the life of the brave young Colonel Cecil Bisshopp.* His loss was deeply deplored, for he had been one of the most daring and best loved soldiers in the service.

*Cecil Bisshopp was the only son of Sir Cecil Bisshopp, Baronet, afterwards Baron de la Zouche. He was born in 1783, entered the army at sixteen, served through the war in Flanders as *aide-de-camp* to General Grosvenor de Walchen; again in Spain and Portugal. He was sent to Canada in 1812, where he displayed great gallantry in several engagements.

In the little deserted and neglected graveyard at Niagara Falls, or Drummondville, which was also the battle-field of Lundy's Lane, a beautiful monument marks his last resting-place. The passing stranger is bidden to pause o'er this shrine where

"Sleeps the young and brave,
And shed one generous tear o'er Cecil's grave."

In the parish church of his far-off English home in Parham, Sussex, is a tablet to his memory thus inscribed:—

"His pillow, not of sturdy oak;
His shroud, a soldier's simple cloak;
His dirge, will sound till time's no more;
Niagara's loud and solemn roar,—
There Cecil lies—say, where the grave,
More worthy of a Briton brave."

CHAPTER XV.

CHAUNCEY'S FLEET—SUMMER, 1813.

ALTHOUGH the Americans still held Fort George, their position was by no means an enviable one. Harassed on all sides by Vincent's troops, who attacked them whenever they ventured beyond their entrenchments, they remained pent-up within the limits of a few acres all through the summer months.

The following letters give some glimpses of what General Vincent, and his little army were doing, through July and August of 1813.

The writer, Thomas Gibbs Ridout, had just been appointed to the commissariat on the Niagara frontier.

His father's diary has this entry:—

YORK, *Wednesday, 7th July,* 1813.

This evening at nine o'clock, my son Tom set out in a boat for the Forty-Mile Creek, on his way to our camp near Niagara.

The first letter from the camp is dated 20th July, 1813.

From Thomas G. Ridout to his Father:—

ST. DAVID'S.

On Saturday, 17th, Henry Nelles and I rode down to the cross-roads, three miles from Niagara, where the Royals, King's, and 600 or 700 Indians are posted. I understood the Americans were advancing into Ball's fields. Immediately the yell was given and Blackbird and Norton set out with their Indians to meet them. Nelles and I rode along, and in a few minutes the skirmish began by the Western Indians getting upon the left flank, and the Five Nations upon the other. The enemy consisted of 500 men. They soon retreated, firing heavy volleys upon Blackbird's party which was the nearest. The road is so straight we could see into town; and Nelles and I rode along with the Indians to within one and a quarter miles of Niagara, when we perceived a large reinforcement join them with a piece of artillery, and they again advanced with a large front, firing grape shot. The Indians scattered in the woods, but we were obliged to keep the road. By this time three companies of the Royals, and a brass six pounder came up and posted on this side of Ball's field, the Yankees on the other side. We fired for some time, when the Americans thought fit to retreat. At one time from the farther end of Ball's field, a mile and a half this way, the road was covered with Indians, officers and soldiers, and horses, and from the Presbyterian church, they must have judged our force at 3,000 men. We had about 1,000. A good many Yankees were killed. One Indian took two scalps. A young Cayuga had his arm and side carried away with a cannon ball, and another had a ball through his arm. Some of the musket balls came pretty close to us.

The cross-roads now are very strong. Dickson is expected here as soon as he returns from the expedition that has gone against Sandusky and Presqu' Isle with 1,500 Indians.

I wish George could bring a little starch with him for the frills of my shirts.

The last week of July was an anxious one for the inhabitants of York.

Chauncey's vessels were cruising about Lake Ontario, ready to attack wherever possible. On the 27th July, his fleet lay off the Niagara river, and on the following day it sailed for the head of Lake Ontario, for the purpose of making an attempt to capture the British stores at Burlington Heights, then defended by a small detachment under Major Maule.

Meanwhile, the ever-watchful Colonel Harvey had taken steps to defend the stores at the Heights, and had ordered Colonel Battersby from York, with a part of the Glengarry corps, to reinforce the guard under Major Maule.

Finding his force insufficent for the attack on Burlington Heights, Chauncey sailed off down the lake to make a second attack on defenceless Little York.

Colonel Scott, who commanded the American land force on the fleet, landed without opposition, took the place, burnt the barracks, storehouses, etc., and carried away a quantity of provisions, chiefly flour. This was on the 1st of August.

The expedition under Chauncey returned to the Niagara on the 3rd of August, carrying with them the sick and wounded American prisoners found in York.

Mr. Ridout's diary has a brief record of this event.

York, 1st August (Sunday).—The Americans returned with their fleet to York, and destroyed the barracks, woodyard, etc.

2nd August (Monday).—The enemy put out into

the lake early this morning, in all, thirteen vessels. 'Tis said our fleet (Sir James Yeo) consisting of six vessels, left Kingston on Saturday last the 31st July.

Another letter from the camp at St. David's, says that the conflagration at York was seen at Niagara, and caused much anxiety there.

From Thomas G. Ridout to his Father at York:—

ST. DAVID'S, *2nd August,* 1813.

I received yesterday letters from you and George, giving an account of the Yankee fleet being off York, threatening it with destruction. Our anxiety has not been less than yours, but since they let you remain unmolested the first day, I think they'll not land until Sir James meets them. The fate of this army depends on this. Its positions are so advanced that a retreat will be impossible without losing half the men. The enemy remain cooped up in Fort George, not daring to stir beyond the common. Everything goe on steadily and regularly. Ten thousand of the enemy will not be able to start John Bull out of the Black Swamp.

Mr. Bissett * went up yesterday to Long Point with £1,000 in specie, to buy cattle for Amherstburg.

I am very much alarmed about York, for a large fire was seen in that direction all last night. The garrison, at all events, must be burnt, with the flour and other provisions Mr. Crookshank has been collecting. Concerning my shirts, the starch has not come to hand.

I keep my things in a pair of saddle bags that Henry Nelles lent me, ready for a march. The military chest is at present run out to $500.

More than $40,000 have been paid out within the last fortnight. Every hour is now of great consequence and I think this week will determine affairs.

* Deputy Assistant-Commissary-General.

Some considerable movement will take place shortly, and I hope to write you of our success. Peggy Nelles has just mended my blue coat and sent it down to me, for which I thank her very much.

In the meantime at York an anxious watch was kept on the movements of the two opposing fleets on Lake Ontario. The Americans were much superior both in vessels and number of sailors.

Mr. Ridout's diary gives an account of what was seen from York during August.

York, 7th August (Saturday).—This morning our fleet, consisting of six vessels, were seen. In the afternoon they passed with a light breeze towards the westward, and in the evening were between the Humber and Etobicoke. The enemy's fleet of fifteen sail were seen on the lake opposite the town about eight or ten miles out. As it was calm, they approached our fleet with sweeps.

Sunday Morning, 8th August.—Not any vessels to be seen.

Sir James Yeo's fleet in 1813 consisted of the *Royal George*, twenty-four guns; *Prince Regent*, twenty-two guns; *Earl of Moira*, twenty guns; *Simcoe*, twelve guns; *Duke of Gloucester*, ten guns; *Seneca*, four guns.

A note is added to the last entry, of what occurred after the fleet left York as follows :—

The enemy retired to the mouth of Niagara on the 8th of August. In the afternoon of the 8th, Sir James Yeo drew them out, and in the night they retreated to the river, in doing which two of their largest schooners upset and went to the bottom. Except thirteen men, all were lost.

The American account of this disaster is that during the evening of the 8th of August the wind came from the westward, freshened, and at midnight was a fitful gale.

Suddenly a rushing sound was heard astern of most of the fleet, and it was soon ascertained that the *Hamilton* and *Scourge* had disappeared. They were capsized by a terrific squall, and all the officers and men, except sixteen of the latter, were drowned.

This was a great blow to Chauncey, for these two vessels, carrying nineteen guns between them, were the best in his fleet.

For two days the rival fleets manœuvred without coming to action, and at last on the morning of the 10th of August, Chauncey formed his fleet in battle order. Nothing was done during the day, but at ten at night Sir James Yeo succeeded in capturing two vessels, the *Growler* and *Julia*, after a severe but short struggle.

Chauncey made no further fight ; but, the gale increasing, he ran for shelter to the Genesee river, and then returned to Sackett's Harbour with the remains of his fleet.

From Mr. Ridout's Diary :—

Wednesday, 11th August.—Early this morning our fleet were seen off shore with two vessels in tow. During the night the wind blew fresh. At midnight (10th of August), Sir James Yeo dashed amongst the enemy's fleet; Commodore Chauncey fled, and left two of his vessels in our possession, which he brought to our harbour.

Friday 13*th.*—Our fleet sailed to Kingston.

To return to the camp at Niagara.

Another skirmish is recounted in the following letter:

Extract from a letter of an officer in the army of St. David's, 24th August, 1813.

A considerable demonstration was made this morning at the dawn of day upon Fort George.

The enemy's picquets were surprised and captured, but no disposition was evinced by the American army to support them, and our advance columns, after having remained for a considerable time in the town of Fort George, and the reconnaissance being completed, were ordered to return to their respective camps. Lieutenant-Colonel O'Neil, with a detachment of thirty of the 19th Dragoons, covered the advance of Lieutenant-Colonel Harvey, and dashed with great gallantry into the town, scouring several of the streets and penetrating as far as the Presbyterian church. Colonel Harvey actually called at his old quarters and recovered a box he had left there, containing several very valuable articles.

The enemy commenced a pretty brisk fire from the garden walls and houses, and opened their batteries upon us, notwithstanding which, our troops, who were extremely unwilling to come away, retired with the greatest order and regularity, and, I am happy to say, with a very trifling loss.

Of the enemy, seventy were made prisoners, and a number killed and wounded.

The officers commanding the picquets made their escape by an early flight. The complete success of the affair, in which the main object has been accomplished, has given additional spirit and confidence to our troops, and must have convinced the enemy that to his entrenchments alone he is indebted for his present security.

From Mr. Ridout's Diary :—

YORK, *26th August.*

Our fleet just dropped anchor off this place, and then sailed for Niagara.

28th August.—Returned and sailed the same evening.

Another letter from camp is dated

30th August. 1813.

From T. G. Ridout to his Father at York :—

I have not received a letter from home since 10th August. Last evening our fleet came over and proceeded to the Twelve-Mile Creek, on the American side, to intercept supplies by water, which the Yankees have daily received.

Allan McNab * has come over to seek his fortune as

---

* The Allan Napier McNab, who was seeking his fortune as a volunteer, was afterwards, as Sir Allan McNab, a conspicuous figure in Canadian history. He was born at Niagara in 1798, and was therefore only fifteen when he volunteered. His grandfather, Major McNab, of the 42nd, or Black Watch, held the post of Royal Forester in Scotland, and resided on a small property called Dundurn at the head of Loch Earn. His father was in the 71st, and served with General Simcoe during the American Revolutionary War, and accompanied him to Canada. The young hero of this sketch had first shouldered his musket at the capture of York; then served as midshipman on board Sir James Yeo's ship; then joined the 100th regiment under Colonel Murray. He was at the taking of Fort Niagara in December, 1813. For his bravery on that occasion he was given an ensigncy in the 49th regiment. He also served at Fort Erie and the attack on Plattsburg at the close of the war.

He was placed on half-pay at the reduction of the army in 1816, and commenced the study of the law, being called to the bar in 1825. He was elected to Parliament in 1829, and was in nine successive Parliaments, part of the time as Speaker of the House. He was knighted in 1838, was Prime Minister in 1854, and was created a baronet on his retirement from the office of premier in 1856.

In 1857, he retired from public life in Canada for a time, and went to England, from which country he returned in 1860, and was appointed to the Legislative Council, and took his seat among the "lords" of Canada.

Sir Allan McNab died in 1863.

a volunteer. I think he'll succeed in the 8th. At present, having no other home, he stays with us.

I suppose you have heard of the great victory gained in Spain on the 21st June, where the French lost 154 pieces of brass artillery, their military chest, etc., and the English lost near 5,000 in killed and wounded.

An Albany paper gives a fine account of Chauncey's "noble conduct." It says that he tried five days to bring the British to action but they always ran away. One night two of his schooners, in carrying a press of canvas in chase, upset, and were lost; and the following night three schooners, too eager in the pursuit, got into the midst of the British, and after maintaining with the most heroic gallantry an unequal contest of forty-five minutes with the *Wolfe* and *Melville* at pistol shot, one went down and the other two struck. Also that Chauncey had only returned to Sackett's Harbour for five weeks' provisions, and would come out and sweep the lake.

De Watteville's regiment is very much wanted here; the 49th are reduced to about 370 men. This morning three companies, amounting to seventy-five, arrived from Burlington. Fifty royal artillerymen have joined by the fleet.

By what I can learn, Sir George's (Prevost) presence here is very little sought for; he has no idea of attacking the Americans on their own ground, but the summit of his wishes is to recover Fort George and there remain. The great officers say that this army will be ruined with petty affairs. Some heavy cannon have arrived at Burlington. The army have been there two days out of whiskey. There is a good deal of ague among the men. The 8th have neither blankets nor great coats, but a large supply has arrived.

FOUR-MILE CREEK, *4th September*, 1813.

By the date of this you will perceive we have changed our quarters for the lake-side. The encampment here is very beautiful, and is formed of the 8th and 104th, part of the 89th and 100th regiments, consisting of 2,000 men. They lie upon the edge of the woods, having large clearings in the front, and the main road crossing the camp by Mr. Addison's, where the General stays. The artillery park is one mile in the rear. Very few troops are left in St. David's.

We came to Thompson's the day before yesterday, and met with rather an ungracious reception. The old fellow said he could not take us in, as his family occupied the whole house, but that we might go into an old house a little distance off, which was inhabited in the early period of the world. Accordingly, we cleared it of rubbish, made a fire, and fried a little beef we had brought with us. In the evening we made a straw bed on the floor. We collect balm in the garden for tea, and carry on an extensive robbery of peas, apples, onions, corn, carrots, etc.; for we can get nothing but by stealing, excepting milk, which is carefully measured. Bread and butter is out of the question, and to-day we sent a dragoon to the Twelve-Mile Creek for these articles and G. to the cross-roads for beef, etc. Lewis cooked some black bread yesterday. Only our chief has been invited to the sanctum sanctorum to partake of delicacies.

We have an iron pot which serves for tea pot, roaster and boiler, and two window shutters put upon three barrels form the table. We have three servants, who eat the remains of our feasts.

I spent a pleasant evening with Colonel Holcroft at the artillery park, and this afternoon I shall spend with Colonel Ogilvie at the 8th camp.

There is an astonishing run of white-cuffed ensigns and lieutenants at the house, and the carpet parlour is adorned the whole day with red. The only domestic on the farm is a miserable little black girl, who is almost worked to death. The army is getting very sickly, forty or fifty men are sent to the hospital every day. There are more than 400 sick, and a great number of officers.

York, being considered the healthiest place in Canada, is to be head-quarters for the medical establishment, you may expect the town to be filled with hospitals and sick. We cannot stand this daily diminution of strength ten days longer. They say that Decatur has succeeded Chauncey, and that we may look for him every hour; also that General Wilkinson has taken the command at Fort George with a considerable reinforcement. Our fleet is just coming over from York; I suppose, with De Watteville's regiment.

Four of the Glengarry's deserted yesterday, and four American dragoons deserted to us. Mr. Stanton bought a pound of tea this morning, the first we have had this long time. We pay out, on an average, £1,500 a day; next week it will be much more, as all the departments for the army will come in with their pay lists. We have now 10,000 barrels of flour in the depots, at $12 per barrel. I believe Allan McNabb will get into the 8th regiment. Shaw and Jarvis have been a year in the 49th.

CHAPTER XVI.

NAVAL FIGHT, LAKE ERIE, SEPTEMBER, 1813.

So FAR the Canadians had succeeded in holding the Americans at bay in the Niagara Peninsula. A great deal depended now in keeping control of Lake Erie, and thereby ensuring the success of General Proctor and his little army in the west.

We left the latter just after his defeat of General Winchester at the River Raisin, January 23rd, 1813. All through the winter and spring Tecumseh and Proctor, with a portion of the 41st regiment, the Essex militia, some artillery, and a force of Indians, varying in number, held back the invaders from crossing on the Detroit frontier. (The American General, Harrison, had taken up his post with a force of 2,500 men at Fort Meigs, on the Miami river.* , Proctor determined to dislodge them. So with a force of 930 men and about 1,200 Indians, collected at Detroit, he set off from Malden (Amherstburg) on the 23rd April, for the mouth of the Miami river, about twelve miles distant from Fort Meigs. His army, in all, a little over 2,000 in number, embarked in brigs and several small vessels,

---

* At the western extremity of Lake Erie.

and were accompanied by two gun-boats and some artillery. On the 26th of April, 1813, they appeared at the mouth of the Miami, about twenty-six miles from the mouth of the Detroit, and on the 28th landed on the left bank of the river, near old Fort Miami, where they established a camp. They next constructed batteries on a commanding elevation opposite Fort Meigs, but the wretched weather and continual rains kept back the work, so that they were not ready to begin operations until the 1st of May.

Fort Meigs was strongly intrenched, and had a good supply of field-pieces, but General Harrison was so doubtful of the result of a siege, that he dispatched messengers to Governor Meigs, of Ohio, to tell him to hasten on reinforcements. General Clay, with 1,200 Kentucky men, he knew were on their way to join him.

For four days shot and shell were hurled by Proctor's batteries upon Fort Meigs with very little effect on the earthworks, though the fire from the fort in reply was weak, owing to the scarcity of ammunition.

On the 5th of May, General Clay, with his reinforcements from Kentucky, arrived from Fort Defiance, in eighteen large scows, and were ordered by General Harrison to make an attack on the British batteries on the western side of the river, while the garrison of Fort Meigs were to attack the Indians on the eastern bank. At first, the advantage appeared to be with the Americans, but Captains Muir and Chandler, 41st regiment, rallied their men, and made a gallant charge with the bayonet. The enemy broke and fled to their boats. A panic seized them. The Indians, who, during the seige of the fort had remained rather silent spectators, now rushed forward and intercepted the retreat.

The reinforcement from Kentucky was almost annihilated. Of the 800 men who had left the boats to attack the batteries only 170 escaped to Fort Meigs. The enemy's loss in this affair, on both sides of the river, was about 1,100 in killed, wounded and prisoners. The Canadian troops lost fourteen killed and forty-five wounded.

The victory for Proctor was stained by the massacre of the flying foe. Tecumseh, we are told, did what he could to restrain his infuriated followers. When he heard of what was being done by them, he rode up at full speed, and, raising his tomahawk, threatened to destroy the first man who refused to obey his orders to desist.

The victory was not altogether satisfactory in its results to Proctor, for the Indian warriors insisted on returning to their homes to indulge in protracted revelry, as was their custom after a great fight. Even Tecumseh's influence was powerless to keep them in bounds.

Proctor, with his weakened force, found himself compelled to re-embark his guns and stores, and return to Fort Malden. He was discouraged on his arrival there by hearing of the fall of Fort George, and also by the refusal of his request for more soldiers. Tecumseh, who had again received large reinforcements of Indian warriors, constantly urged him to renew the attack of Fort Meigs, but he had lost heart, and though an expedition was fitted out, nothing was done. On the 1st of August an attempt was made by Proctor against Fort Stephenson, at Sandusky, but it resulted in failure, and cost the lives of several brave men.

Both sides were now, at the close of the summer, resting on their arms, waiting for the fitting-out of their respective fleets to contest the dominion of Lake Erie.

The Canadian fleet on Lake Erie was under the command of Captain Robert Barclay, one of Nelson's heroes, who had fought and lost an arm at the battle of Trafalgar.

His squadron consisted of the *Queen Charlotte,* seventeen guns, Captain Finnis; *Lady Prevost,* thirteen guns; brig *Hunter,* ten guns; *Little Belt,* three guns; *Chippewa,* one gun, and the *Detroit,* the flag-ship, of nineteen guns, which was not ready for action until September. In all, six vessels and sixty-three guns.

The American fleet was under the command of Commodore Perry, and consisted of the flag-ship *Lawrence,* twenty guns (named in honor of Captain Lawrence of the *Chesapeake,* who had been killed in action with H.M.S. *Shannon,* off Boston harbour, in June, 1813);

15

the *Niagara*, twenty guns; brig *Caledonia*,* three guns; schooner *Ariel*, four guns; *Scorpion*, two guns; *Trippe*, one gun; *Tigress*, one gun; *Porcupine*, one gun; and the *Ohio*, not in action. Nine vessels, fifty-two guns.

The weight of metal was with the Americans, although they had a smaller number of guns, the difference being, Americans 928 pounds, Canadians 459 pounds.

Perry's fleet had been fitted out in the harbour of Presqu' Isle, and during the month of July had been closely blockaded there by Barclay's squadron. A sand-bar at the mouth of the harbour prevented the American larger vessels from sailing out without first removing the cannon. This, of course, could not be done in the face of the enemy.

About the 1st of August Commodore Barclay sailed away to obtain provisions from Long Point, and during his absence Commodore Perry seized the opportunity to unload his vessels and place them safely over the sand-bar. It was a critical moment for the American fleet, for if Barclay had returned while the vessels were on the bar he would have had an easy victory. It is said a public dinner given to him and his officers by the citizens of Port Dover prolonged his absence. He arrived back just as the *Niagara* was safely moving into deep water. Once free to roam the lake, it was

---

* The *Caledonia* was captured from the Canadians on its way down from Detroit, October 9th, 1812.

Perry's turn to annoy Barclay, who sailed to Amherstburg, there to await the completion of his largest vessel, the *Detroit*.

At last September came, and all felt the decisive moment was near. Proctor's troops were suffering for want of supplies, and a communication with Long Point had to be opened at all hazards. So perfectly destitute of provisions was the post that there was not a day's flour in store.

On the morning of the 10th September, Barclay sailed out from Amherstburg, a light breeze blowing from the south-west. The enemy were lying five or six miles away, near Put-in Bay, and an action was inevitable. Both commanders knew that on this contest the fate of their armies on shore depended. Although Barclay's fleet had sixty-three guns, it was lamentably deficient in sailors, having only fifty experienced men between the six vessels. The rest of the crew were 240 soldiers and 80 Canadian volunteer seamen, who had no proper training in the use of the ropes and guns. Perry had nine vessels with fifty-nine guns, and his vessels were fully manned by nearly 600 of the pick of the American merchant marine.

It was to Barclay's advantage to fight at long range. Perry's tactics were to bring the ships to close quarters. At about eleven o'clock on the morning of the 10th September, the fight began, and for four hours the battle raged. At first the advantage was altogether with the Canadians. Barclay's fire had raked the

Lawrence, Perry's flag-ship, so badly that she lay a disabled hulk. Of the 103 men that had composed her crew when she went into action, twenty-two were killed and sixty-one wounded. At last, when the American commodore saw that his ship was so dismantled as to be of no further service, he determined to leave it, and to make for the *Niagara*, his largest vessel, which had up to that time been uninjured.

Wrapping his flag around him, he ordered his boat to be lowered, and with four stout seamen at the oars, he made the dangerous passage in the face of a tremendous fire. He was met at the gangway of the *Niagara* by the astonished commander of that vessel. "How goes the day?" asked Elliott. "Bad enough," replied Perry; "why are the gun-boats so far astern?" "I'll bring them up," said Elliott. "Do so," said Perry. So the captain of the *Niagara* pushed off in a small boat to hurry up the lagging vessels.* Now the fortunes of the day changed. The wind veered, and for lack of seamen Barclay's vessels became unmanageable.

The rudder of the *Lady Prevost* was disabled; the *Detroit* and the *Queen Charlotte* became entangled. Barclay† and Finnis,‡ their commanders, were both

---

* Lossing, "Hambleton's Journal."

† Robert Barclay was a Scotchman, and attended the school at Kettle, of which Bishop Strachan was the master. In a charge delivered by the Bishop in 1860, he thus speaks of him: "Commodore Robert Barclay, afterwards so unfortunate on Lake Erie, from causes over which he had no control, was another of my pupils. He was a youth of the brightest pro-

wounded, the latter mortally; the former had his thigh shattered, and a shot in the shoulder disabled his only arm. Close and deadly was the fire from the American vessels. All Barclay's officers were wounded or killed, and three-fourths of the men. Resistance was no longer possible. It was about three in the afternoon when the flag of the *Detroit* was lowered, and when the smoke of the battle cleared away, a sad scene of carnage was revealed. The vessels of both squadrons were dreadfully shattered, especially the two flag-ships. Sixty-eight men were killed and 190 wounded during the four hours the battle lasted. The Americans lost 123, twenty-seven of whom were killed; the Canadians, 135, forty-one of whom were killed.

When some months afterwards Barclay (who had been placed on parole and then exchanged) was brought before a court of inquiry to answer for the loss of his fleet, his judges were moved to tears as they looked at the mutilated form of the hero who had fought so well.

mise, and often have I said in my heart that he possessed qualities which fitted him to be another Nelson, had the way opened for such a consummation."

‡ The loss of Captain Finnis was deeply deplored by Barclay, who thus writes to Sir James Yeo, on September 13th, three days after the battle: "Too soon, alas! was I deprived of the services of the noble and intrepid Captain Finnis, who, soon after the commencement of the action, fell; and with him fell my greatest support."

Sir James Yeo wrote of the ill-fated action in his official despatch to Sir George Prevost: "Though His Majesty's squadron were very deficient in seamen, weight of metal, and particularly long guns, yet the greater misfortune was the loss of every officer, particularly Captain Finnis, whose life, had it been spared, would, in my opinion, have saved the squadron."

This victory on Lake Erie was most important to the Americans. Both armies were anxiously awaiting the result of the encounter. If Barclay had been successful, Proctor's army would have been enabled to obtain its needed supplies and reinforcements, and so could have held the western frontier. Perry's success enabled Harrison to seize Detroit, to recover Michigan, and to press on and once more invade the Western Peninsula. The Americans were intoxicated with success. "Canada must now be ours," was their exultant cry. Medals were struck in honour of their victory. There were illuminations all over the land, and honours and rewards were heaped upon Perry and his officers.*

Washington Irving wrote : "The last roar of cannon that died along Erie's shore was the expiring note of British domination."

The cannon roar on that fateful day on Lake Erie was heard at an incredible distance. At Cleveland, seventy miles away, the people thought at first it was thunder, but seeing no clouds, concluded that the two squadrons had met. The listeners could easily distinguish the sound of the heavier and lighter guns.

Lossing records the fact that a man who lived on the New York State line, heard at his house the cannonading on the lake, 160 miles distant.

---

* The captured squadron was valued at $225,000. Commodore Chauncey, Commander-in-Chief of the lakes, received one-twentieth ; Perry and Elliot each drew $7,140 ; Congress voted Perry $5,000 additional ; each commander of a gun-boat received $2,200 ; each midshipman, $800 ; each marine and sailor, $200.

It is a curious fact that, on the day of the fight, Mr. Ridout's diary has this entry :—

York, Friday, 10*th September.*—About eleven a.m., loud firing was heard, and continued about an hour. It seemed to be towards Niagara; the wind was westward, with thick rain.

The diary continues :—

Saturday, 11*th September.*—Heavy firing said to have been heard on the lake nearly opposite Hamilton, which continued four hours, supposed to be between the fleets.

The firing heard on the 11th September is accounted for by an action that took place on Lake Ontario, between Sir James Yeo and Commodore Chauncey. On that day Sir James' fleet lay becalmed off the Genesee. Catching a gentle breeze from the north-west, Chauncey bore down upon it, and was within gun-shot distance, when Yeo's sails took the wind, and their vessels being swifter sailers, escaped, not, however, without sustaining considerable damage, during a running fight for more than three hours.

The diary continues :—

Thursday, 16*th September.*—A heavy storm of wind and rain began ; no certain news respecting the firing.

Lake Ontario during the month of September, 1813, was the scene of many a lively contest. On the 18th, Commodore Chauncey sailed for Niagara, for the purpose of conveying troops to Sackett's Harbour, and was followed by Sir James Yeo. An exciting fight took place between the fleets. The *Pike, Madison* and *Sylph*, American, engaged the *Wolf*, Sir James' flag-ship, the *Royal George* and some smaller vessels. At last the *Wolf* was found to have sustained serious injury, and pushed away before the wind, crowded with canvas, and gallantly protected in her flight by the *Royal George*. A general chase was commenced, and the pursuit was continued towards Burlington Bay for two hours, when Chauncey called off his vessels. The American Commodore thought that if he had received proper support, he might have captured and destroyed the British squadron, but the wind was increasing, and he dared not run into any harbour for shelter, so he sailed away for Niagara, where he lay during a gale that lasted forty-eight hours. The exciting chase was known by the name of the "Burlington races."

So slow was news in arriving from the western frontier, that it was not until the 16th September that intelligence of the battle on Lake Erie reached York.

The following note is in Mr. Ridout's diary :—

York, 16th September.—On Friday, the 10th September, a battle was fought on Lake Erie, near the Islands, between our half-manned fleet of six sail, and the enemy's fleet of nine sail, which lasted four hours, when neither fleet could act any longer, at which time the American gun-boats came out and attacked our fleet. In their defenceless state we had the mortification to be compelled to surrender.

It is possible that the firing heard by Mr. Ridout and others at York, on the morning of the 10th September, was from the guns on Lake Erie. The wind from the west and the heavy atmosphere makes it probable that the sound was carried an immense distance.

There is no record of any other fight that day on Lake Ontario to account for the firing heard at York.

In the camp at Niagara during the month of September, 1813, things were not prospering. Fever had broken out; the men, weary with inaction, badly fed and ill-paid, were deserting day by day, and the news of the loss of the fleet on Lake Erie brought gloom and consternation.

From Thomas G. Ridout to his brother George at York :—

HEADQUARTERS, NEAR NIAGARA,

16th September, 1813.

I received your letter yesterday by Starr Jarvis, who has come here to be our waggon-master. To-morrow we shall have 20,000 hard dollars in silver and £5,000 in paper money, and in about eight days shall receive in army bills £20,000.* The Commissary-General is going to the Mediterranean, and Mr. Couche will take his place.

Gee cooks and waits upon us, and a little French dragoon helps him. We burn rails, steal apples, pears and peaches at a great rate. Old Lion sometimes growls at the rails going so fast, but can't help himself. He thinks me the most innocent of the lot.

---

* The large expenditure of money during the war was of undoubted benefit to those engaged in trade. Therefore, from a monetary point of view, the war was not an unmixed evil.

Desertion has come to such a height that eight or ten men go off daily.

The army is not quite so sickly as it was.

We have heard nothing of the fleet since she left last Friday. A schooner went into the river (Niagara) yesterday afternoon. The Americans have been busily employed for some days past in transporting all their heavy guns and baggage across the river. Their deserters come in every day. They say that 4,000 men are in Fort George. The other day, a Yankee picket shot two of our deserters dead. One of the 49th attempted to swim over by Queenston, but was killed by the sentry.

As soon as the rainy weather comes we shall move to the Mountain, for the troops cannot remain in their present encampment by the Black Swamp.

From Thomas G. Ridout to his Father at York:—

HEADQUARTERS, 21*st September*, 1813.

Things are going on very badly. It is too true that our fleet on Lake Erie is taken, and Proctor is left at Amherstburg without provisions, guns or men. Most of the cannon were mounted on board the ships; £20,000 is on the way to pay the debts at Amherstburg, and we have $40,000 in gold and silver on the way from Kingston, besides £20,000 in bills. Assistant-Commissary-General Dance has gone to take charge at Burlington, with three clerks.

The militia are all called out to build barracks at Lundy's Lane, Queenston and Chippewa, and also at Burlington Heights, which, I believe, is to be headquarters this winter. Nichol has gone up to bring the Long Point militia down. General De Rottenburg went up to the head of the lakes to-day. General Vincent commands at the Cross-Roads; I think he is the best of the two. Mr. Couche has had a notification that he must hold the military chest, etc., in readiness, as a movement would shortly take place, somewhere on the Mountain, it is expected. The 8th have lost two officers within a week—Captain Kingsley, the paymaster, of a fever, he was a very gentlemanly, good fellow, and Lewis; Fitzgibbon has got well again.

The last thing seen of the fleets on Lake Erie was at the islands near Amherstburg. After the battle twelve vessels were seen very quietly together. Captain Barclay was ordered out with six vessels, half manned, very much against his will, to fight the Americans, who consisted of nine vessels every way superior. The consequence was that he was taken, and all that country must fall, and that before long, for we have just heard 10,000 Ohio militia are on their march to Detroit. Colonel Hamilton has moved up to Turkey Point. The 2nd battalion of the 41st are on their way from Kingston.

We are in the same state at the old house as ever. I carry on the foraging. To-night our dragoon is to make a grand attack upon the onions. The nests are kept very nice and clean from eggs. The dragoon has just come in with a fine musk melon and a peck of onions. We feed a turkey every day at the door, which is doomed for our Sunday dinner. Sometimes a cow happens to get milked over night, for the old lady is getting to be very stingy of the milk.

Colonel Coffin went in yesterday with a flag of truce, and the Americans told him that our whole fleet was taken on Lake Erie, after a most desperate engagement. Our second ship went down in the battle, and every man on board their flag-ship was either killed or wounded. Had it not been for some gunboats that came up at the close of the engagement, we would have gained the day; so roughly had our six little vessels handled them. They say it was the most severe action fought this war; great numbers fell on both sides.

From Thomas G. Ridout to his Father at York:—

ST. DAVID'S, *October 2nd, 1813.*

I wrote a letter three or four days ago telling you that we had changed our quarters, and that the whole department was ill, Mr. Couche much the worst. He has kept his bed for several days and has not heard a word upon business. Jones and myself are his nurses, with the assistance of the old people in the house. His servant-man is as ill as his master. This afternoon fever and headache attacked me. Mr. Couche has given Jones and me charge of the military chest, the key of which I wear in my pocket, and I pay out the money. We have to account for $27,000 paid since we had the management.

The people flock so after money that I am obliged to have a sentry at the door to let but one person in at a time, and when they do enter, they must not speak ten words, so now they hold us in great awe. The Americans have possession of our side as far down as Samuel Street's, and have plundered all the loyal inhabitants of their property.

The greater part of the settlement being Dutch Mennonites, are friendly to the enemy, and assist them in everything. We have lately taken a number of their waggons.

We expect some serious movement every hour, as the enemy are in great force at Fort George. A number of bateaux, about sixty, loaded with men now accompany their fleet, to make some landing above us, I have no doubt. We are driving all the cattle from this part of the district towards the head of the lake. The Chippewa and Short Hill country is stript of cattle, and to-day they have been driving them from the vinicity of the camps. The waggons stand ready loaded with the baggage which moves in the rear. I am sure we shall march soon.

What is to be done with Mr. Couche, I know not; but he must go along. I believe the rainy weather has set in, for it has rained all day.

CHAPTER XVII.

TECUMSEH—BATTLE OF THE THAMES, OCTOBER, 1813.

AFTER the defeat of Barclay on Lake Erie, Forts Detroit and Amherstburg became untenable for the Canadian troops, and were abandoned. General Proctor first destroying the magazines, barracks and public stores. General Harrison's reinforcements amounted to 7,000 or 8,000 men, including 4,000 volunteers from Kentucky. Commodore Perry, with his fleet, conveyed all the American troops to the Canadian shore, except the dragoons, who were to meet them at Malden.

General Harrison, finding the forts abandoned, left Colonel McArthurs in command, and hastened to follow the retreating army.

Tecumseh had urged upon General Proctor the advisability of meeting the invaders as they landed below Amhertsburg, and, if overpowered, to take up another position on the Canard; if driven from that, to go up the River Thames, retiring with supplies protected and drawing the Americans far into the interior, when all the forces of the upper Province, such as could be brought from Burlington Heights and other posts, could join them, and harass the enemy continually, and compel them to retreat. This advice met with no response. Proctor ordered a rapid flight.

Tecumseh, it is said, rose from the council, dashed his sword on the table, and denounced Proctor as a miserable old squaw.

Proctor wished to appease him, and told him that he could not meet Harrison's troops on landing, as they had all the ships and great guns, and could fire with the "double balls," as the Indians called the shells.

Therefore, he proposed to continue the march, and fight them out of reach of the ships.

Tecumseh saw that Proctor did not want to fight, so proclaimed that he would march in advance and select the battle ground.

History has it recorded, that when, at last, General Proctor was forced to give battle on the ground chosen by Tecumseh on the River Thames, at the first charge the British General fled, leaving his heroic ally to breast the onset alone.

General Harrison, six days after the battle of the Thames, wrote to the Governor of Ohio, dated Detroit, October 11th, 1813 :—

Nothing but infatuation could have governed General Proctor's conduct. The day that I landed below Malden, he had at his disposal upwards of 3,000 Indians. The Indians were extremely desirous of fighting us at Malden. I enclose you Tecumseh's communication or speech to Proctor.

Tecumseh to General Proctor :—

AMHERSTBURG, *September 18th*, 1813.

In the name of the Indian Chiefs and warriors to Major-General Proctor, as the representative of their great Father, the King. Father listen to your children, you have them all before you.

When war was declared our Father stood up and gave us the tomahawk, and told us he was then ready to strike the Americans, that he wanted our assistance, and that he would certainly get us our lands back which the Americans had taken from us. Listen! Our fleet has gone out; we know they have fought; we have heard the great guns. Listen! the Americans have not yet defeated us by land; neither are we sure they have done so by water.* Father, you have got the arms and ammunition which our great Father sent to his red children. If you have an idea of going away, give them to us, and you may go, and welcome; our lives are in the hands of the Great Spirit. We are determined to defend our lands, and, if it be His will, we wish to leave our bones upon them.

On the morning of the 4th October, Harrison and his troops had nearly come up to Proctor's retreating army. The latter had reached Chatham, where a stream called McGregor's Creek flows into the Thames. There Proctor promised Tecumseh he would make a final stand. "Here," he said, on his arrival, "we will defeat Harrison or lay our bones." These words pleased the warrior, and he said, "When I look on these two streams I shall think of the Wabash and the Tippecanoe."

* Tecumseh had been kept in ignorance of the defeat of the 10th September.

The last stand was not, however, made here, but some miles farther on.

At two o'clock on the 5th October Harrison's army had nearly come up to the fugitives. When about three miles from Moraviantown, Harrison's scouts learned that Proctor and Tecumseh were awaiting him there, drawn up in order of battle.

The ground chosen by Tecumseh was well selected. On the left was the River Thames, with a high and steep bank. On the right a marsh running parallel with the river about two miles. The whole space between the river and the swamp was covered with beech, sugar maple and oak trees.

The 41st regiment was posted near the river. The artillery commanded the road. The Indians were in the woods on the right. Tecumseh commanded in person. Harrison ordered the mounted Kentucky riflemen to make the first charge. They were accustomed to riding in the woods, and their arms were no impediment. A volley from the Canadian troops caused them to hesitate a moment, but at the second volley the American cavalry dashed in and broke the line of their opponents. All was now confusion. Five minutes after the first shock Proctor's troops were flying in all directions. We are told that the General, without making an attempt to rally his men, fled in his carriage,* hotly pursued by the enemy, who made

* An American officer (Sholes) writes : "I had a very pleasant ride back to Detroit in Proctor's beautiful carriage. I found in it a hat, a sword and a trunk. The latter contained many letters in the handsomest writing I ever saw, by Proctor's wife to her dear Henry."

many prisoners.   On the right the American advance
was more hotly contested.   The Indians, led by
Tecumseh, fought with the enthusiasm of desperation.
They waited until the enemy were within a few paces
of them, and then hurled on them a deadly shower of
bullets.   In this part of the field the undergrowth was
so thick that the mounted riflemen could not advance.
They were therefore ordered to carry on the fight on
foot.   The battle-cry of the Kentucky men was:
" Remember the River Raisin."   For awhile victory
hung in the balance, but at last the great leader,
Tecumseh, fell, and then his followers gave way and
scattered through the woods.

Among the spoils secured by the Americans were
the brass cannon of Revolutionary fame, which had
been retaken by Brock at Detroit, also the small arms
which had been captured by Proctor's troops at Detroit, and Frenchtown, and the Miami.   The pursuit
of Proctor was continued until dark, but he succeeded
in escaping.   He abandoned his carriage, left the
road, and escaped by a by-path.

Proctor had, as an excuse for his conduct, that he
had to face an enemy greatly his superior in numbers,
provided with cavalry, of which he was destitute, also
that his troops were worn out with their hasty march,
and had suffered much in a long service of fifteen
months on guard at the frontier.

On his trial by court-martial, which took place in
December, 1814, it was found that he had not re-

16

treated with judgment, nor had he judiciously disposed of his forces. He was sentenced to be suspended from rank and pay for six months.

George IV. was very severe upon the unfortunate Proctor, and censured the court for mistaken lenity. He expressed his regret that any officer of the length of service, and the exalted rank of General Proctor, should be so extremely wanting in professional knowledge, and deficient in those active, energetic qualities which must be required of every officer.

The few who escaped being made prisoners after the battle of the 5th October, fled in confusion through the unbroken wilderness towards Lake Ontario.

They reached Ancaster, seven miles west of Burlington Heights, on the 17th October, their number, including seventeen officers, amounted to only 256.

The victors remained in possession of the ground, and on the 7th October, General Harrison left for Detroit with his army, taking the property they had captured, and the prisoners.

On the way back, a furious storm wrecked several of the vessels from the Thames, and much of the captured property was lost. Harrison and Perry had planned the re-taking of Michillimackinac, but the furious storms, and near approach of winter, caused them to abandon that enterprise.

General Harrison then prepared to go down the lake, and join the American forces on the Niagara frontier.

The campaign on the bank of the Thames was the last in which General Harrison was engaged. His friends had expected him to be made Commander-in-Chief of the American army, but jealousy and the disfavour of the Secretary of War made urther military service so unpleasant, that he resigned his commission in May, 1814.*

On the return of the Kentucky volunteers after the battle of the Thames, half a dozen of them were impressed with the belief that they had each slain the great chieftain. The description given by them of the personal appearance of the warrior did not, however, correspond with the personal appearance of Tecumseh.

It was considered probable that he had been severely wounded, and borne from the field.

The contest had been so short and sharp, that no one seemed to have a clear idea of what happened during the charge.

One thing is certain, that, when Tecumseh was shot down, dead or alive, his body was carried from the field by some of his devoted followers. It was thought possible that he was only wounded, and that he might appear again, but silence and mystery have always surrounded his end. No certain information has ever been obtained of his death. His tribe and friends

---

*William Henry Harrison, a descendant of a celebrated leader in Cromwell's army, was elected President of the United States in 1840, and died a month after his inauguration. His grandson is the present President, 1890.

appeared unwilling to admit that he had been slain by the white man. Their pride prevented them giving any replies to questions on the subject.

They were asked :—*

"What has become of Tecumseh ? "
Raising the right hand to heaven, with an expression of deep sorrow,
"Gone!"
"Did you see him on the day of battle ? "
"Yes."
"When did you see him the last time ? "
"Just as the Americans came in sight, he with his young braves passed rapidly up and down the line, spoke to every old warrior ; saw every one ; said, 'Be braves, stand firm, shoot certain.'"
"Did you hear after the battle that he was killed or badly wounded ? "
No answer.

And so, like King Arthur of old, in "that last weird battle of the West," he passed unseen "to the Island valley, where falls not hail, or rain, or any snow."

*Hatch's Chapter of the War.

CHAPTER XVIII.

CHATEAUGUAY—CHRYSLER'S FIELD—OCTOBER, NOVEMBER, 1813.

OCTOBER did not begin auspiciously for the Canadian troops. Sickness, disaster and defeat had followed them closely. Times were certainly gloomy, and the struggle that had gone on without interruption for fifteen months seemed hopeless, and the abandonment of Upper Canada was considered probable.

On the 14th October, General Proctor was still at the Grand river with the small remnant of his demoralized troops. Three hundred of his men had been made prisoners at Moraviantown, and he was gathering the rest of the stragglers together. General Vincent, with his division, had left the vicinity of Fort George, and was once more in his stronghold at Burlington Heights.

The next letter is from the camp, dated Burlington, 14th October, 1813.

From Thomas G. Ridout to his Father :—

Yesterday I received your letter of the 10th. The times are so gloomy that I know not what to say. We shall soon retreat to Kingston. Every preparation is making. The Americans with 1,000 men have advanced as far as the Twenty. Last night 600 men marched to drive them back. General Vincent complains of De Rottenberg* leaving him in this eventful period, when every difficulty stares him in the face. The troops are recovering their health. I am afraid you will have to go to Quebec. It must be before the army retreats, or not at all. There will be no getting down with them. George must stay at home to protect all left behind. I hope you will take John with you.

I am Couche's secretary, cashier, etc. Young Jones was left behind sick. I have now £9,000 in charge. I have been busy since seven this morning, it is now twelve o'clock at night.

Proctor has more than 200 of his regiment collected, he is still at the Grand River with them.

BURLINGTON, 16th October, 1813.

DEAR FATHER,—I wrote to you the other day from this place, which letter I suppose you have received. I was in such a hurry I could hardly tell you anything. We had a most dreadful time from the Cross-Roads (Homer). Upwards of 300 men were straggling upon the road and waggons loaded with miserable objects stuck fast in mud-holes, broken down and unable to ascend the hills, and the men too ill to stir hand or foot. One thousand Western Indians arrived last night from Detroit, besides 2,000 women and children. Poor creatures! What will become of them? It is said the great Tecumseh is killed. The Indians have made horrid work with Harrison's army, killing several hundred.† We are sending all the heavy baggage to York, but do not think Sir George will allow this army to retreat. In two days Mr. Couche and I set off for Quebec. Mr. Dance wanted

---

* General De Rottenberg had left for Kingston, where an attack was expected.

† This must allude to the massacre at Fort Meigs.

his brother with Mr. C. but he said he would not part with me. I shall ride one of his horses down. If the army retreats 8,000 barrels of flour, besides immense stores, will fall into the enemy's hands.

The troops have left the Forty. Vincent is waiting for orders from below before he retreats. It is said that Evans, Muir and Chambers are killed.* For these four days I have worked from six in the morning till ten at night. Mr. Couche will soon be Commissary-General.

I suppose you have heard of Lord Wellington's defeat in Spain, when he lost 7,000 men.

York will be left in a dreadful state if we retreat. We shall stay two days with you.

Mr. Ridout's diary :—

York, 20th October, 1813.—Thomas came home on his way to Montreal. He accompanies Ed. Couche, Deputy-Commissary-General, as his cashier. He remained with us all the day of the 21st, and set out with Mr. Couche for Kingston and Montreal early on Friday morning, the 22nd October. His brother George accompanied him as far as Scarboro'.

Formidable preparations were now being made for the capture of Montreal, where the American soldiers were promised good winter quarters.

General Wilkinson, the rather incompetent commander-in-chief of the American army, had the control of about 16,000 men on the northern frontier, including General Hampton's division. The first plan proposed was the capture of Kingston. This did not strike General Wilkinson favourably, who, in

* Gallant officers of the 41st.

August, before the defeat of the Canadians on Lake
Erie and at Moraviantown, wrote thus to the Secretary of War :—

Will it not be better to strengthen our force already
at Fort George ; cut up the British in that quarter,
and should General Harrison fail in his object, march
a detachment and capture Malden? After which,
closing our operations on the peninsula, descend
like lightning with our whole force on Kingston, and,
having reduced that place, and captured both garrison
and shipping, go down the St. Lawrence and form a
junction with Hampton's column, if the lateness of
the season should permit ?

The Secretary of War objected to any further
movement on the peninsula, as it would only " wound
the tail of the lion," and General Wilkinson left the
Niagara district for Sackett's Harbour, in August,
without any definite plan being decided on.

On his way, he sent from Albany his first orders as
commander-in-chief to General Hampton.

This aroused the anger of the old aristocrat Hampton, who resented any interference from Wilkinson,
and henceforth cherished an intense hatred against
him.

In September, it was decided by the Americans to
leave an efficient garrison of 600 troops in Fort
George, and to take the remainder of the Niagara
division of the army in Chauncey's fleet, to join in an
attack on Montreal.

When General Vincent withdrew to Burlington

Heights after Proctor's defeat, Colonel Winfield Scott, who had been left in command of the Americans at Fort George, with about 800 regular troops, left the defence of the fort to General McClure, commanding the New York militia, and crossed the Niagara river on the 13th October, on his way to join Wilkinson's army at Sackett's Harbour. When Scott left Fort George, it was believed that all the British troops had been called from the western end of Lake Ontario to reinforce the garrison at Kingston. These orders had indeed, been sent by Sir George Prevost to General Vincent, as soon as the Commander-in-Chief heard of General Proctor's defeat at the battle of the Thames. However, Vincent, Morrison and Harvey were not men disposed to retire. A council of war was held at Burlington Heights, and it was determined not to abandon the Niagara Peninsula.

The American General, McClure, was sending out foraging parties from Fort George, and greatly annoying the inhabitants in the vicinity. So Colonel Murray, of the 100th, was despatched with about 400 men to drive them back. This was successfully done, and soon the Americans were hemmed within their own lines, and the Canadian troops once more took up their position at Twelve-Mile creek (St. Catharines).

General Wilkinson was now (October, 1813), concentrating his force at Grenadier Island, which is situated eighteen miles below Sackett's Harbour, between that place and Kingston. His plan was to descend the St. Lawrence in bateaux and gun-boats, to pass by the forts, and after forming a junction with Hampton, to proceed and take possession of the Island of Montreal.

Storm followed storm on Lake Ontario and the St. Lawrence. Snow fell to the depth of ten inches, and the American troops, encamped on Grenadier Island, suffered severely.

They remained there until the 1st November, with the exception of General Brown's brigade, some light troops, and heavy artillery, which moved forward on the 29th October, and took up their position at French Creek, now Clayton.

Chauncey, in the meantime, endeavoured unsuccessfully to blockade the Canadian fleet in Kingston harbour.

General Wilkinson arrived at French Creek on the 3rd November.

On the morning of the 5th November, a clear bright crisp day, the whole flotilla of 300 boats moved down the river.

As soon as the American movements were ascertained, General De Rottenberg sent a flying column down the St. Lawrence to intercept them. But few men could be spared for the daring enterprise, and the corps of observation, as it was called, comprised in all not more than 800 men, accompanied by a few gun-boats. It consisted of the remains of the 49th regiment, some Canadian Fencibles, the second battalion of the 89th, and three companies of Voltigeurs, the whole force under the command of Colonel Morrison, aided by the Deputy Adjutant-General, Colonel Harvey—the hero of Stoney Creek.

The Commissariat Department, under Mr. Couche, accompanied, or rather followed this column, and the following letter from Mr. Ridout gives an account of the march down the river :—

KINGSTON, 1st *November*, 1813.

DEAR FATHER,—We have had a most harassing journey of ten days to this place, where we arrived last night in a snow-storm. It has been snowing all day, and is now half a foot deep. The journey has knocked Mr. Couche up. He is in the next room with a fever. Frequently I had to go middle deep in a mud-hole, unload the waggon, and carry heavy trunks fifty yards, sometimes waist-deep in mire, and reload the waggon. One night it upset going up a steep hill in the woods. Gee and I carried the load up to the top, whilst Mr. C. rode on three miles in the rain for a lanthorn. About eleven o'clock we got in, when we missed a trunk with 500 guineas in it. Mr. Couche and I immediately rode back about two miles and found it in a mud-hole.

The Yankees lie with their whole fleet and 12,000 men over on Grenadier Island. Yesterday they sent down to scour the river ten gun-boats and forty Durham boats full of men. At Cornwall they captured a convoy of boats and merchandise to a great amount.

These Durham boats have letters of marque and reprisal, so the river is completely theirs. I know not how we are to get from them.

Accounts have just arrived from Montreal, saying that 400 of our troops have defeated General Hampton's army of 4,000 men. Kingston is well fortified, and I think would withstand a large force.

The fleet lie about Snake Island. There are about 2,000 troops here. The gates are shut every night at sunset. Two fine blockhouses are built back of the town, with water and ditches round them, and the works carried from one to the other. Along the bay a breastwork of empty barrels is made.

The defeat of Hampton's army, mentioned in this letter, was one of the most romantic achievments of the war, and most important in its results. All the posts in Western Canada, with the exception of Mackinaw, had fallen into the hands of the Americans. They had not only recaptured Michigan, but the result of the battle of Moraviantown had given them control of the garden of Upper Canada. Everything pointed to the early conquest of that Province, and the authorities at Washington now planned a vigorous invasion of Lower Canada.

General Hampton began his advance on the 20th of September, surprised a Canadian picquet at Odelltown, and then took the road to L'Acadie. He had to pass through a swamp for upwards of fifteen miles, before reaching the open country. Colonel De Salaberry, with the aid of his Voltigeurs, had done his best to make the road a bad one. He had felled trees, and dug holes, and placed every obstruction in the way. At last Hampton moved with his whole force towards the head of the River Chateauguay.

De Salaberry having ascertained the road by which

Hampton was to advance, took up a position in a thick wood, on the left bank of the river, six miles above its junction with the English river. Here he threw up breastworks of logs. His front and right flank were covered by extended abattis, and his left rested on the river. In his rear, the river being fordable, he covered the ford with a strong breastwork, defended by a guard, and kept a picquet of Beauharnois' militia in advance, on the right bank of the river, lest the enemy should mistake the road, and crossing the ford under cover of the forest, should dislodge him from his position.

On the 22nd September, Hampton sent General Izard to force a militia picquet at the junction of the rivers Outaite and Chateauguay, and there the main body of the Americans arrived on the 22nd September. Two days later, the enemy repaired the road, and brought forward ten pieces of artillery to within seven miles of De Salaberry's position.

Hampton had discovered the ford, and sent Colonel Purdy with a strong body of infantry on the evening of the 25th September, to fall upon De Salaberry's rear, while the main body were to assail in front. Purdy's brigade lost themselves in the woods, and wandered about all night. On the morning of the 26th September, Hampton appeared in the front, with about 3,500 men. A picquet of twenty-five Canadians was driven in, but it only fell back on a second picquet, where a most resolute stand was made. De Salaberry heard the firing, and advanced to the rescue. He had with him Ferguson's company of Fencibles, Chevalier Duchesnay's and Juchereau Duchesnay's company of Voltigeurs. He posted the Fencibles in extended order, every man being an arm's length from his neighbour, the right touching the woods, in which some Abenaquis Indians were distributed. Chevalier Duchesnay's company was in skirmishing order, in line extended from the left of the Fencibles to the Chateauguay; and Juchereau Duchesnay's company, and thirty-five militia were ranged in close order along the margin of the river, to prevent a flank fire from the enemy.

The Americans advanced steadily within musket shot, and De Salaberry commenced the action by discharging his rifle. In order the deceive the enemy, the greatest possible noise was made, purposely, by buglers stationed here and there in the wings, the centre and the rear of the Canadian force. The enemy wheeled into line and began to fire in volleys, but threw away their bullets as the battalions were not fronting the Voltigeurs or Fencibles. As some of the skirmishers retreated, the enemy moved forward. Again the Canadian buglers sounded the advance, and the notes of martial music echoed through the woods as if 20,000 men were being marshalled for the fight. At this crisis, Colonel McDonell, of the Glengarries arrived on the scene with some reinforcements, and at the same time Purdy's detachment of American infantry, long lost in the woods, was guided to the ford by the firing and music. He drove in a Canadian picquet which was on the opposite side of the river, and was pushing for the ford, when De Salaberry ordered Captain Daly with the light company of the 3rd battalion of Canadian militia to cross the river, and take up the ground abandoned by the picquet. This was done gallantly, and the American advance guard was driven back. As they appeared again, De Salaberry ordered Juchereau Duchesnay to be up and at them, and his men, rising from their place of concealment, poured in a fire on Purdy's brigade, as effectual as it was unexpected. The Americans reeled back, turned and ran. Hampton seeing Purdy's discomfiture, slowly withdrew, leaving De Salaberry with his 300 Canadians in possession of the position with all the honours of victory.

For his skilful management of this affair De Salaberry was loaded with honours, his officers and men publicly thanked, and five pairs of colours were presentled to the five battalions of Canadian embodied militia which had taken part in the fight.

Charles Michel d'Irumberry de Salaberry, Seigneur de Chambly et de Beulac, was born at the manor house of Beauport, November 19th, 1778. He entered the British army at an early age; served eleven years in the East Indies, and distinguished himself in command of a company of grenadiers in the expedition to Martinique, in 1795. He was *aide-de-camp* to General de Rottenburg, in the Walcheren expedition and held a post of honour during the siege, and at the capture of Flushing. Returning to Canada as a staff-officer, under General de Rottenburg, he was chosen by Sir George Prevost to raise a regiment of light infantry among the French-Canadian population, a task which he accomplished most successfully. His regiment was known as the Voltigeurs, and throughout the war they were distinguished for their bravery and devotion.

De Salaberry afterwards laid down the sword for the pen. He became a senator, and was called to the Legislative Council in 1818. He died at Chambly on the 26th February, 1829.

His escutcheon bears the motto becoming to the perfect knight, " *Force a superbe, mercy a faible.*" —(From Morgan's " Distinguished Canadians.")

The next letter, of the 9th November, tells of Wilkinson's descent of the St. Lawrence, with 10,000 men; and we can well imagine the scene was an impressive one to the young Canadian, as he watched the passing of that fleet of 300 boats down the river.

Of all the events of that eventful year, none was more truly heroic or more worthy of praise than Morrison's march to intercept the invaders of Montreal.

The new Republic then seemed on the point of overwhelming its weak half-brother. Upper Canada was almost in the grasp of the enemy. There was nothing to stay their victorious progress except a little band of cool, brave men. As Colonel Harvey says in his letter describing the battle of Chrysler's Field, " We had nothing to trust to but every man doing his duty."

It seemed as if only a miracle could prevent the annihilation of the Canadian troops.

What were Wilkinson's hopes and plans may be seen from his letter to General Hampton, dated

HEAD-QUARTERS OF THE ARMY,

Seven miles above Ogdensberg,

November 6th, 1813.

I am destined to and determined on the attack of Montreal, if not prevented by some act of God, and to give security to the enterprise, the division under your command must co-operate with the corps under my immediate orders. I shall pass Prescott to-night, because the stage of the season will not allow me three days to take it. I shall cross the cavalry at Hamilton, which will not require a day, and shall then press forward and break down every obstruction to the confluence of this river with the Grand river, there to cross to the Isle Perrot, and with my scows to bridge the narrow inner channel, and thus obtain foothold on Montreal island, at about twenty miles from the city; after which, our artillery, bayonets and swords must secure our triumph, or provide us honourable graves.

Inclosed you have a memorandum of my field and battery train, pretty well found in fixed ammunition, which may enable you to dismiss your own; but we are deficient in loose powder and musket cartridges, and therefore hope you may be abundantly found. On the subject of provisions, I wish I could give as favorable information; our whole stock of bread may be computed at about fifteen days, our meat at twenty. In speaking on this subject to the Secretary of War, he informed me that ample magazines were laid up on Lake Champlain, and therefore I must request you to

17

order forward two or three months' supply by the safest route, in a direction to the proposed scene of action.

(Signed)

JAS. WILKINSON.

Hampton's answer, received a few days later, ran as follows :—

HEAD-QUARTERS, November 8th, 1813.

SIR,—I had the honour to receive at a late hour last evening, your communication of the 6th. The idea suggested of effecting the junction at St. Regis was most pleasing, as being the most immediate, until I came to the disclosure of the amount of your supplies of provisions. Colonel Atkinson will explain the reason that would have rendered it impossible for me to have brought more than each man could have carried on his back; and when I reflected that in throwing myself on your scanty means, I shall be weakening you in your most vulnerable point, I did not hesitate to adopt the opinion, that by throwing myself upon my main depot, where all the means of transportation had gone, and falling on the enemy's flanks and straining every effort to open a communication between Plattsburg and Caughnawaga, or any other point you may indicate on the St. Lawrence, I should more effectually contribute to your success, than by a junction on the St. Regis.

The way is in many places blockaded and abattised, and the road impracticable for wheels during winter; but by the employment of pack-horses, if I am not overpowered, I hope to be able to prevent you from starving.

I have ascertained and witnessed the plan of the enemy is to burn and consume everything in our advance.

My troops and other means will be described to you by Colonel Atkinson.

Besides their rawness and sickness, they have endured fatigues equal to a winter campaign, and are sadly dispirited and fallen off.

This discouraging epistle was received by General Wilkinson on his arrival at Cornwall.

In the next letter from Thomas G. Ridout we have a vivid description of Wilkinson's flotilla descending the St. Lawrence.   It is dated

PRESCOTT, 9th November, 1813.

I am so far on the journey.   Yesterday we got thirteen miles below this, and were obliged to return on account of the landing of the American army half a mile below us on our side.   We had the most narrow escape of being taken.   Mr. Green only rode on a few hundred yards farther, and was taken prisoner.

It was a very grand sight to see an army of 10,000 men going down the Gallette rapids.   They fired at us several shots, taking our waggon for artillery, I suppose.   Every boat had a gun mounted, and carried about sixty men.   About 180 immense boats went down full of men, besides schooners with provisions. Yesterday Colonels Harvey and Pearson left this with 1,500 regulars and eight gun-boats in pursuit, determined to attack the enemy wherever they are to be found.   They got to Lake St. Francis last night. Unless this armament is destroyed, Montreal will go; but we have every reason to believe its entire destruction will take place in three or four days.   The Americans landed 800 men under Forsythe, within half a mile from where we slept, and have destroyed the bridges down the river.

Prescott is very strong and would stand a regular siege.   It is supplied with two months' provisions.

To-morrow we again prosecute our journey down. Colonel Harvey promised to clear the road.

The Americans seem confident of taking Montreal. I never witnessed such a beautiful sight as the army going down the rapids. Had we not fortunately stopped where we did, but gone farther as intended, nothing would have saved us.

I went down to inquire about Mr. Green's fate yesterday morning, but was glad to return after going two miles, for their boats rowed directly into the shore, so I galloped off.

Extract of a letter from Lieutenant-Colonel Harvey, Deputy Adjutant-General, dated, Banks of the St. Lawrence, Chrysler's, 12th November, 1813 :—

At two o'clock yesterday, after having apparently embarked and proceeded downwards, the enemy suddenly showed his columns in the woods in our front, consisting of three heavy ones (apparently brigades), of infantry, a considerable amount of cavalry on the road on his left, and riflemen on his right and in his front. Our position, fortunately, was not more extensive than our little band could well occupy, and dispositions were therefore easily made.

The ground was perfectly open. The troops disposed in the following manner : The flank companies 49th, detachment of Canadian regiment, and Voltigeurs, with one field-piece, under Lieutenant-Colonel Pearson, on the right, a little advanced on the road. Three companies 89th regiment, with a gun supporting the advance, formed in echelon with it on its left. The 49th and 89th regiments thrown more to the rear, with a gun, formed the main body and reserve, and extended almost from the road to the woods on our left, which were occupied by our Indians. As the enemy advanced, I plainly saw we had nothing to trust to but " every man doing his duty." I was convinced we had, with 800 men, to meet, in the open field, a force of not less than 4,000, and strong in an arm of which we were wholly destitute—cavalry. Our light troops—Voltigeurs—were thrown forward and showed a good countenance, but were, of course, immediately driven back; and the enemy advanced at the *pas de charge a la Francaise*, which was quickly changed by a well-directed fire from our field-pieces, to one more comporting with the dignity of the American nation.

I then recommended to Colonel Morrison to advance the line in echelon of battalions.   On arriving within musket distance the enemy's columns halted, and commenced a heavy but irregular fire, which our battalions returned with infinitely more effect by regular firing of platoons and wings.   The superiority of this fire, aided by that of our three field-pieces, which were admirably served, gave, after a severe contest, the first check and repulse to the enemy, and his columns fell back, only, however, to advance again in a more determined manner, supported by three or four field-pieces, and by his cavalry formed for a charge on our left.   Having again opened his fire upon us, I perceived that it would be impossible, in our advanced position, to stand long against the grape from his field-pieces, which it was accordingly determined to charge.   The 49th was moved on against the field-guns opposite to them, the 89th in echelon supporting; and though this charge was not executed as intended, nor as far as the proposed point, it nevertheless decided the fate of the day, as the enemy immediately fell back, leaving in the possession of the three companies of the 89th regiment, on the right, one of his six-pounders, with its tumbril, etc., which they had spiritedly charged, after having repulsed a treble charge of the enemy's cavalry.   Some efforts were still kept up, but the fire of our platoons and guns, and above all, the steady countenance of the troops, finally drove the enemy out of the field; and about half-past four o'clock he gave up the contest and retreated rapidly through the woods, covered by his light troops.

The enemy's loss in this severe action in killed, wounded and prisoners, may be safely estimated at 600 or 700 men. Nearly 180 of the dead were counted on the field; upwards of 100 prisoners are in our hands, and the number of slightly wounded who were carried off is very great. They were commanded by General Boyd in person.

British loss—killed, officers, 1; men, 21; wounded, officers, 10; men, 137; missing, men, 12; total, officers, 11; men, 170.

Names of officers killed and wounded :—

49th regiment—Captain Nairn, killed; Lieutenants Morton, Richmond and Holland, slightly wounded; Lieutenants Jones, Bartley and Claus, severely.

89th regiment—Captain Brown, wounded severely; Ensigns Brown and Leader, wounded slightly.

Canadian regiment — Lieutenant De Lorimier, severely wounded (since died); Ensign Armstrong, dangerously.

Loss of the enemy from 600 to 700, in left on the field, killed and wounded, 180 prisoners and one field-piece.

(Signed),

J. HARVEY, D.A.G.

From Thomas G. Ridout to his Father in York :—

MONTREAL, *November 20th*, 1813.

We arrived here on the 18th on horseback, having left all the luggage in Fort Prescott; we stay at Holmes', but intend taking private lodgings.

I suppose you have had a full account of Colonel Harvey's gallant affair of the 11th at Chrysler's. I was on the field of battle next morning, and it was covered with Americans killed and wounded; we had buried some, and about eighty lay dead, some scalped. Some horses were intermingled among them. We had eleven killed on the field and 135 wounded, some of whom died since. Poor Captain Nairn was killed at the close of the battle, almost the last shot fired. It was fought at Chrysler's house on a level piece of ground half a mile square. Our army were drawn up in a solitary line of 1,000 men, from the woods to the river. The enemy issued out of the woods in two large columns of 2,000 each, besides 300 horse, who kept in rear. After two hours' sharp firing our men retreated into a ploughed field, 200 yards back, while a six-pounder with grape and canister threw the American columns into disorder, assisted by the 49th, who fired as on a field day, by divisions and companies, thinning the Yankees at every platoon. When they began to give way in good order, our fellows gave three cheers and closed upon them. They immediately broke and ran as fast as possible for their boats, about a mile distant. Owing to our small force, now reduced to 800 men, they were not pursued more than half a mile. About eighty prisoners were taken, a colonel and some officers. It is said that one of their generals has since died of his wounds.

The 49th had sixty men killed and wounded, six officers. Young Claus has had his leg amputated below the knee. Two others are dangerously wounded, and two have died. That same night the enemy embarked in their boats and descended the Long Sault to Cornwall, and joined the other division. The next day they crossed over to Salmon river, and are now making their approach to Montreal through the Chateauguay country, while Hampton does the same by Chambly. We have 6,000 regular troops besides militia to oppose them, and there is not the least danger for this place. The 49th are to winter here. They are now reduced to 200 effective men.

There is a regular and strong fort built at the Coteau du Lac, which cannot be taken except by a regular siege.

I have not seen a stack of hay or wheat in Lower

Canada, and the barns appear to be only half full. There are also few or no cattle. Flour is now $20 per barrel, and bread 2s. per loaf; 1,500 marines are now at Chambly. The crew of the *Eolus* have gone up to Kingston. Had the Yankees continued with their expedition night and day down the river, they would have taken Montreal by surprise. It was a most powerful flotilla—some boats carried 100 men, all with artillery on board.

If the papers come out to-day, I will send you a copy. Sir George, in general orders, has reprobated the conduct of Proctor and his officers in very severe terms. Do make inquiries about Jones, my comrade, I am afraid he is a prisoner. Good fortune attends me, for there never was a more narrow escape than when the Yankees landed twelve miles below Prescott. We slept within 200 yards of them. Mr. Green was taken prisoner three minutes after he had left us. Next morning they departed, and Mr. Couche sent me down to reconnoitre and inquire for him. I rode down two and a half miles, but the whole river above and below was covered with their boats; some pulled towards the shore where I was, and came within fifty yards, when a man came running to me and told me by all means to make my escape, for that six boats had landed above me. I instantly galloped back, and passed before they reached the road, as they had landed on a small wooded point 300 yards away. The man told me afterwards that I had hardly got out of sight, when they took three prisoners.

The American general reported killed was General Covington. He was buried at French Mills, Salmon River, called also in his honour Fort Covington.

After the battle of Chrysler's Field, the Americans made a hasty retreat to their boats, and the stricken expedition proceeded as quickly as possible down the

river to the rendezvous at Cornwall, where General
Brown's division anxiously expected them. Here
Wilkinson received the mortifying intelligence that
Hampton declined to meet him as requested at St.
Regis. This was, indeed, a dilemma for the Americans. The Canadian gun-boats were closely following
them. To retreat up the rapids was an impossibility.
To retrace their steps by land on the Canadian
side was also impossible, in the face of Morrison's
little army and the numerous batteries on the shore.
Wilkinson did not dare, with his disheartened troops,
to make the promised dash on Montreal. So he held
a council of war on the 13th November, which
decided that it was expedient to remove the army
from Canada into winter quarters at French Mills,
on the Salmon river. Thus, in disaster and disgrace,
ended the expedition which had promised so much,
and the fact remained indisputable that the invasion of
the Invincible Armada of the St. Lawrence was a
failure.

CHAPTER XIX.

FIRE AND SWORD—DECEMBER, 1813.

IN December, 1813, Lieutenant-General Gordon Drummond* assumed the command in Upper Canada, in place of General de Rottenburg. He at once proceeded to the head of Lake Ontario, with the view of regaining possession of Fort George. When the news reached that place of the failure of Wilkinson's and Hampton's expedition on the St Lawrence, General McClure determined to abandon the post and place his garrison in Fort Niagara. Before leaving, however,

---

* General, afterwards Sir Gordon, Drummond, who distinguished himself as a commander in Upper Canada during the campaign of 1814, was a Canadian by birth, having been born at Quebec in 1771, where his father was Paymaster-General of the forces. Gordon Drummond entered the army as ensign in 1789, had rapid promotion, and was made Lieutenant-Colonel in 1794, and given the command of the 8th regiment. He served with distinction in Holland, and Egypt, and the West Indies. In 1811 he was appointed to the staff in Canada ; returned to England in 1812 ; and was sent out again at the close of 1813 as second in command to Sir George Prevost.

His vigour and promptitude were invaluable to Canada at this crisis. Though wounded at Lundy's Lane, he still kept the command until the close of the war, when he succeeded Sir George Prevost as Commander-in-Chief and Governor-General of the Canadas.

He held this post until 1816, and then retired into private life, and resided in England until his death in 1854, in the eighty-fourth year of his age.

on the 10th December, a bleak, cold winter day, he inhumanly set fire to the town of Newark.†

Hitherto the war had been conducted without any startling outrages on either side; but, by this cruel act, 450 women and children were left homeless and shelterless in the snow. One hundred and fifty houses were reduced to ashes. Only half an hour's warning had been given to the defenceless inhabitants. Mr. Merritt in his narrative says: " My old quarters, Gordon's house, was the only one standing." Colonel Murray, of the 100th, was at Twelve-Mile Creek when he heard of the conflagration. He pressed on eagerly, hoping to surprise the retreating garrison. He was a little too late, but in the hurry of departure the Americans failed to blow up, as they had intended, the fort and barracks; and that night once more the British flag floated over old Fort George, and once more British troops slept within its walls.

† The Episcopal church, St. Mark's, first built in 1802, was occupied by the American troops when they held the place, and was set on fire with the rest of the town in 1813. The body of the church was burnt down, but rebuilt after the close of the war, and the venerable old tower, which escaped the flames, still stands, strongly buttressed, a sacred memorial of the sufferings of days gone by. A large and beautiful burying-ground surrounds the church, shaded by magnificent old trees. It is crowded with stately monuments and humble head-stones, and the graves near the old tower lie thick and close together, many of the tombstones bearing the names of officers and militiamen. When the American soldiers were quartered in the church they cut up their rations of meat on some of the great flagstones which covered the graves, and the scars and chippings made by the cleavers can still be plainly seen. But, happily, the verdure of many springs, the fading leaves of many autumns, and the snows of many winters have covered these scars and healed the bitter feelings they once awakened, leaving only a generous pride in the valour and fortitude of the men who saved the independence of their country.—(From " Picturesque Canada.")

"Let us retaliate by fire and sword," we are told that Murray said to Drummond, as they gazed on the smoking ruins of the town.

"Do so, swiftly and thoroughly," said the commander; and bitter, indeed, was the vengeance taken.

On the night of the 18th December, the flank companies of the 41st and 100th, under Colonel Murray, with some militia, artillery and the Grenadier company of the 1st Royals, crossed the River Niagara, and were quietly put on shore at the Five-Mile Meadows, three miles above the fort. The midnight expedition proceeded with the greatest caution. Every order was given in a whisper, neither musket nor sabre clanked, and with noiseless steps, Murray and his soldiers advanced. The sentries were seized before they could give the alarm, and the Canadian troops succeeded in entering Fort Niagara before a drum had rolled or bugle sounded.

General McClure had left for Buffalo a few days before, and the defence of the fort had been entrusted to Captain Leonard, with about 400 effective men, besides invalids. Only a feeble resistance was made by the surprised garrison, and the conflict was over before they were fairly awake. Only twenty-nine escaped; 344 were made prisoners, and about eighty killed and wounded.

The fort proved a valuable prize. The spoils consisted of twenty-seven pieces of cannon, 3,000 stand of arms, and many rifles; an immense amount of ordnance and commissariat stores; clothing and camp equipage of every description; all sorely needed then at Newark.

A discharge from one of the largest cannon was the signal of success to General Riall, who, in the meantime, had marched to Queenston, with the 1st battalion of the Royals, part of the 41st regiment, and a number of Indians. At dawn, Riall, with his troops, crossed the Niagara at Lewiston, and took possession of the batteries there. Now came the vengeance for the burning of Newark. The troops and Indians were let loose on the frontier. Lewiston, Youngstown, Tuscarora Village, Schlosser and Manchester were laid in ruins.

The Commander-in-Chief, Drummond, determined to proceed still further in his work of destruction. He pressed on to Chippewa, and fixed his headquarters there on the 28th December.

About 2,000 American troops were then collected at Black Rock and Buffalo, under the command of General McClure, besides a considerable number of irregular troops, disorganized and confused. Drummond ordered Riall to cross the river at midnight, on the 29th of December, with four companies of the King's, the Light company of the 89th, under Colonel Ogilvy, and 150 men of the 41st, with a large body of militia volunteers. About a thousand in all. Such was the impetuosity of the attack that the Americans were driven from their batteries at the point of the bayonet, and their own guns turned on them as they fled. Riall then continued the pursuit of the retreating troops to Buffalo, where they rallied and gained some reinforcements of fresh infantry.

The Canadian troops still pushed on, and succeeded in capturing some guns, when the enemy broke and fled to the woods. General Riall now gave orders to destroy four armed vessels (part of Perry's squadron),* at anchor a short distance below Buffalo. This was done under the direction of Captain Robinson, of the King's, Colonel Ogilvy having been wounded.

And now the torch was applied again, and soon Buffalo and Black Rock, deserted by their inhabitants, were smoking ruins. Clothing, spirits, flour, public stores, anything that could not be carried away, were ruthlessly destroyed.

At Buffalo, only four buildings were left standing. At Black Rock, only one house escaped.

The Americans lost in this attack about 400 killed and wounded, and 150 prisoners. The Canadian loss was thirty-one killed, seventy-two wounded, including four officers.

The almost universal condemnation of General McClure for the destruction of Newark, and the greater enormities committed in retaliation, caused Sir George Prevost to hasten before the world with an assurance that he would endeavour to stop that sort of warfare.

In a proclamation issued 12th January, 1814, after

---

* The *Ariel, Little Belt, Chippewa* and *Trippe*

justifying the retaliation thus far, he said : " To those possessions of the enemy along the whole line of frontier, which have hitherto remained undisturbed, and which are now at the mercy of the troops under his command, His Excellency has determined to extend the same forbearance and the same freedom from rapine and plunder which they have hitherto experienced ; and from this determination the future conduct of the American Government shall alone induce him to depart."

The last two entries in Mr. Ridout's Almanac for 1813 are :—

Sunday, 19th December.—Fort Niagara was taken by us.

Wednesday, 29th December. — Black Rock and Buffalo were taken and burnt, in retaliation for the enemy's burning Niagara.

The campaign of 1813 had now closed, and its result, as given by the Americans themselves, was, that not one advantage had been obtained by them, to atone for the blood and treasure which had already been exhausted.

The capital of Upper Canada (York) had been taken. It was scarcely captured before it was abandoned.

The bulwark of the Province, Fort George, had been carried; but its defenders were suffered to escape after being defeated, and the conquerors were soon after confined to the works of the garrison, and closely

invested there for more than six months. The long-
contemplated attack upon Montreal was frustrated.
Kingston still remained a safe and advantageous harbour for the Canadian fleet; and Fort Niagara, which
might have been obstinately defended, was yielded
with scarcely a struggle.

In the course of the summer of 1813, the Americans
possessed every position between Lake Ontario and
Lake Erie, on both sides of the Niagara. In the winter of the same year, they not only lost their possessions on the Canadian side of the stream, but were
deprived of every post on their own side.

CHAPTER XX.

THIRD YEAR OF WAR—LACOLLE, OSWEGO, 1814.

THE third year of the war had begun, and still peace seemed to be as far off as ever.

It is well to remember that the defence of Canada had for two years been entrusted to the militia and fencible corps of the country, fighting side by side with the few regular troops stationed on the frontier.

In all the battles that had been fought in those two years of hard fighting the same names appear over and over again. Among the regulars and militia were the 41st, the 49th, the 89th, the 8th King's, the 1st Royals, De Watteville's, the Glengarries, the Voltigeurs, the Lincoln and York and Essex and Kent militia.

On them fell the burden and heat of the day, and looking back on that long-kept-up struggle against fearful odds, on the hardships endured, and the difficulties faced, it must be acknowledged that the defenders of Canada were gallant men, led, for the most part, by wise and skilful commanders. It was not until the close of the summer of 1814 that Wellington's troops poured into the country.

18

The Americans were now learning wisdom by experience. They found that numbers were of no avail against skill and patriotism.

The lessons learnt at Detroit, and Stoney Creek, and Chrysler's Field, and Chateauguay, had made an impression at last, and the first thing they set about in 1814, was the improvement in the *personnel* of their commanding officers, and the better drilling of their troops. Hull had disappeared after Detroit; Van Rensselaer, after Queenston; Dearborn was in retirement; Hampton had left the service in disgrace; Winchester, Chandler, and Winder were still prisoners of war at Beauport, Quebec.

New blood was needed to lead their troops. In January, 1814, Brigadier-Generals Brown and Izard were commissioned Major-Generals, and the former, on Wilkinson's retirement, became chief commander of the northern division of the American army. Colonels Macomb, Bissell, Scott, Gaines and Ripley, were appointed Brigadier-Generals.

At York, there is again a meeting of Parliament for the third time since the declaration of war, and again the opening Speech is a congratulatory one on the success of the campaign of 1813. On the 15th February, 1814, it meets, for a short session. His Honour Gordon Drummond, then being President, administering the Government of Upper Canada, Lieutenant-General commanding His Majesty's forces within the same.

After the usual preliminaries, the Speech goes on to say :—

At the moment they (the Americans) were exulting in the assurances of their commander, that the conquest of the Canadas was achieved, they were arrested in their progress to invade our sister Province, and their collective force discomfited by a handful of troops, who drove them in dismay to take refuge on their own shores.

That with no less gallantry in another quarter, a small band of British soldiers attacked and carried by storm the fortress of Niagara, the strongest and most formidable they held on our frontier.   In advancing to this enterprise, the troops beheld with indignation the smoking ruins of the town of Newark, which an atrocious policy had devoted to the flames.   Resentful of the misery brought upon the innocent, but too credulous inhabitants, who had remained to the last moment under promise of protection to their persons and property, the army inflicted a severe retaliation, in the entire destruction of the whole frontier, from Lake Erie to Lake Ontario.

Thus the valour of our soldiers and citizens has proved what can be effected, in a good cause, by men who have nothing in view but their own honour and their country's safety.

It has been more a subject of regret than surprise to have found two members of the Legislative body in the ranks of the enemy.

The two members of the Legislature named in the last paragraph as traitors, were Jos. Willcocks, whose name has appeared before in these chronicles, and Benj. Mallory, an American by birth and sympathy. These men raised what they were pleased to call a Canadian regiment, which fought on the Yankee side, but it is certain no native Canadians were within its ranks. Willcocks, who was the self-appointed colonel, met with a tragical end at Fort Erie.

In January, 1814, Thomas Gibbs Ridout received his commission as Deputy Assistant-Commissary-General.

The first letter of the year is,

From T. G. Ridout to his Father in York :—

QUEBEC, *January 6th,* 1814.

It was with great pleasure I received this day your letter of the 20th December. We had already heard of the glorious success of our army against Niagara, and rejoice with you on that brilliant day. Yesterday the Commissary-General, with Sir George Prevost, Bart., etc., appointed me to be a Deputy Assistant-Commissary-General to His Majesty's forces. The appointment will go home to be confirmed by the War Office, and the commission will come out in the spring.

I have risen over the heads of eighty-nine clerks in the short space, of seven months. My promotion has been most rapid. My pay is now more than £500 a year. I am getting a coat made and shall sport an epaulet. Some time this winter I shall join the army at Fort George, as they intend employing me in the Upper Province. Mr. Couche and I dined with Commissary-General Robinson last Sunday. Mrs. Robinson sent me tickets for the grand garrison ball to-morrow night.

It is refreshing to hear of a little gaiety in the midst of "war's dread alarms." No doubt the belles of Quebec then, as now, were quite ready for a dance with the defenders of their country.

From T. G. Ridout to his Father in York :—

Quebec, 10th *January,* 1814.

Your letter of the 1st I have this day received. The late success of our troops over the enemy on the American frontier is a most glorious affair. We have just heard of the second defeat at Black Rock, and the conflagration of Buffalo and other places.

We have now made up all our accounts to the amount of a million. I can assure you my labour has been incessant, such as I never went through before. In two or three weeks I am to proceed to Upper Canada, and take charge of a post ; Cornwall, I believe, or Prescott, but I had rather go up to Niagara, and shall try for it. I am now well acquainted with the duties of the commissariat, having learned more with Mr. Couche than seven years' experience in an office could have taught me.

Mr. Couche took me out to-day in his tandem cariole. We drove to the Falls of Montmorenci. They can now cross from the Isle of Orleans to the north shore.

The next letter is,

From T. G. Ridout to his Father in York :—

Prescott, 19th *January,* 1814.

I arrived at this post last evening from Quebec, which I left on the 13th inst. To-morrow I return to Cornwall to take charge of my new post. There are 1,600 troops there to be fed, and my duty will be hard, for the country is so excessively poor that our supplies are all drawn from the American side of the river. They drive droves of cattle from the interior under pretence of supplying the army at Salmon river, and are so allowed to pass the guards, and at night cross them over to our side. I shall also be under the necessity of getting most of my flour from their side.

The Commissary-General told me that as Cornwall was the most arduous post and full of difficulties, he would entrust me with the care of it.

General de Rottenburg went to Montreal yesterday. Mrs. Strachan is better, Mr. Strachan arrived at Cornwall on the morning of the 17th. Colonel Chapin passed by to-day with a fair wind, bound to Quebec jail, where he will most likely winter.

Brother Jonathan evidently was not deterred by feelings of patriotism from earning an honest penny by feedin his country's enemies.

The Colonel Chapin mentioned was Colonel Cyrenius Chapin, of the New York volunteers. He had been taken prisoner at Beaver Dams, on the 25th June, 1813, but had escaped on his way to York. He was again taken prisoner at Buffalo, on the 30th December, 1813.

The story of Chapin's escape after the battle of Beaver Dams is rather amusing. He, and some other prisoners, were being conveyed to York by water. There were two boat loads. In the first was Colonel Chapin, Captain Showers, who was in charge of the prisoners and the principal part of the guard. The second boat, which was rowed by the American prisoners, was ordered to keep some distance in the rear. Chapin managed to signal to it to come closer, and while he was telling an amusing story to the Captain it came up under the stern of the forward boat. It was immediately ordered back, when Chapin, in a loud voice, commanded his men not to move. In a moment all was confusion. Captain Showers was felled by a blow from the Colonel. The rest of the guard were overpowered and secured, and to give Colonel Chapin's own words, "I succeeded to the command of our fleet of two bateaux. We shifted our course, crossed Lake Ontario, and with the boats and prisoners arrived next morning safe at Fort Niagara."

From Thos. Ridout to his son T. G. Ridout :—

YORK, 21st *January*, 1814.

We received yesterday with great joy your letters of the 8th and 10th inst. We had seen three or four days ago your appointment in the General Orders. We have just had accounts of the total defeat of Bonaparte at Leipsig in October, and of the armistice between us and the United States.

Pray buy me a Quebec almanac for the present year, and make inquiry also if any stationery came out for me last year as Surveyor-General. I believe it is generally sent to the care of Commissariat Department at Quebec, and forwarded by it. The President's office stationery has been sent to Kingston, but no other that I can learn.

I hope you have written, or will soon write, to Mr. Crookshank. He informed me of your appointment. Write also to Dr. Strachan, who is much gratified at your good prospects. He set out about a week ago with Mr. Wood for Cornwall, where Mrs. Strachan is. He intends to return by the opening of our Parliament here, on the 15th of next month.

It is with the greatest satisfaction and delight my mind rests on your new appointment. You have entered into life on a very conspicuous and great theatre, and where your services must be seen and felt extensively. The well providing of a portion of His

Majesty's forces at this important period is committed
to your care. The labours you go through in your
office are only to be known by that officer to whom you
transmit your accounts, but the exertions you employ
in furnishing the troops with the necessaries they
depend on you for, will be best appreciated by them.
In this the King's service is best promoted by a
knowledge of the country in which you are stationed,
and its resources; the employing of intelligent, honest,
active and conciliating persons to collect your supplies,
and an obliging, as well as a rigid, exactness on your
own part. The *suaviter in modo* with the *fortiter
in re* will smooth your greatest difficulties.

Is it a fact, that the misfortunes which attended our
fleet on Lake Erie, as also that of the Western army,
was really owing to want of due exertions without doors
of the commissariat in that quarter ?

I have heard that such is the case ; it will be worth
your investigation.

From S. Ridout to his Brother Thomas G. Ridout :—

YORK, 24*th January*, 1814.

We congratulate you most sincerely on your good
fortune, and well I know you deserve it.

We have no news here of any consequence except
our affairs in the North of Europe, which have been
brilliant beyond description, but of this you are
already informed.

I think Jonathan must curse his stars, and wish the
war had never taken place, but Jemmy Madison's
vanity will probably induce him to make another
attempt to recover his disgrace ; but of the result I
entertain no apprehension.

It is said that an expedition is ordered against Fort
Malden and Amherstburg, which places, I hope soon
to hear, are again in our possession. And who knows
but what Detroit may share the same fate !

From Thomas G. Ridout to his brother John, late Midshipman
on the "Royal George," who had been taken prisoner at York
and put on parole :—

CORNWALL, 31st *January,* 1814.

As I am now settled as long as the army remains here, and am much in want of assistance, I have obtained the Commissary-General's leave to have you with me as my second-best clerk, therefore you must set out immediately for this post and bring your head, hands and feet along with you, for the public service.

I expect to go up as soon as the army moves from here. We are now 1,400 strong. The Yankees on the other side are 4,000, but they are afraid to attack us. The marines and 103rd are here.

Forsythe has been destroying all the boats up the river, to prevent any supplies coming over.

General Wilkinson, who had not at that time been superseded in the command, was still in his winter quarters on the Salmon river.

Lieutenant-Colonel Forsythe was one of the most dashing officers of the American army. He commanded a corps of riflemen, and had been conspicuous throughout the war for his daring bravery.

He lost his life on the 22nd June, 1814, on the Champlain frontier—shot by an Indian in an insignificant skirmish.

Towards the close of January Wilkinson received orders from the War Department to break up the post on Salmon river. Early in February the movement was made. The flotilla was destroyed, and the barracks were consumed. General Brown, with a large portion of the troops, marched up the St. Lawrence to

Sackett's Harbour. The remainder accompanied General Wilkinson to Plattsburg on Lake Champlain.

What the Canadians were doing at the time is told in the following letter :—

From Thomas G. Ridout to his Father in York:—

CORNWALL, *9th February,* 1814.

It is now twelve o'clock, and I have been actively employed since eight a.m. Only think of 1,700 rations per day, and no one but myself and a store-keeper. My disbursements since the 24th January have amounted to £4,000.

Colonel Morrison commands this post. We are on the alert, expecting the Americans, who are upon some movement. All their artillery, except a few pieces, and the whole of their baggage, has been sent away.

The only thing that troubles me is a quantity of specie that I have. If John was here, in case of an alarm, I would put him into a sleigh with it and one set of my accounts to make off; I must remain with the army.

I have paid very large sums in specie for secret service, this being the fountain head of all correspondence with the enemy. Reuben Sherwood is very active in that way. He has been twice taken, but made his escape.

Two nights ago, with thirty of the marines, he crossed over to Hamilton, marched ten miles into the country, and captured a great quantity of goods, which I have now in charge. To-morrow a board of survey is to be held on them.

The story of Sherwood's raid is as follows :—When the Americans were at Cornwall, in the autumn of 1813, under Generals Brown and Boyd, previous to recrossing the river, they plundered some merchants of all their goods, wares and merchandise, *en route* for Upper Canada.

Colonel Morrison had stipulated for their restitution, but the American Government had failed to keep this agreement, and the goods were about to be sold for the benefit of the United States.

To prevent this, Captain Sherwood, of the Quarter-Master-General's Department, suggested the idea of plundering them back again. Accordingly, Captain Kerr, with a subaltern, twenty rank and file of the marines, and ten militiamen, with Sherwood, crossed the ice on the 6th February, during the night, from Cornwall to Hamilton, N.Y., with horses and sleighs innumerable. The merchandise, or a great part of it, was secured, packed up and carried off. The inhabitants made no opposition, and indeed, rather enjoyed the joke at the expense of the Yankee officers, who were charged with the sale of the stolen goods.

From Thomas G. Ridout to his brother George at York:—

CORNWALL, 19*th February*, 1814.

3 *a.m.*—John arrived yesterday, and in an hour he accompanies me to Salmon river and from there into the States. We are in pursuit of the Yankee army, and will go to Plattsburg. Everything has been bustle all night. Half an hour ago the army moved off. In the course of the day we shall be joined by 3,000 troops. I have a great deal of gold and silver wherewith to make purchases in Vermont. I have sixty sleighs loaded with provisions.

Nothing of importance occurred during February on the St. Lawrence. The Niagara frontier was quiet. The Americans had, as yet, made no attempt to regain their lost possessions there. On the western frontier there were some slight skirmishes. An attempt had been made by the enemy to take Port Talbot, on Lake Erie, and an expedition was also sent against another outpost at Delaware, on the River Thames.

For the defence of this district there were part of the Royal Scots, Light Company of the 89th, and the Kent militia, under Captain McGregor.

An engagement took place at the Longwoods, twenty-two miles from Delaware, on the 4th March, 1814, between some Kentucky volunteers and the Kent militia. McGregor and his men made an heroic charge up an ice-covered hill, where the enemy was posted. They fought more than an hour, till darkness came on, when the engagement terminated. Its only result being the loss of some brave men.

Mackinaw still remained unmolested in the hands of the Canadians. It was of immense importance to hold it, as it was the key to the vast traffic in furs with the Indians of the North-West.

From T. G. Ridout to his Father in York:—

CORNWALL, *24th March,* 1814.

I am now busily employed in finishing my accounts, as we expect to move shortly from this place. I have found out the fate of your box of stationery. It came up to Cornwall last December, and laid a long time in the commissariat stores here unnoticed, until January last, when Mr. Tuttle, Deputy Assistant-Commissary-General Osborne's storekeeper at Prescott, took it up with him to that place, where it has furnished the Commissariat Office there with the finest stationery in the country.   It is now nearly expended.

There are now only 200 men left here, and shortly there will be none. I have had a great deal of trouble settling with 300 or 400 Scotchmen, for the expedition to Malone.   The river will soon break up.   I am afraid the Yankees will be too strong for us in the spring on the lake.   I hear they are building a seventy-four at Sackett's Harbour.   You mentioned to John he had better read history.   At present he has no time for it, being employed with me from eight in the morning till eleven at night, without intermission, Sundays and every day.   A person in the commissariat should never read ; I have not done so since I began.

In the month of February I issued 70,000 pounds of flour, and other provisions in proportion, so you may think we were not idle.

On the 30th March Generals Macomb and Wilkinson crossed Lake Champlain on the ice, with about 4,000 men, to Odelltown, to assault our troops stationed at Lacolle Mills.*   The latter was a strong stone tower, and was defended by Major Hancock and about 200 men.   The walls of the mill were eighteen inches in thickness, and the windows were barricaded with heavy timbers, through which were loop-holes for muskets.   The Americans opened fire on the tower, but their missiles were harmless, and the whole Ameri-

* On Lacolle creek, a small tributary of the Sorel, three or four miles below Rouse's Point.

can line, being in open field, was exposed to a galling fire. The small garrison was soon reinforced by some Grenadiers of the Fencibles and Voltigeurs.

The Americans got into the woods with a view of surrounding the mill, and simultaneously assaulting it from all sides. The fire from the mill, however, was so hot and well-directed, that the enemy were forced to retreat in confusion.

The Americans kept up a cannonade for about two hours without the slightest effect, and, wearied and disheartened, were at last compelled to fall back on Plattsburg.

The enemy lost in this attempt to carry a stone tower, bravely defended, 13 killed, 123 wounded, and 30 missing. The Canadians lost in a dash to capture the American guns 10 killed and 46 wounded, including two officers.

After the fiasco at Lacolle, the military career of General Wilkinson closed.

The next letter is from

Surveyor-General Ridout to his Son :—

YORK, *10th April,* 1814.

The ice went out of the bay two days ago. At the extremity of Gibraltar Point, a blockhouse is erected, to annoy the enemy if he attempts to enter the harbour ; and we are, in other respects, much better prepared than last year. Our vessels at Kingston were to be launched to-day. 'Tis said the American ship *President* is launched at Sackett's Harbour, therefore, we may soon expect to see both fleets on the lake.

During the winter, both the American and Canadian fleets had been strengthened. At Sackett's Harbour, Chauncey was busy collecting stores, and building new gun-boats and a large frigate. In Kingston, Sir James Yeo was also busy preparing for the spring campaign. Both commanders were waiting anxiously for the ice to break up in the harbours.

The command of Lake Ontario was considered an object so important by the two Governments, that they withdrew officers and men from the ocean to assist in the lake service.

From T. G. Ridout to his Father at York :—

CORNWALL, 11*th April*, 1814.

Yesterday all the troops left this place for Prescott, and I am now commanding officer. About the time you will receive this letter, I am afraid the Yankees will pay you another visit. I dread the consequences.

I expect bateaux in a few days from Lachine, as the river is open. We drive a pretty good trade with the Yankees from Salmon river.

From Thos. G. Ridout to his Father :—

CORNWALL, 1*st May*, 1814.

Colonel Morrison commands this district from Brockville to the Cedars. I am immediately under the command of Major Clifford, 89th regiment, who is stationed here with 250 men of that regiment. I have spent at this place already £17,000.

Every day twelve bateaux arrive here from Lachine on their way to Kingston, with provisions and naval stores, and we have troops stationed along the river to protect the communication.

The campaign opened with the opening of navigation in May.

Sir James Yeo, with the co-operation of General Drummond, planned an attack on Oswego, with the view of destroying the naval stores, which were collected there for the equipment of the American fleet at Sackett's Harbour.

General Drummond sent on board the fleet six companies of De Watteville's regiment, the Light companies of the Glengarry militia, some Royal marines and artillery, with two field-pieces, a rocket company, and some sappers and miners.

The expedition left Kingston on the 4th of May, 1814, and arrived off Oswego at noon the following day. There was blowing a gale of wind, so it was thought expedient to keep off the port till the weather calmed.

On the morning of the 6th May, a landing was effected in the face of a heavy fire of grape and round shot from the enemy's batteries, and of musketry from a detachment of Americans posted on a hill, and partly sheltered by a wood.

The Canadian troops charged the battery and captured it, the enemy leaving about sixty wounded men behind them in their hurried retreat. The stores in the fort were taken, the fort itself was dismantled, and the barracks were destroyed.

A number of officers were wounded of the attacking party, and eighteen rank and file killed and sixty wounded.

Unfortunately the naval stores were not captured, as they had been placed for safe keeping at the falls of the Onondaga, some miles above Oswego.*

The troops were re-embarked, and the fleet sailed for Kingston, on the 7th of May.

On the 10th of May, the anxious inhabitants of York were still ignorant of what had happened at Oswego, although firing had been heard from that direction.

From Thomas Ridout to his Son:—
YORK, 10th May, 1814.

The wind blows strong from the east, and we are in hourly expectation of hearing what has been done by our fleet and troops on Friday last, supposed to be at Oswego.

Everything is quiet on the Niagara frontier. The Western District and District of London are, for the present, abandoned. If we meet with success on this lake we shall soon mount upwards.

It is bleak and cold to-day. Yet I think this year we shall have some peaches. The blossoms begin to appear.

I have lost about 800 rails by the Indians.

The next letter gives an item of news about prices of provisions, also that reinforcements were beginning to arrive in the country :—

From Thomas G. Ridout to his Father in York:—
CORNWALL, 15th May, 1814.

Beef is seven and a-half cents per pound, and flour seventeen and a-half dollars per barrel. News has arrived that the 16th and 90th regiments have

---

* On the 29th May, Sir James Yeo made another attempt to capture these coveted naval stores, but without success.

19

landed at Quebec, besides a corps of riflemen and some very fine artillery. Fourteen transports and a frigate had come up.

The firing you heard on the 6th May must have been from Oswego. I saw a letter of that date from Sackett's Harbour, which describes them to be in great dread of our troops; that the war party had gained a majority in all the States as yet returned, and that there is no prospect of peace this summer. Bonaparte, it is said, has gained some advantages over the allies, and there will be no peace this year in Europe.

Major Clifford commands this garrison, with 250 men of the 89th regiment.

The Commissary-General has informed me that a regiment will be stationed here, but don't say anything about it. I am to furnish them with provisions, *from the Yankees*, for which I shall be well supplied with specie.

The next letter gives a graphic description of how the army was supplied with provisions, "from the Yankees," and the extraordinary spectacle is presented of two officers, one civil and the other military, supplying the wants of their country's foes.

From Thomas G. Ridout to his Father in York:—

CORNWALL, 19*th June*, 1814.

Three companies of the Canadian regiment are coming here to relieve the 89th, who will move upwards. Two hundred and fifty artillery marched for Prescott yesterday morning. I have contracted with a Yankee magistrate to furnish this post with fresh beef. A major came with him to make the agreement, but, as he was foreman to the grand jury at the court in which the government prosecutes the magistrates for high treason and smuggling, he turned his back and would not see the paper signed.

CHAPTER XXI.

FORT ERIE, CHIPPEWA, LUNDY'S LANE, 1814.

To RETRIEVE the consequences of the last disastrous campaign, to regain possession of the posts in Canada which had been lost, to drive the Canadians from Fort Niagara, and to command the frontier on both sides of the river, were the objects of the next campaign.

About the end of June, 1814, the American troops were concentrated at Buffalo and Black Rock, on the Niagara frontier. The army was commanded by General Brown, an officer of experience and judgment, and with him were Brigadier-Generals Scott and Ripley.

General Winfield Scott had taken special care to discipline thoroughly the troops under his command. During the spring and early summer, they were kept under arms from seven to ten hours a day. The result was, that when they took the field, they manœuvred in action, and under fire, with the accuracy of parade.

On the 1st July, General Brown received orders from the American Secretary of War to cross the Niagara river, to capture Fort Erie and march on Chippewa, where, at the mouth of the creek, some fortifications had been thrown up, to attack Fort George with the co-operation of Chauncey's fleet, and to seize and fortify Burlington Heights at the head of Lake Ontario. The plan looked very well on paper; and had it been carried out successfully, the Americans would not only have held the Niagara peninsula in their grasp, but would have easily accomplished the conquest of a large portion of Upper Canada.

It must be remembered that at this time, July, 1814, there were only about 3,000 Canadian troops spread over the frontier from York to Long point, Lake Erie. There were so few men available for the different posts that it seems almost incredible what was accomplished by that scanty force. It was necessary to have garrisons in Forts George, Niagara, Erie, and Mississauga.* The important position of Burlington Heights had to be defended. Detachments also had to be placed to guard provision depots at Twelve and Twenty-mile creeks. York was in an exposed position, liable to attack at any moment from Chauncey's fleet. Port Dover, on Lake Erie, was also in need of protection, as there was a danger that troops might be landed there, and gain the rear of General Riall's division by the western road.

Detachments had to be posted at the crossing of the Grand river (Brantford), also at Delaware, to guard the advance of the enemy by way of the Thames.

* Fort Mississauga was built early in 1814, after the burning of Newark by the Americans.

The constant duty and insufficient food had caused a great deal of sickness in camp. General Drummond had reported to the Commander-in-Chief that half the men were unfit for service. The 8th were so enfeebled that they had been ordered to Lower Canada, in hopes of regaining their strength. They had only, however, proceeded as far as York, when they were ordered back, to join General Riall at Chippewa.

On the 3rd July, 1814, two brigades embarked from the American shore in obedience to General Brown's orders. The first, under General Winfield Scott, crossed the Niagara about a mile below Fort Erie; the second, under General Ripley, crossed the river about the same distance above.

Fort Erie, at the foot of Lake Erie, nearly opposite Buffalo, where the River Niagara is about a mile in width, was then garrisoned by 170 men of the 100th and 8th regiments, under the command of Major Buck. It was the most serious impediment in the way of the invasion of Canada in that quarter, but was in a weak condition, and ill-provided to stand a siege. As soon as the Americans landed, they began to erect batteries, and an eighteen-pound cannon was placed ready for action on an eminence called Snake Hill. Brown then demanded the surrender of the fort, giving the commander, Major Buck, two hours for consideration. Although it might have been defended for a short time, the commandant decided to surrender to the American general, and at six o'clock in the evening, the soldiers marched out, stacked their arms, became prisoners of war, and were sent across the river.

During the morning, some cannon had been fired from the fort, which killed four Americans, and wounded several others. One Canadian soldier was killed when the pickets were driven in. These were the only casualties.

General Riall was much chagrined when he heard of the surrender of the fort, as he was on the point of sending forward several companies to reinforce it.

The invaders now determined to approach Chippewa, where General Riall was entrenched on the north bank of the creek of that name.

On the 4th July, General Scott received orders to advance to Street's Creek, two miles from the British works.

At midnight, the main body of Brown's army came up, accompanied by the commanding general.

That night both armies slept within two miles of each other.

Early in the morning of the 5th July, skirmishes began between the two camps, and a desultory fire was kept up by pickets and scouts.

At last, in the afternoon, General Riall, who had been reinforced by the arrival of the 8th regiment from York, determined to come out of his entrenchments, and attack in force the invading army.

The Americans were, however, well prepared to

receive him, and a vigorous and desperate engagement followed. Soon General Riall found his men falling round him in numbers too great to leave him any hope of victory. He was, therefore, after more than an hour's desperate fighting, compelled to retire to his entrenchments beyond the Chippewa.

There was, on both sides, in this short engagement, an immense loss, in proportion to the numbers engaged. The Americans acknowledged 328 killed, wounded and missing. General Riall's returns were 139 killed, 320 wounded, forty-six missing, total 505. Among the wounded were the Marquis of Tweeddale, Lieutenant-Colonel Gordon, Captain Holland, the *aide-de-camp* to the General, seven captains, and seventeen lieutenants.

In this battle the 1st Royal Scots, the 19th Light Dragoons, the 100th, and the 8th were engaged, and the Lincoln militia greatly distinguished themselves.

Of the 2nd Lincoln, the Colonel, Thomas Dickson, was wounded, and Major David Secord then took command, and led his men with great bravery.

It is said that the Canadian force looked like the wing of a regiment, in comparison to the Americans.

The strong reserve which General Brown was able to bring forward, made it impossible for General Riall to maintain the conflict against a force so superior in numbers.

How the news came to York is told in the following letter.

We can imagine what the scene must have been that midsummer night, as the boats came in from Niagara, bearing their freight of wounded and dying men.

Almost every house in the little town must of necessity have become a hospital.

From Surveyor-General Ridout to his Son at Cornwall:—

YORK, *Sunday,* 10th *July,* 1814.

We have appearances now of very troublesome times. On Tuesday last, about four in the afternoon, General Riall crossed the Chippewa with his forces, and attacked the enemy whose numbers, as it appears by a letter written the same morning by Major Glegg, he was totally unacquainted with. The enemy was posted above Pine Grove, Mr. Street's place, and they were covered by thirty-six pieces of cannon. The woods on their left swarmed with their numbers, nor would they suffer our men to approach them. The action continued about one hour and a half, when we were compelled to retreat over the Chippewa bridge, leaving many wounded. Fort Erie was on the same day attacked by them and carried. Major Buck, who commanded the place, is killed, Captain Dawson wounded, and all the men—two companies—killed, wounded or taken prisoners. The 100th regiment, commanded by the Marquis of Tweeddale, who had joined it that morning, has greatly suffered; of 600 men who went into the field, only 146 came out.* The Marquis is wounded in the thigh and leg. He arrived here last night on one of our vessels, and is now at Judge Campbell's. Lieutenant Lyon, who attracted the notice of the Marquis by his bravery, and who was

* Three or four days after this sanguinary conflict, the enemy were employed burying their own dead and burning those of the British. (Thomson's History of the War.)

posted on our left near the Niagara river, with the company he commanded, which consisted of twenty-eight privates, four non-commissioned officers and three officers, only brought six out of the field. He was wounded near the close of the action by a grape-shot, which went through his right thigh a few inches above the knee, passing all the arteries, and the surgeon, on examining it was astonished at his wonderful escape. He came here with his wife last night, and they are now at our house. I have not yet seen him. About 140 wounded were also landed here last night about nine o'clock, and five or six officers whose names I have not yet learned. Yesterday morning the enemy advanced towards Fort George and Niagara, and when our vessels came out of the river, they were seen in great numbers at the Two and Four-Mile creeks. They are said to be from 7,000 to 9,000 strong, well appointed and disciplined.

Captain Hey of the 100th is very dangerously wounded. The ball entered at the groin and came out in the opposite direction. Captain Sherrard of the 100th is also very much wounded in four places, yet there are hopes of him. Our force at Burlington is but weak, and this place has only the Glengarries of 400 strong, and it is said they have orders to embark this morning for Fort George, so that this place will be abandoned, except by a few inefficient local militia; for all those in the neighbourhood are called out, to the great and sure loss of the harvest, if they are not relieved. It is said that provisions at Niagara have become very scarce, and are now served out at half-allowance. Unless, therefore, some of the thousands now in the Lower Province are speedily sent up and arrive, with all necessaries, and that the enemy's fleet be kept in check, the game is up in this quarter. A few days will, I think, determine our fate.

The enemy's fleet are expected at Sackett's Harbour this day. If so, we shall probably soon see them.

Hope yet remains; Providence may again interpose and save us, as last December, contrary to all human expectations.

After the battle of Chippewa, General Riall gave orders to retire under shelter of Forts George and Mississauga until reinforcements should arrive.

On the withdrawal of the Canadian troops, General Brown moved within a mile and a half of those posts; his army in a crescent, his right resting on the Niagara river, his left on Lake Ontario.

Then began a system of pillage on the unfortunate inhabitants.

A story is told that a certain American general, with a party of about 200 mounted men, appeared before a small farm-house near Fort George, occupied by a few women and children, where some goods had been stored for safety. The general took possession of these and divided with his followers, reserving for himself a set of silver spoons, a great coat to fit over his own, and as much of a chest of tea as he could carry off in a flannel shirt sewed up at one end for the purpose. So equipped, the gallant general marched off; then next met and took prisoner a young man named Thompson, whom he robbed of his silver watch, but afterwards, approaching too near the picquets, was himself mortally wounded, and taken by the same young man to his father's house, where he died. The officer next in command, with a finer sense of honor, restored to its owner the stolen watch.

On the 19th July the pretty little village of St. David's, near Queenston, was wantonly burnt by some American troops. To the credit of General Brown, Colonel Stone, the officer who had incited the outrage, was immediately dismissed from the United States service.

In spite of the strict watch kept by the American picquets, General Riall contrived to march part of his force, a few ammunition waggons, and two six-pounders, to a rendezvous for reinforcements at the Twelve Mile Creek.

General Brown, in the meantime, had been daily expecting the arrival of Chauncey with his fleet, and on July 13th wrote him this imploring letter :—

Meet me on the lake shore north of Fort George with the fleet, and we will be able, I have no doubt, to settle a plan of operations that will break the power of the enemy in Upper Canada, and that in the course of a short time. I doubt not my ability to meet the enemy in the field, and to march in any direction over his country, your fleet carrying for me the necessary supplies. We can threaten Forts George and Niagara and carry Burlington Heights and York, and proceed directly to Kingston and carry that place.

For God's sake, let me see you.

However, Commodore Chauncey was safely block-aded in Sackett's Harbour by Sir James Yeo, therefore General Brown, apprehensive, by his own account, of an attack on the rear of his army, and of communication with his encampment being cut off, fell back to Queenston on the 22nd July, to protect his supplies.

He then determined to disencumber the army of its heavy baggage and march against Burlington Heights. In order to draw from Fort Schlosser a supply of provisions necessary for the expedition he retired, on the 24th July, to the junction of the Chippewa and Niagara.

In the meantime General Drummond had been vainly urging Sir George Prevost to send more troops for the relief of the Niagara frontier. The latter insisted that the chief attack would be on the Champlain border, and although Wellington's troops were now arriving in the country, none were available for Drummond's command. That gallant soldier therefore hastened back to Niagara, bringing with him only a portion of the 89th regiment, under Colonel Morrison, the hero of Chrysler's farm.

General Drummond arrived at Fort George at dawn of the 25th July, and learnt immediately of the withdrawal of the American army. At that date the Canadian troops were scattered over twenty or thirty miles of country, but ready at a short notice to concentrate at any given point. All the active militia had been called out, and had nobly responded to the call. General Riall, who was at Twelve-Mile creek, had, early on the morning of the 25th, sent forward Colonel Pearson's brigade, which included the Provincial Dragoons, the Glengarries and incorporated militia, to reconnoitre the American camp at Chippewa, and watch its movements. They took up their position on the high ground near Lundy's Lane, and in the afternoon were joined by General Riall, and Lieutenant-Colonel Drummond of the 104th.

In the meantime the American Commander-in-Chief at Chippewa, having received intelligence of General Drummond's arrival at Niagara, and of an expected attack on his supply-camps at Lewiston and Schlosser, ordered General Winfield Scott to advance rapidly and menace the forts at the mouth of the river. This order was issued between four and five o'clock of the afternoon of July 25th, and within twenty minutes Scott had all his troops in motion. He pushed on towards the Falls, impressed with the belief that a large force of the enemy was on the other side of the river, and not directly before him.

The battle of Lundy's Lane, so important in its results, was, therefore, unpremeditated on both sides.

General Drummond, who had only arrived in the Niagara river at daybreak of the 25th, acted with his usual energy, and determined to march at once from Queenston to Niagara Falls, in order to join General Riall there. He first sent Colonel Tucker, with about 400 men, across the river to capture the supply-camp at Lewiston, which was successfully accomplished after a slight skirmish, and the troops then recrossed the river at noon, and joined the main body under General Drummond and Colonel Morrison, the whole colmmn consisting of about 800 men. This was composed of the 89th, detachments of the Royals and the 8th, and two twenty-four-pound field-pieces. Although but seven from Queenston to the Falls, it was a toilsome march on a hot summer day to men who already had done a good day's work. Their experienced commander knew there was no time to spare for rest, and that, scanty as was the reinforcement he brought, it was sorely needed at this crisis by General Riall.

Word came to him late in the afternoon that the Americans had left Chippewa, and were marching towards the Falls. At about six in the evening, General Drummond arrived with his brigade at the junction of the Queenston Road and Lundy's Lane. To his dismay, he met General Riall retiring from his strong position on the hill in the face of the advancing columns of the Americans. Without a moment's hesitation, Drummond countermanded the retreat, and placed his guns in position on the hill. The men were formed as they came up in order of battle, ready to receive the enemy. The line was a crescent, the left resting on the Queenston Road, the artillery in the centre, strongly posted on the hill near the little church and graveyard, which still marks the spot. The discrepancies in the account of numbers engaged on both sides is almost ludicrous, each historian claiming that their side fought against double the number.

It is certain, that at this early part of the engagement, Drummond had about 1,600 men, and Scott, the American general, about 1,800. The arrival of reinforcements increased the respective sides to about 4,000 Americans and 3,000 Canadians. A little before sunset the battle began, which raged until midnight, with a fury unequalled during the war. Through the long summer twilight, on the roads, overhung as now by lovely orchards, in the copses and on the hill-side, the

> " Roar of baleful battle rose,
>   And brethren of a common tongue
>   To mortal strife, like tigers, sprung."

Early in the engagement General Riall was wounded, and as he was proceeding with an escort to the rear, he fell into the enemy's hands, and was, with his escort, taken prisoner. His capture was a curious accident. One of his *aides* saw a flanking party of the enemy, which had unperceived almost gained the rear of the Canadians, to the left of their line, and mistaking them in the darkness for a company of our own troops, called out, "Make room there men for General Riall!" The officer commanding immediately said "Ay, ay, sir," and then directed the men, with fixed bayonets, to surround the general and his officers, and make them prisoners. As Riall was badly wounded, no resistance was made, and he was delivered over to General Scott, who treated him with great consideration. The American company, quite elated with their prize, charged back through the British line and joined their comrades.

At nine o'clock there was a pause for a short time,

and the long-looked for reinforcements appeared, for both sides: General Porter's brigade, with General Ripley and General Brown for the Americans, and Colonels Scott and Gordon, with about 1,200 men, for the Canadians. This latter force consisted of part of the 103rd and 104th, and Royal Scots, and had left their quarters at Twelve-Mile Creek in the afternoon, but when well on their way had been met by a courier from General Riall, ordering them to retreat, as he was about to retire on Queenston. They had gone four miles back, when another courier came from General Drummond, ordering them to advance at once to Lundy's Lane. It was nine o'clock before these troops, wearied with their march of twenty miles, appeared on the scene.

In spite of the darkness, which was illumined only by the faint moonlight, and the flashes of musketry, the struggle began again in all parts of the field with redoubled fury.

The key of the position was the hill, and the American general saw that he could not hope for success until the height should be carried and the guns taken. He, therefore, gave orders to Colonel Miller, of the 21st United States infantry, to charge the guns with his regiment, and the order was gallantly obeyed. The American soldiers moved steadily up the hill, concealed by an old fence, on which was a growth of shrubbery. They approached undiscovered so near the Canadian batteries that the gunners were shot down to a man in the act of loading, and by an impetuous rush the Americans succeeded in obtaining possession of the guns.

Now began a hand-to-hand struggle for the mastery, and the bayonet was used with frightful effect. A line formed for the protection of the cannon opened a destructive fire on Miller's column, and Drummond's men closed round the guns, determined to contest their possession. In the darkness, confusion and carnage reigned supreme, as both sides struggled to hold the crest of the position. In all parts of the field the stubborn fight was carried on, and mingled with the shout of command, the roar of artillery, and the clashing of steel, was the thunder of that mighty cataract whose waters rolled so near.

The officers of both armies exposed themselves recklessly, and led their troops with equal bravery. Of the Canadians, the 89th and Royal Scots lost half their men, and the Glengarries, Lincoln and York militia, and Provincial Dragoons suffered severely. Colonel Morrison, of the 89th, was wounded, and carried from the field. General Drummond had his horse shot dead beneath him, and received a bullet wound in his neck. With heroic courage he concealed his hurt and still fought on, reforming his shattered battalions, and leading them to a renewed charge on the enemy. More than half of his troop were of the volunteer militia, and that night brought desolation to many a home in Canada.

20

On the American side, the loss too, was severe, and the wounded included three of the generals—Porter, Scott and Brown. On the latter's retirement from the field, the command devolved on General Ripley.

The American regiments were now weakening in all directions, and it was impossible for their officers to rally them. Ripley, therefore, with Brown's permission, decided to withdraw to Chippewa, and at midnight the battle ceased and the Americans retired, leaving the field and the guns, with the exception of one six-pounder, in the possession of the Canadians. There was no attempt at pursuit that night, and Drummond's wearied troops sank to rest among the dying and the dead.

General Brown had ordered Ripley to resume the fight for the guns at daybreak, but that cautious commander deemed discretion the better part of valour, and, instead of advancing, retreated in great confusion to Fort Erie, destroying on the way the bridges, and throwing the heavy baggage into the rapids above the Falls.

It has been the fashion of American writers to claim this battle as a victory, and as such, under the name of Niagara Falls, it is emblazoned on their flags. It is difficult to see on what grounds they base their claim. It is true they fought gallantly, and, for a time, held the guns on the hill; but they failed to keep the advantage they temporarily gained, and their precipitate retreat the next day was a proof that they felt themselves defeated.

The number of the killed was so great, and the heat of summer so excessive, that the British were unable to bury friend and foe alike ; and, accordingly, on the second day, sent a message to the enemy to send back a detachment to bury their dead. This duty the American general was unable to fulfil, leaving it to General Drummond to order the burning of the bodies of some 200 Americans.

It is surely not the custom of the victors to allow their dead to be buried by the vanquished.

General Ripley was called severely to account for his retreat, and was superseded in the command of the American army by General Gaines, who was summoned from Sackett's Harbour to take command until General Brown should recover from his wounds.

A letter from General Brown to Commodore Chauncey, dated Buffalo, September 6th, 1814, does not give one the impression that he considered the battle of the 25th July a success. It runs thus :—

The Government led me to believe that the fleet under your command would be upon Lake Ontario to co-operate with my division of the army the first week in July. I have deemed it fit and proper to let the nation know that the support I had a right to expect was not afforded me. From the 9th of July to the 24th the whole country was in our power, from Fort George to Burlington Heights, and could the army have been supplied with provisions from the depots provided on the shores of Lake Ontario, we should not have doubted our ability to carry the Heights, when we could have returned upon Fort George and Niagara, or advanced upon Kingston with the co-operation of the fleet.

I have endeavoured to execute the orders given me, success has not attended my endeavours. (From manuscript letters in Library of Parliament, Ottawa).

The official reports of losses at the battle of Lundy's Lane, or Niagara, are as follows :—General Brown's report gives for the Americans, killed, 171 ; wounded, 570 ; missing, 117 ; total, 858.

General Drummond's report is :—Killed, 84 ; wounded, 559 ; missing, 193 ; prisoners, 42 ; total, 878.

Among the prisoners taken on both sides were Captain Loring, A.D.C. to General Drummond, and Captain Spencer, A.D.C. to General Brown. Both general's agreed to depart from the usages of War, and to exchange their *aides* without waiting for the usual formalities. Captain Loring was sent back to his general, but poor Captain Spencer, who was mortally wounded, died the day he arrived at Fort Erie.

From Thomas Ridout to his Son at Cornwall :—

YORK, *2nd August*, 1814.

The enemy have been defeated with great loss at the battle of Lundy's Lane, on the 25th July. The particulars you will, perhaps, see about this time.

Your good friend, Colonel Morrison, has been severely wounded in the arm, and has gone to Kingston or Montreal.

We are greatly, but agreeably, surprised at not having seen any of the enemy's fleet. Surely there must exist some wonderful and important cause for their continuance in harbour.   Sometimes it is reported they are out, sometimes that they want seamen.

It is reasonable, I think, to suppose that the peace of Europe will induce all the foreign seamen in the enemy's service to wish themselves at home.   At all events, though frequently alarmed, we are all whole; and I hope in a few days that there will be a sufficient number of men at this post to repel the enemy in case of an attack.

CHAPTER XXII.

FORT ERIE, LAKE ONTARIO, LAKE HURON, AUGUST, 1814.

AFTER the battle of the 25th July, only a few days of needful rest were taken by our army, and its indefatigable commander. Although suffering severely from his wound, General Drummond prepared his plans for the pursuit of the Americans, and their investment in their harbour of refuge at Fort Erie.

General Ripley was so impressed by the severe handling his troops had received at Lundy's Lane, that he implored General Brown, who was at Buffalo, disabled by his wounds from taking the field, to abandon the inhospitable shores of Canada. However, this was not permitted by the American Commander-in-Chief, and Ripley received orders to entrench his army on the lake shore above Fort Erie, to strengthen the old works and to construct new and more extensive ones, preparatory to an expected siege. From the 27th July, 1814, to the 2nd August, the troops were employed day and night, casting up entrenchments, constructing redoubts, and preparing abattis. Up to this time Fort Erie had been but a small and weak affair, but it now began to assume a formidable appearance. On the extreme right of the American encampment, and near the lake shore, a strong stone work had been erected, and two guns mounted on it. This was called the Douglas battery. From the left of the battery to the right of the old fort, continuous earth-works were thrown up, seven feet in height, with a ditch in front and slight abattis; and from the fort, and in a line nearly parallel with the lake shore, strong parapet breast-works were commenced with two ditches and abattis in front. At the south-western extremity of this line of works, on a natural sand mound called Snake Hill, a sort of bastion, twenty feet in height, was cast up, and five guns mounted on it. This was named Towson's battery. From this battery to the lake shore, near which lay at anchor three armed schooners (the *Porcupine*, *Somers* and *Ohio*), was a line of abattis, thus completing the enclosure of the American camp, with defences on land and water, within an area of about fifteen acres.

These works, with the exception of old Fort Erie, were incomplete on the 2nd August. On that day General Drummond, who had been reinforced by De Watteville's regiment and some artillery, made his appearance.

The Canadian troops advanced steadily, drove in the American picquets, and in the woods, two miles from Fort Erie, formed a camp and commenced casting up lines of entrenchments and constructing batteries in front, at points from which an effectual fire might be poured upon the American works.

As it was thought important to capture the batteries at Black Rock, on the opposite side of the river, General Drummond sent over on the night of the 3rd August, Colonel Tucker with some of the 41st, in nine boats, to attempt to take them.

However, the Americans were prepared to receive them, and such a destructive fire was poured on the boats at dawn, that the expedition fell back on Squaw Island, and then recrossed the Niagara, to join the main body in the investment of Fort Erie.

General Drummond had opened fire on the 3rd August, but, until the 7th, cannonading was seldom heard, as both sides were labouring hard. Drummond constructing works for a siege and assault, and Ripley in preparations for a defence.

The Americans were now thoroughly dispirited, and kept within the limits of Fort Erie as far as Snake Hill. On the 5th August, General Gaines arrived from Sackett's Harbour to take command in place of General Ripley, and his presence revived the courage and confidence of the beleaguered army.

Early on the morning of the 7th August, the besiegers began hurling a tremendous storm of round shot on the enemy, and from that day until the 13th, a constant fire was kept up on the American works.

On the night of the 12th August, a clever capture of two of the enemy's gun-boats—*Ohio* and *Somers*—was made by Captain Dobbs of the Royal Navy, with seventy-five men.

The prizes were taken to Chippewa, and secured there. The third gun-boat, the *Porcupine*, slipped its cable and escaped to Presqu' Isle.

On the 13th August, General Drummond completed the mounting of all his heavy ordnance, and made preparations to carry the fort by storm.

All day of the 14th the cannonading was kept up, but with very little effect on the strong works.

The firing ceased at seven, and the garrison, exhausted with constant watchfulness, slept on the night of the 14th the sleep of weary men.

There was silence in both camps till midnight—the calm before the storm.

General Drummond had determined on a night assault, and taking advantage of a dark, cloudy night, silently and warily his little army moved out of its entrenchments for the attack.

The troops were divided into three divisions. The first under Colonel Fischer of De Watteville's regiment, consisting of the King's, De Watteville's and the flank companies of the 89th and 100th regiments, with some militia, was directed against Towson's battery on Snake Hill. The second division under Lieutenant-Colonel Drummond of the 104th, consisted of the 41st and 104th regiments, and some seamen and marines under Captain Dobbs, who had made the successful capture two nights before. This division was directed against old Fort Erie.

The third division, under Colonel Scott of the 103rd,

consisting of part of that regiment and two companies
of the Royal Scots, advanced towards the Douglas battery and the connecting entrenchments. It was
about two o'clock of the morning of the 15th August,
when the several divisions began the attack. The
alarm of their approach had been given by the American picquet guard, and soon the garrison was on the
alert.

Up in the gloom Colonel Fischer's division came
dashing on, and charged furiously upon Towson's
battery. The gunners had been warned in time, and
immediately two twenty-four-pounders from the battery sent forth a stream of flame from the summit of
Snake Hill, and revealed the position of the Canadian
troops to the garrison.

While part of Fischer's column was attempting to
scale the embankment at Towson's battery, another
party forming the reserve, while marching too near
the lake, found themselves entangled between the
rocks and the water, and in the darkness, were thrown
into such confusion that it was impossible to form
them. They were exposed to a galling fire, and many
of them were killed or severely wounded.

Soon a tremendous fire from the guns in the fort
and from the entrenchments on the shore of the lake
announced that Scott and Drummond had commenced
their assault. The column under Scott was repulsed,
but Colonel Drummond's division, under the impetuous lead of their heroic commander, succeeded in

penetrating the enemy's works. They were met gallantly by the American soldiers within, and twice were repulsed, but could not be kept in check. In the meantime, Scott's column had rallied, and the fort was assailed from all quarters at once. Colonel Drummond and a hundred of the artillery, taking advantage of a thick fall of gunpowder smoke, went silently around the ditch, and, with scaling ladders, ascended the parapet and gained a secure footing there. The enemy were driven from their posts at the point of the bayonet. Colonel Drummond performed extraordinary acts of valour, encouraging his men, and leading them in the hottest of the fight. It was a repetition of the midnight contest on the hill at Lundy's Lane, and again the bayonet was used with terrible effect.

The American general sent reinforcement after reinforcement to assist in driving the British troops from the bastion, but in vain.

Just at the moment of victory, a terrific explosion took place in the centre of the bastion. A jet of flame, mingled with fragments of earth, stone and bodies of men rose in the air, and the greater number of the brave men, who had just entered the fort, were literally blown to pieces.

An eye-witness (American) says, The cause of the explosion has never been officially explained. History ascribes it to accident. If it was design, I think the end justified the means. It was that mysterious explosion which saved our little army.

Is it possible that some soldiers in the fort, who saw the American cause was lost, took this desperate means of destroying their opponents?

Be it as it may, accident or design, the result was disastrous to the Canadians. The few officers who had survived the explosion could not rally their men. Both the commanding officers had been killed in that terrible contest in the fort. Drummond by a bayonet wound, Scott by a musket ball, and as day dawned on the scene, the shattered troops retired to their entrenchments.

The loss to the Canadian force was much greater than that of the Americans.

In General Drummond's official report, the returns are:—

Killed—2 lieutenant-colonels, 1 captain, 1 lieutenant, 1 sergeant, 1 drummer, 51 rank and file; total, 57. Wounded—1 deputy assistant-quarter-master-general, 1 major, 8 captains, 11 lieutenants, 2 ensigns, 1 master, 12 seamen, 20 sergeants, 2 drummers, 250 rank and file; total, 308. Missing—1 deputy assistant-quarter-master-general, 1 captain, 3 lieutenants, 2 ensigns, 1 midshipman, 1 adjutant, 7 seamen, 41 sergeants, 3 drummers, 479 rank and file; total killed, wounded and missing, 904.

Among the killed on the American side was the renegade member of the Assembly, Jos. Willcocks.

The ill-fated and much lamented Lieutenant-Colonel William Drummond, 104th, a nephew of General Gordon Drummond, who had done good service to Canada in numerous engagements, was buried by the Americans near Towson's Battery. From his pockets were taken his papers, among them this secret order in Colonel Harvey's handwriting :—

" The Lieutenant-General most strongly recommends the free use of the bayonet."

Through this paper, General Gaines says, is the mark of the fatal bayonet thrust.

Colonel Scott, of the 103rd, who had also distinguished himself on many a field, was buried the same evening by his own men, in the presence of the only three officers of his regiment, who came out of the fort unhurt.

Fischer's division at Snake Hill had only been partially successful. They had, indeed, turned the enemy's battery, but the flank companies were stopped by an impenetrable abattis, and the column of support had been hopelessly entangled among the rocks in the lake.

Among those of the militia mentioned in despatches as distinguished for their gallantry, were Captain Powell, of the Quarter-Master-General's Department, and Sergeant Powell, of the 19th Dragoons; Lieutenant-Colonel Pearson and Lieutenant-Colonel Battersby, of the Glengarries, and Captain Walker, of the incorporated militia.

A letter from York of the 9th August, tells what was going on there while Drummond and his men were entrenched at Fort Erie.

Chauncey's fleet had broken through the blockade at Sackett's Harbour, and were sailing on Lake Ontario, to the constant menace of the little town.

It may be gathered from the letter, that in the midst of war's alarms, ordinary affairs were carried on. The courts were held as usual, and those who one week buckled on their swords, another week wore the barrister's gown.

From Surveyor-General Ridout to his Son at Cornwall:—

YORK, *9th August.*

On Saturday last, the 6th inst., I hastily enclosed to your care a letter I had written to my brother, informing you, at the same time, that the American fleet were off this place. They made their appearance on the preceding day, about ten sail, standing toward Niagara, with a fine easterly breeze, and at no great distance from that shore. I had gone down to the Bay and was standing near Coxe's door conversing with Captain McDonell, who had lost his left arm at the battle of Lundy's Lane, when I felt a violent concussion of the air, and, presently after, heard an explosion towards Niagara, much greater than the explosion of our magazine. On looking over the lake where the enemy's vessels were, I saw a prodigious cloud of smoke rising to a great height. I then concluded, and do now, that one of the enemy's vessels was blown up, but of this we have not received any information. When I enclosed my letter the American fleet were lying off this place about eight miles, and the *Lady of the Lake* was attempting to come into this harbour as a flag of truce; but, not permitting such insidious policy, a shot from one of our batteries was fired at this vessel. She then hoisted her proper colours, and fired at the garrison, and afterwards, another shot.

We fired three or four more, but all fell short of her. She put out to join her fleet, and a visit was expected from them. At this time we had only a few convalescent and lame soldiers and 200 or 300 of the sedentary or home militia. In the course of the afternoon 300 men of the first detachment of the 82nd came in, having marched at the rate of four miles an hour, and on Sunday the residue of that regiment came in also. This morning a part of that corps have proceeded to Niagara by land, and the 1st division of the 6th are expected in the course of the day. Four of the enemy's vessels are now in sight, about eight miles off. On Friday, Saturday and Sunday people were busy moving their effects to the country. On Saturday I removed the remainder of my office papers and some family necessaries. With much difficulty I walked as far as Sam's, having been laid up some days with a lumbago. I came in this morning.

George* went from home yesterday. He attends the court at Ancaster as Acting Solicitor-General.

Judge Powell is gone on that circuit.

John Robinson goes the Eastern Circuit with Judge Campbell.

Sam † took sixty-one prisoners in charge for Kingston on Saturday. He set out by land with twenty-four militia as guard.

Peter Robinson ‡ is come from Mackinaw, from whence he escaped through a fleet of ten sail who are besieging it. He says that they will not, in his opinion, be able to reduce it, and that there are plenty of provisions for our troops in the place. I have not had any news from Fort Erie, only, it is said that General Drummond is highly displeased with the 41st.

* Lieutenant George Ridout, York militia. † Samuel Ridout, Sheriff.
‡ Brother of John Beverley Robinson.

From Surveyor-General Ridout to his son Thomas at Cornwall :—

YORK, *Sunday Afternoon, 14th August,* 1814.

I wish you would subscribe for the Quebec *Mercury*, printed and published by S. Carey. I think it the best Canadian paper.

Colonel Hamilton, who lately commanded the 100th regiment, and is now Inspecting Field Officer, came here last night with his family, and occupies Mr. Campbell's house in his absence. He says it is reported above that the American generals Brown and Scott, have died of their wounds received on the 25th. The coolness of General Drummond on that memorable night, and the performance of all his duties are beyond all praise. His wound in the neck was very severe, and has been very troublesome, but is now doing well. Three of the American fleet are seen from here almost every day. They consist of two brigs and a schooner. It is reported the other part of the fleet are gone over the lake. 'Tis said the residue of the 89th are coming hither, as well as the remnant of the 100th.

The report of the death of the American generals was not correct. General Brown recovered enough to take the field again in September. General Winfield Scott's wounds were more serious.

The reference in the letter of the 9th to Peter Robinson's escape through the enemy's fleet, takes us back to Lake Huron and the white cliffs of Mackinaw.

Although the Americans had, in 1813, recaptured Detroit and Michigan, and now controlled the upper lakes, the little island fortress of Michillimackinac still defied them.

In May, 1814, a reinforcement of Canadian militia and a few regulars were sent there, under Lieutenant-Colonel McDouall, who also had in charge twenty-four bateaux. This reinforcement arrived safely at the island on the 18th May. Early in the spring the Americans had planned an expedition on the upper lakes, but for various reasons, the sailing of their squadron was delayed, and the fort at Mackinac remained for some time unmolested.

Colonel McDouall, however, did not remain inactive. Early in July, he sent off Colonel McKay, of the Indian Department, with 650 men—Fencibles, Volunteers and Indians—to reduce Prairie du Chien, a village at the junction of the Ouisconsin and Mississippi. There was a small fort there, also two block-houses, and a gun-boat of fourteen guns. McKay, a sturdy Highlander, demanded an immediate surrender. This was refused, so he opened fire on the gun-boat, which cut her cable and ran down the stream. McKay then threw up a mud battery, and prepared with his one gun to bombard the fort. The enemy, seeing the earthworks, imagined that the Canadians were well supplied with artillery, and without waiting for a single round, sent out a white flag, and McKay took possession of the fort.

The effect of the capture was of service in securing the continued allegiance of the Indians.

In the meantime an American squadron had been fitted out under the command of Arthur St. Clair. It

21

consisted of the *Niagara, Caledonia, St. Lawrence, Scorpion* and *Tigress*, vessels which had taken part in the battle of Lake Erie the preceding year.

This expedition left Detroit about the middle of July. The land force was under the command of Colonel Croghan, and consisted of 500 regulars U. S. A., 250 militia, and a regiment of Ohio volunteers. They first sailed for Matchedash, Lake Huron, where there was a British post, but fogs, and the lack of good pilots for the dangerous channels, caused them to abandon their designs in that quarter. They then sailed for the deserted fort of St. Joseph, which they committed to the flames. Then they proceeded to the village of Sault Ste. Marie, where they arrived on the 21st July, 1814. This place, where the North-West Company had large stores, and which was the centre of traffic with the Indians, was also laid in ashes.

They then sailed for Michillimackinac, where they arrived on the 26th July. The little garrison was quite prepared for their reception. The guns of the vessels could not be used with effect on the high position of the fort, and Croghan determined to land in the rear, or western part of the island, under cover of the guns of his fleet. From the 26th July to the 4th August, the vessels had lain waiting for a chance to land the men, and it was through this fleet that Peter Robinson escaped.

On the 4th August, Croghan succeeded in landing, but was received by a storm of shot and shell from a

battery on the shore, and from the garrison under Mc-
Douall, and a hot fire from the Indians stationed in the
thick woods. The enemy fell back and fled to the
boats, with the loss of seventeen killed, and a large
number wounded. Croghan and St. Clair then abandoned the attempt to take Michillimackinac, and after
hovering for several weeks on the lake, they returned
empty-handed to Detroit.

At Fort Erie the siege still continued. After the
disastrous explosion on the 15th August, General
Drummond retired to his entrenchments to await
reinforcements, and to construct new batteries. The
struggle soon began again, and through the remainder
of the month, almost daily, hot shot, shells and rockets
were thrown into the fort, much to the annoyance of
the Americans. On the 28th, a shell fell through the
roof of General Gaines' quarters, and exploding at his
feet, injured him so severely that he was compelled to
give up the command and retire to Buffalo.

While these events were happening in Upper Canada,
the war was raging fiercely on the American seaboard.

On the 24th August, 1814, Washington, the capital
of the United States, was entered, taken by the combined forces of General Ross and Admiral Cockburn,
after a sharp engagement at Bladensburg, where the
only resistance was made.

The victors destroyed by fire the capitol, the public
buildings, the President's house, the arsenal and two
frigates, also an immense amount of military stores.

The destruction of so much valuable property was severely censured at the time, and deemed more suited to a barbaric age than to the warfare of a civilized people.

It is true that General Ross first demanded an indemnity, but, this being refused, the torch was applied.

In the meantime, while blood and treasure were being thus wasted, the Peace Commissioners had assembled at Ghent, and were trying to reconcile differences and to put an end to the desolating ravages of war.

CHAPTER XXIII.

PLATTSBURG, LAKE CHAMPLAIN, SEPTEMBER, 1814.

TROOPS were now pouring into Canada. The downfall of Napoleon, in May, 1814, and his retirement to Elba, had released from service on the Continent, a number of English regiments ; and several thousands of Wellington's veterans were despatched to Canada, during the months of July and August, 1814, to reinforce the army there.

With 14,000 veteran troops at his command, Sir George Prevost thought the moment had come to strike a decisive blow, by invading the enemy's territory.

Stoney Creek, and Chrysler's Field, and Lundy's Lane, had proved what could be done with a mere handful of troops under the leadership of men like Harvey, and Morrison, and Drummond.

The unfortunate expedition to Plattsburg was now about to show how useless the best troops in the world may be in the hands of an incompetent general.

A letter from Thomas G. Ridout speaks of the arrival of more regiments, and also of the expected movements on Lake Champlain.

From Thomas G. Ridout to his Father in York :—

CORNWALL, *25th August,* 1814.

I received yesterday your letter of the 19th inst., giving an account of the melancholy affair at Fort Erie. We have not yet had the particulars. I am very sorry for Colonel Scott's death.

General Kempt, with three regiments and a brigade of artillery, will be here to-night, or to-morrow morning.

The 70th and part of the 16th are now here, waiting for orders to march upwards.

Nothing done yet on Lake Champlain.

The General Kempt, afterwards Sir James Kempt, mentioned in the letter, was one of Wellington's best officers, and had greatly distinguished himself in the Peninsular war.

After serving on the staff in Canada during 1814, he went back to Europe, and was severely wounded at the battle of Waterloo.

He returned to America, in 1820, as Governor of Nova Scotia, and, in 1828, became Governor-General of Canada, which post he held for two years.

Another letter from the young commissariat officer gives further information of the movement of troops just prior to the battle on Lake Champlain.

From Thomas G. Ridout to his Mother in York :—

CORNWALL, *1st September,* 1814.

General Kempt will fix his head-quarters at Cornwall on Tuesday next, with about 4,000 troops.

The 37th are expected this evening, the 9th in two days, and the 81st to follow immediately.

The American army* have left Lake Champlain, and are now at Four Corners, where we were last winter, advancing upon Ogdensburg and Sackett's Harbour. They are to occupy Ogdensburg with about 4,000 men, and have hired barracks for that purpose.

Our frigate† is now on two rafts at Prescott, waiting for convoy to go to Kingston, for the Americans say they will attack her.

The 70th regiment are now here, with a brigade of flying artillery. They are ordered to be ready at a moment's warning, and the Commissary-General has notified me that the army must want for nothing.

There is one of Lord Wellington's brigades of artillery stationed here, consisting of brass six-pounders, 180 horses, 120 artillerymen, and 80 drivers. They give a great deal of trouble, and consume two tons of hay per day, and 50 bushels of oats. I am getting sixty tons of hay from the Yankees in bateaux, but am afraid of great difficulty in December.

In August, 1814, the right wing of the American army were encamped at Champlain, on the River Chazy, under the command of General Izard. Under him were Generals Winder (taken prisoner at Stoney Creek, and lately exchanged), and Brigadier-General Macomb.

At the end of August, General Izard was ordered to co-operate with the army on the Niagara frontier. He therefore, very unwillingly, set out for Sackett's Harbour with about 4,000 men, leaving General Macomb in command at Plattsburg, with an army of about 3,500 men, 1,500 of whom were invalids.

On the day that Izard left his camp at Champlain,

---

* The division under General Izard.   † The *St. Lawrence*, of 100 guns.

the British troops advanced from Odelltown, and occupied the abandoned camp.

On the 3rd September, 14,000 picked British troops were gathered there under the immediate command of General Sir George Prevost.

The different brigades were led by Generals Brisbane, Power and Robinson, heroes of the Peninsular War, well-inured to fighting, and accustomed to command.

On the 5th September, they had advanced to within eight miles of Plattsburg, while Macomb's army were doing what they could to obstruct the progress of the invading army, by felling trees and breaking up the bridges on the road. During this advance several skirmishes took place.

On the 6th, there was a sharp engagement with the enemy about a mile and a half from Plattsburg bridge, at Halsey's Corners, where the Americans had thrown up a battery commanding the road. Three times the battery hurled its deadly shot at the advancing troops, but without effect. The British bugles sounded, and the men, throwing away their knapsacks rushed forward at double-quick, and charged with the bayonet.

The Americans fled to the town across the Saranac, whose bridges they tore up, using the timbers as breast-works.

Nothing could have prevented the capture of Macomb's army, had Sir George now pushed his whole force on. He paused, however, and spent five days erecting batteries, and throwing up breast-works.

He was possessed with the idea that nothing could be done without the co-operation of the fleet, although the men under his command were in sufficient numbers to have carried the works alone.

In the meantime the American general was not idle, and kept his troops constantly employed finishing his line of redoubts.

Up to the 11th September the assault of Plattsburg was delayed, waiting for the arrival of the squadron on Lake Champlain, whose co-operation, Sir George thought, would enable him to capture both the American fleet and army.

The British fleet consisted of the frigate *Confiance*, 38 guns (scarcely finished and manned by sailors who had just arrived a few days before from Quebec); the *Linnet*, a brig of sixteen guns; two sloops, *Chub* and *Finch*, formerly United States *Growler* and *Eagle*; thirteen gun-boats or galleys, numbering in all ninety-five guns and 1,050 men. Captain Downie commanded the squadron.

The American fleet lay in Plattsburg Bay, and consisted of the flag-ship *Saratoga*, twenty-six guns; the brig *Eagle*, twenty-six guns; *Ticonderoga*, seventeen guns; the *Preble*, seven guns, and ten gun-boats carrying eighty-six guns in all, and manned by 882 men, under the command of Commodore McDonough.

The weight of metal was about equal.

General Prevost ordered a combined attack to be made by the land and naval forces, and early on the morning of the 11th September the fleet came in sight, Captain Downie having hurried forward in obedience to General Prevost's command.

At the same time three brigades, under Generals Power, Brisbane and Robinson, pressed forward, in order to force the fords of the Saranac, climb its steep banks, and scale the American works, while the British batteries were ordered to open a brisk fire on the fleet and town.

As the *Confiance* appeared round Cumberland Head the *Saratoga* opened fire with fearful effect. Captain Downie, with great coolness, waited until he had secured a desirable position for his ship, and then levelled his guns at the *Saratoga*. The sixteen twenty-four-pounders of the *Confiance* were discharged at once, raking the American flag-ship from stem to stern and laying low half her crew.

The battle now became general between the larger vessels, and the slaughter on both sides was terrible. Early in the engagement Captain Downie fell, and the command of his vessel was taken by Lieutenant Robertson.

While the deadly duel was going on between the two flag-ships, the *Chub* had received a broadside from the *Eagle*, which so crippled her that she drifted helplessly into the enemy's lines, and was taken.

Soon afterwards, the *Finch* struck on some rocks, and was forced to surrender. The British gun-boats now entered vigorously into the action, and caused the *Preble* to cut her cable and make for the shore, where she was of no further use. They then made a furious attack on the *Ticonderoga*, and nearly succeeded in boarding her. The *Eagle* was exposed to the combined fire of the *Confiance* and *Linnet*, so fled to a safer position, between the *Saratoga* and *Ticonderoga*, where she was able to pour in a fresh fire on the gun-boats and the *Confiance*.

So deadly had been the fire between the two large frigates that the *Saratoga* had not a single starboard gun left, and the *Confiance* was not much better.

Victory still hung in the balance, when, as in the battle on Lake Erie, a piece of skilful seamanship on the part of the Americans turned the fortune of the day.

The *Saratoga* cut her cable and wound round, so as to bring a new broadside on the *Confiance*, who vainly attempted to perform the same manœuvre.

In a few minutes the British ship was obliged to strike its colours, followed soon after by the *Linnet*, whose commander said he was not supported by the gun-boats.

Three of these had sunk, the remainder bent their sweeps and escaped down the lake, the American vessels being in too crippled a state to follow.

Commodore McDonough wrote to the American Secretary of War :—

There was not a mast in either squadron that could stand to make sail on ; the lower rigging being nearly all shot away, hung down as if it had been just placed over the mastheads.

Midshipman Lee, of the *Confiance*, wrote : --

Our masts, yards and sails were so shattered, that one looked like so many bunches of matches, and the other like a bundle of rags. I don't think there are more than five of our men out of 300 but what are killed or wounded. Never was a shower of hail so thick as the shot whistling about our ears. There is one of the marines, who was in the Trafalgar action with Lord Nelson, who says that was a mere flea-bite in comparison with this.

For over two hours this naval battle raged, witnessed from the headlands of the Vermont shore by hundreds of spectators, who greeted the victory with shouts.

It was these shouts that reached the ears of Sir George Prevost, and filled him with consternation and dismay.

Although his splendid troops had advanced with all necessary despatch, and part of them had successfully forded the Saranac and scaled the heights, Sir George Prevost withdrew them, at the moment of their victory, and ordered a precipitate retreat.

The army fell back in sullen submission to his command. So indignant was General Robinson that he broke his sword, declaring he could never serve again.*

Sir George's own despatch says :—

Scarcely had His Majesty's troops forced a passage across the Saranac, and ascended the height on which stand the enemy's works, when I had the extreme mortification to hear the shout of victory from the enemy in consequence of the British flag being lowered on board the *Confiance* and *Linnet*, and to see our gun-boats seeking safety in flight.

Sir James Yeo expressed his opinion very freely in a letter to the Admiralty Office, dated September 24th, 1814.   He says :—

It appears to me that Captain Downie was urged, and his ship hurried into action, before she was in a fit state to meet the enemy.   I am also of opinion that there was not the least necessity for our squadron giving the enemy such a decided advantage by going into their Bay to engage them ; even had they been successful, it would not in the least have assisted the troops in storming the batteries, whereas, had our troops taken their batteries first, it would have obliged the enemy's squadron to quit the Bay, and given ours a fair chance.

A desultory fire was kept up until sunset from the British batteries, when Sir George ordered a rapid retreat into Canadian territory.   He left behind his

---

* General Robinson, afterwards Sir F. P. Robinson, was a son of Colonel Beverley Robinson, of New York, a U. E. Loyalist, and a relative of the late Sir John Beverley Robinson, Bart., Chief Justice of Upper Canada. General Robinson was afterwards acting-Lieutenant-Governor of Upper Canada for a short time, until the return of Governor Gore, in 1816.

sick and wounded, with a request that they might be generously treated by General Macomb. Quantities of stores fell into the hands of the Americans.

One bright spot in this disastrous affair, is the kind and humane treatment, which the wounded and prisoners received from Commodore McDonough and General Macomb.

In the hasty flight, numbers of men deserted to the enemy, and the cup of disgrace was filled to overflowing.

For the failure of this expedition Sir George Prevost was called to account. He resigned his governorship as soon as the war was over, and hastened to England to answer the charges brought against him, but died before the court-martial took place. His widow pressed for an inquiry, with the result that in consideration of the many services he had rendered in Canada, and his good qualities as a civil governor, he was exonerated from blame, and the Prince Regent bestowed on his family, as an honour,* some additional armorial bearings.

* The honour bestowed was the right to add supporters to the coat of arms, together with the motto, *Servatum Cineri*.

" The supporters, the proper badges of nobility, give the honour of the peerage, without the rank, to which the fortune left by Sir George was not equal, though his merits were."—*Gentleman's Magazine, January, 1817.*

CHAPTER XXIV.

LAST DAYS OF THE WAR—AUTUMN, WINTER, 1814-1815.

THE news of the success of the American army of the North at Plattsburg quickly reached Fort Erie, where General Brown and his troops were still held at bay by grim Sir Gordon Drummond.

After General Gaines' mishap in August, General Brown, though still unrecovered from his wounds received at Lundy's Lane, had come back to take command at the fort, and arrived there on the 2nd of September.

Both sides had received reinforcements, but there had been no serious fighting since the 15th of August. General Brown's return infused new spirit into the garrison, and the American victory on Lake Champlain so elated his men that he determined upon a grand attack on the Canadian entrenchments.

The Americans had now twenty-seven heavy guns mounted at the fort, and a force behind them of about 4,000 men.

General Drummond's camp was on an open plain, almost surrounded, except on the river side, by thick woods, and beyond the range of shot and shell from the fort. His army was divided into three brigades;

one of these, daily relieved by another, was constantly on duty at the batteries. The works had now been extended to within four or five hundred yards of the old fort, and at that distance two batteries had already been completed, and a third was nearly finished. Heayy rains had flooded the flat ground on which Drummond's camp was situated, and typhoid fever had broken out among his troops.

General Brown's army chafed under their inaction, and were getting tired of being cooped up within the narrow limits of the fort.

A sortie was, therefore, planned, and the day fixed for it was the 17th September. The plan was, as General Brown writes, " To storm the batteries, destroy the cannon, and roughly handle the brigade upon duty, before those in the camp could be brought into action."

The American general made his plans with great secrecy, not even disclosing them to his own officers. He waited until a reinforcement of 2,000 militia, under General Porter, arrived from Buffalo, and then announced his intentions. They were not received favourably by some of the other generals. Ripley thought the enterprise was a hopeless one, and said he should be well satisfied to escape from the disgrace which, in his judgment, would fall upon all engaged.

Towards noon of the 17th September, taking advantage of a thick fog, which obscured their movements, the Americans advanced from the fort in three brigades. The first, led by General Porter, was to move from the extreme left of the American camp, by a circuitous road through the woods, and attack the Canadians on their right flank. The second division, under General Miller (who had led the attack up the hill at Lundy's Lane), was ordered to move by way of a ravine, between Fort Erie and the Canadian batteries, and attack their centre. The third division, under General Ripley, was posted as a reserve near the fort, out of sight.

The first division reached a position within a few rods of the Canadian right before their movements were even suspected, and commenced the assault at once.

The Canadian troops were so completely taken by surprise that they fell back, leaving the Americans in possession of the ground. Batteries three and four were stormed, and after a close contest of thirty minutes were carried, the blockhouse in their rear captured, the garrison made prisoners, and the magazine blown up. This success was obtained at fearful cost to the Americans, their three principal leaders of divisions, General Davis, Colonel Gibson and Colonel Wood, being mortally wounded, and a number of their men killed.

In the meantime General Miller had advanced on the Canadian centre, carried the first and second batteries with the blockhouses in rear ; and so, within forty minutes, four batteries, two blockhouses, and the

22

whole line of Drummond entrenchments, were in possession of the Americans.

Just at this moment General Ripley was ordered up with his reserve, and received such a severe wound that he was carried from the field to the fort.

So far the sortie had been successful, but the victors were not long allowed to hold their spoils.

The story of how the batteries were re-taken is best told by General Drummond, and General De Watteville, in their despatches.

Extract of a letter from Lieutenant-General Drummond to Lieutenant-General Sir George Prevost :—

CAMP BEFORE FORT ERIE,

September 19th, 1814.

My letter to your Excellency of the 17th gave a short account of the result of an attack made by the enemy on my position on that day.

I have to add, that as soon as the firing was heard, I proceeded towards the advance, and found the troops had moved from camp, and the Royals and 89th had been pushed, by Major-General De Watteville, into the wood on the right towards No. 3 battery, and that the 82nd was moving to the support of the batteries on the left. At this moment it was reported to me that the enemy had gained possession of the batteries Nos. 2 and 3, and that our troops were falling back— a report which the approach of the fire confirmed ; (your Excellency will have in recollection that the whole line of operations lay in a thick wood). I immediately directed Lieutenant-Colonel Campbell to detach one wing of the 6th regiment to support the 82nd in an attack which I ordered to be made for the recovery of battery No. 2. I threw forward the Glen-

garry light infantry into the wood in front of the
centre, to check the advance of the enemy, and support
the troops retiring from that point.   Both these movements were executed to my entire satisfaction, and
being combined with a judicious attack made by
Lieutenant-Colonel Gordon with part of the first
brigade, consisting of the 1st battalion of the Royal
Scots supported by the 89th, the enemy was every-
where driven back, and our batteries and entrenchments regained, not, however, before he had disabled
the guns in No. 3 battery and exploded its magazine.
The enemy did not attempt again to make a stand,
but retreated in great disorder to the fort, and was
followed by our troops to the glacis of that place.

I myself witnessed the good order and spirit with
which the Glengarry light infantry, under Lieutenant-
Colonel Battersby, pushed into the wood, and by their
superior fire drove back the enemy's light troops.

I cannot sufficiently appreciate the valuable assistance which I have received from Lieutenant-Colonel
Harvey, Deputy Adjutant-General, during the present
service, and which has been of the more importance,
as, from my own state of health, of late (in consequence of my wound), I have not been able to use
those active exertions which I otherwise might.   To
Major Glegg, Assistant Adjutant-General; to Captains
Chambers and Powell, Deputy Assistants Quarter-
master-General; to Captain Foster, Military Secretary;
Lieutenant-Colonel Hagerman, Provincial *aide-de-
camp*, who have rendered me every assistance in
their respective situations, my best acknowledgments
are due.

The enemy, it is now ascertained, made the sortie
with his whole force, which, including the militia
volunteers, by which he has lately been joined, could
not consist of less than 5,000.   About 200 prisoners
fell into our hands, and I cannot estimate the enemy's
loss in killed and wounded at less than that number.

The dreadful state of the roads and of the weather, it having poured with rain almost incessantly for the last ten days, renders every movement of ordnance or heavy stores exceedingly difficult.

By great exertions, the commanding artillery officer has succeeded in moving the battery guns and mortars, with their stores, etc., towards the Chippewa, to which place I mean to withdraw them for the present.

General De Watteville's report gives substantially the same account of the attack and repulse, and ends by saying, that by five o'clock the entrenchments were again occupied, and the line of picquets established as it had been previous to the enemy's attack.

An extract from a letter of one of the officers engaged says :—

The companies of the 6th and 82nd did wonders. The bayonet was lavishly dealt in the enemy's ranks. .   .   .   .   . Our loss has been heavy, about 100 killed and nearly 500 wounded and missing.

Most are of De Watteville's, who have been surprised in the trenches. Of that fine regiment, fourteen officers are killed, wounded and missing.

Typhoid fever was now proving a more formidable foe even than the Americans, and General Drummond found it necessary to change his camp.

He writes from

DISTRICT HEAD-QUARTERS,

FALLS OF NIAGARA, *September 24th*, 1814.

The troops fell back at eight o'clock on the evening of the 21st, to the position alluded to in my letter of that date, and bivouacked for the night under torrents of rain.

Soon after daylight on the 22nd, the enemy discovered our movements, and pushed out his picquets posted on the plain opposite Black Rock, and immediately retreated, after exchanging a few shots, without attempting to molest us. Having waited until two o'clock (as well for the purpose of giving battle to the enemy, should he have ventured out, as of giving time for the movement of all encumbrances behind the Black Creek), I ordered the troops to retire across Frenchman's Creek, and the bridge over that creek to be destroyed.

A cavalry picquet was left to watch this brigade, and the troops then proceeded to take up the cantonments. The whole of the movement has this day been completed, and the troops are now in comfortable quarters, where it is my intention to give them a few days' repose.

No further sorties were made from Fort Erie, although General Izard's division of 4,000 men arrived there on the 10th October, after a toilsome march through the wilderness from Genesee river, which they left on 24th September, to Lewiston, where they arrived on the 5th October. General Izard placed his camp two miles north of Fort Erie, and being senior to General Brown, the latter retired to his old post at Sackett's Harbour.

General Izard was now in command at Fort Erie of more than 8,000 men, and a battle might have been expected. However, beyond a trifling skirmish at Lyon's Creek, near Chippewa, where the Americans succeeded in destroying some flour at a mill, nothing was done.

The American account says that General Izard clearly perceived that further offensive operations on the peninsula so late in the season would be imprudent, and, perhaps, extremely perilous to the army. Soon afterwards the whole American force crossed the Niagara river, and abandoned Canada.

Fort Erie, the scene of so much hard fighting, was mined by them before leaving, and on the 5th November, 1814, it was blown up and laid in ruins.

The capture of the British fleet on Lake Champlain, on the 11th September, was the last event of importance on the Lower Canadian frontier, and the sortie and repulse of the Americans at Fort Erie on the 17th September, closed the campaign on the Niagara frontier.

The only event recorded in October was a raid of 700 Kentucky volunteers, under General McArthur, who crossed from Detroit into Canada on the 26th of October, and made a dash through the western peninsula. The object of the expedition was the capture of Burlington Heights, but after plundering a few of the inhabitants of the country, and burning some houses in Oxford, they met with such sturdy opposition from a number of militia and Indians at " The Crossings," Grand river, that they did not pursue their journey farther eastward, but turned down the Long Point Road, and returned to Detroit by way of Port Dover and St. Thomas, pursued part of the distance by a company of the Glengarries and some of the 41st, under Major Muir.

General Drummond's work as a military commander was now nearly over. After a short stay in the camp at Chippewa he withdrew his troops to Fort George, but General Izard's retirement from Fort Erie had banished any expectation of an attack from that quarter.

On Lake Ontario Sir James Yeo's grand ship, the *St. Lawrence*, 100 guns, had just been launched, and once more that gallant commodore was lord of the lake, and troops and supplies could now have been easily brought to Drummond's army at Niagara.

The war was, however, practically over.

It was terminated by the Treaty of Ghent, at which place the Peace Commissioners for Britain, and the United States, had been engaged in prolonged negotiations from the 6th August, until the Treaty of Peace was signed on the 24th December, 1814. The Treaty was not ratified by the United States until February, and all through the month of January, 1815, the boom of cannon resounded along the sea-board.

The Americans went to war ostensibly to secure immunity from Search and Impressment, yet after nearly three years of fighting, they joyfully approved of the conclusion of a treaty, which was absolutely silent on that important point.

The Treaty contained provisions for the settling of disputed boundaries by commissioners, and an agreement that, in the interests of humanity and justice, both nations should use their best endeavours for the entire abolition of the Slave Trade.

The Treaty required the ratification of the American Senate, which was unanimously given on 17th February, 1815.

A letter from Thomas G. Ridout gives the date of the arrival of the news of the Peace at Montreal :—

CORNWALL, 27th *February*, 1815.

Yesterday morning I received letters from Montreal stating that the Treaty of Peace had been ratified, and the guns of that place had, in consequence, been fired as a rejoicing at the event. General Brisbane received the express on the *lines* (boundary), and it would reach Quebec the night of the 25th.

All stores are stopped at Montreal, and nothing but provisions will now be sent up.

By a General Order issued on the 1st March, 1815, the Canadian militia were ordered to disband on the 24th of the same month.

The war-worn citizen soldiers returned to their homes, for which they had fought so well. Yet their ranks were sadly thinned. Under the green leaves of shot-riven woods, beneath the grasses of many a quiet hill-side, and in the village churchyards along all that historic frontier, were left behind those who had laid down their lives for Canada.

A few words must be said of the after career of the young Commissary, whose letters form so large a part of this volume.

Thomas G. Ridout continued in the Commissariat until 1820, when he retired on half-pay. In 1821 he was offered a permanent post in the service by the Commissary-General, but declined, as he was then engaged in helping to organize the Bank of Upper Canada, the pioneer bank of the Province. In 1822, he was appointed its first cashier, and continued in that position until shortly before his death, in 1861.

The admirable qualities that he possessed as a youth, which were displayed in his devotion to the duties that devolved upon him during the important years described in this volume, shone out through his whole life, which was a useful and laborious one.

As a conscientious servant, and as a man of business, Mr. Ridout had few equals. His whole object was to perform fearlessly and honestly his duty, and to advance the interests of the institution placed under his control.

Mr. Ridout never entered what is called public life, never sought a seat in Parliament, or even took an active part in politics; but in his career can be traced the wonderful monetary and commercial progress of the country. He took a deep interest in the public welfare, and assisted in furthering those enterprises calculated to promote the prosperity of the Province.

In politics, Mr. Ridout's views were liberal, and it would be difficult to find a more loyal subject to the Crown, or a more staunch supporter of those British institutions under which we are so happily governed.

He was a distinguished member of the order of Free Masons, Master of St. Andrew's Lodge, in which he succeeded his father; and among Royal Arch Masons he will be especially remembered, as the founder, and for nine years, the first Principal of St.

Andrew's Royal Arch Chapter.   As a Masonic Knight Templar, his valuable services will be remembered in the introduction of the Order into Canada.

Of unbending integrity and sterling honesty, Mr. Ridout was respected by all, and being possessed of an amiable and generous disposition, he had many warm and attached friends—we may add, he was without an enemy.—(From Toronto *Leader* and *British Herald*, July 31st, 1861.)

———————

HON. THOMAS RIDOUT.

Surveyor-General of Upper Canada, and Member of His Majesty's Legislative Council.

Born, Sherbourne, Dorsetshire, England, 17th March, 1754.

Died, 8th February, 1829.

APPENDIX.

Narrative of the Captivity among the Shawanese Indians, in 1788, of Thomas Ridout, afterwards Surveyor-General of Upper Canada, from the Original Manuscript in Possession of the Family.

An Account of my Capture *by the Shawanese Indians, dwelling on the River Ohio in North America, and of my residence amongst them during the Spring and part of the Summer of the year 1788.*

I HAD arrived at Philadelphia from Europe in February, 1787, in order to collect debts due to me by several persons in the United States, and being informed that many of my debtors had gone with their families to the new settlement of Kentucky, near the falls of the River Ohio, in the month of December of the same year I set out from Annapolis, in Maryland (where a brother of mine resided), for Fort Pitt, intending to go from thence to Kentucky as soon as the ice should break up in the spring, and the river became navigable; and I had agreed with a Mr. Samuel Purviance, of Baltimore, who possessed large tracts of land in Kentucky, to meet him in January at Fort Pitt, and go together to Kentucky. I received letters of introduction from *General Washington, Colonel Lee, of

* Notes from Mr. Ridout's Diary:—" General Washington had furnished me with letters of introduction to General Scott and Colonel Marshall, and Colonel Henry Lee, an original character, who lived in one of my brother's houses, sent me letters of introduction to Governor Arthur St.

Virginia, and other gentlemen, to their friends in the western
settlements, and having collected £300 or £400 worth of merchandise from some of my debtors in lieu of cash, which was
not at that time to be obtained, and forwarded it to Fort
Pitt by means of horses, I set out myself on horseback and
alone from Hancock, a town in Maryland, on the River Potomac,
about five miles from the warm springs in Virginia, on the
first day of January, 1788.

The snow at this time was about three feet deep, and the
weather clear and very cold. To Old-Town on the Potomac,
is about thirty-six miles, and from thence to the entrance of the
Alleghany Mountains about thirty miles, the same road that
General Braddock cut through the mountains to enable him to
pass on to Fort Pitt, and near which latter place he met with
so great a defeat. On the evening of the second day of my
departure I entered the mountains and slept at one Greig's.

I proceeded on my way early next morning, and passed but
one house during the day. The weather was extremely cold,
the snow deep and but little beaten by travellers—the road
lay through dismal vales and over frightful precipices, the
gloominess of which was heightened and increased by large
cypress trees, whose branches overhung. This particular place
is known by the name of the "Shadow of Death,' a name
very applicable. Towards the evening I met seven or eight
men riding furiously, more than half-drunk, and yelling like
savages.

I, not before it was dark, arrived at a solitary house, but
where the accommodations were tolerable; and was informed
that I should not see another house till towards the evening of

Clair, to Brigadier-General Harmer, General Wilkinson and Hon. John
Armstrong."

"I received also the following memorandum from General Washington,
who requested me, if possible, to send him the things mentioned, as they
were intended for the gardens of the King of France:—The seeds of the
coffee tree, pappa tree, cucumber tree, blackberry tree, wild cherry tree,
black-eye tree, wild rye, buffalo grass, crown imperial, cardinal flower,
Shawanese salad, wild lettuce, tulip-bearing laurel, and the seeds of everything curious which the western country of America produces.

the next day. This night the weather was excessively cold. In the morning I took an early breakfast, and proceeded on my solitary journey through the mountains, the snow being about four feet deep. In the afternoon, becoming very cold and weary, I looked out very anxiously for the house where I was to stop, and at last, to my infinite joy, discovered it at no great distance ahead. It proved very comfortable, which was the more relished when contrasted with the gloominess of the surrounding scene.

The next morning I continued my journey, and about noon arrived at the summit of the famed Laurel Hill, from whence all the country to the Ohio, more than sixty miles distant, lay before me. The day was clear, and the scene, though wild, was magnificent. I descended gradually on a straight road, and soon found myself amongst other mountains, which the extreme height of the Laurel Hill (the western extremity of the Alleghany) had before reduced to hillocks. On the evening of this day I reached Red Stone old fort, lying on the River Monongahela, which unites with the Alleghany river at Fort Pitt, and forms the Ohio. I crossed the Monongahela, which is here about 400 yards wide, and slept at a Dutchman's house. During the night there fell near two feet depth of snow, and the roof under which I slept being old and bad, a great quantity was on my bed when I awoke.

The road I had to travel this day was difficult to find, and without any track. In the course of the day I went five miles out of my way, and it was not till nine o'clock at night, and very dark, that I came to a house, which was a very grateful sight to me, as I expected to be reduced to the necessity of roving in the woods all the night. My horse partook of my alarm, for he trembled under me.

The inhabitants of this house were the most rude and savage in their manners I had ever met with, but the risk and dangers I had escaped reconciled me to my fare.

The next day I had company to Fort Pitt, where I arrived about two o'clock in the afternoon, crossing the Monongahela again on the ice; the river here is about 500 yards wide. I lodged at a house of a Mr. Ormsby, where I found my friend Mr. Purviance, who had arrived a few days before. I received many civilities from the inhabitants of this place, who form a very agreeable society among themselves. Here I remained till the 12th of March following, when I embarked in one of the boats built at Red Stone for the conveyance of passengers etc., to the falls of Ohio; two days before, the ice of the river broke up with a tremendous noise, and the waters rose in the space of three days twenty feet perpendicular. Mr. Purviance and myself, with one John Black—his servant—together with our horses and baggage, embarked at Fort Pitt. Many other boats were preparing to set out on the same route; although the ice was yet floating in large masses, we committed ourselves to the furious current. At a town called Wheeling, about 100 miles down the river, we were to take in the other passengers and their baggage. The second day, in the afternoon, we stopped at Wheeling, and immediately took on board those who were waiting for our arrival. We were in all about twenty persons and sixteen horses. The boat was exceedingly deeply laden. A boat, laden as we were, put off with us for Kentucky.

These boats are flat-bottomed with upright sides and stern, and the front turns up like a skate; they seldom use any sail, but are steered by means of a long oar from the stern, and two or three oars are occasionally used to conduct them, for the stream, which runs at the rate of about five miles an hour, carries the boat with great rapidity. They maintain their course night and day. We stopped the day after we left Wheeling, for a few minutes, at the mouth of the Muskingum river, where was a small fort called Fort Harmer, and a garrison of about fifty men. We then proceeded on our way, and our course being nearly south-west, we soon found the weather grow very mild and pleasant, and the trees putting forth their leaves. At the Great Kanawa, which is on the east side of the Ohio, as the Muskingum is on the west, we saw eight or ten houses, and went on shore for a few minutes. The soil is of a black, deep mould. The Ohio continues nearly of the same breadth, that is about three quarters of a mile, still rising and flowing in a majestic stream. In the night we were almost upon an island before we discovered our danger. With the greatest exertions we got clear of it, although not without touching once or twice. The next day it rained throughout, and just at the close of the evening we reached the first settlement in Kentucky, called Limestone. Here we went on shore, and almost all of the party left us the next morning, taking their route by land to their respective homes. They pressed me greatly to accompany them, as I had letters from General Washington to his friends, Colonel Marshall and others, who resided in this settlement. I had my baggage brought on shore, and purposed going by land to Lexington, and from thence to the falls of Ohio; but finding that it did not suit Mr. Purviance to take this route by land, and unwilling to leave him, I returned with my baggage to the boat, and set out with him, our man, J. Black, and two other men. The other boat, whose company was also reduced to five or six persons, set out for the falls early that morning. We followed in the afternoon. The distance from the falls to this place was 170 miles. The weather was remarkably pleasant, and the moon being now full and the nights serene and clear, added greatly to the agreeableness of our voyage. The spring, too, began to show itself, and the trees, especially those on the river, were already in leaf. Not often had I felt so much satisfaction or delight of heart as I did on the second morning, which was Good Friday. I had breakfasted, and with a map and travelling compass, was computing the bearings and distances to the place called the Big Bones, which I reckoned to be about ten miles distant. Some of the bones here found, are to be seen in the British Museum. They belong to an animal whose species is now extinct, but supposed to be the same as that mentioned by Cæsar in his " Commentaries."

Our tranquility, however, was soon to give place to the greatest anxiety and alarm, for on turning a point which opened to our view a considerable extent of the river, we saw, at some distance on the Indian or west side of it, a boat like our own amongst the bushes, which appeared to be the same which had left Limestone a few hours before we did. Whilst we were conjecturing the cause of such apparent delay, we perceived several people running about the shore, and a boat to put off full of people, whom we soon, to our surprise and terror, discovered to be Indians, almost naked, painted and ornamented as when at war.

They soon came up with us, and about twenty leaped into our boat like so many furies, yelling and screaming horribly, brandishing their knives and tomahawks, struggling with each other for a prisoner. A young man, painted black, first seized me by the arm, when another, an elderly man, who seemed to be a chief, took me from him; this Indian was of a mild countenance, and he gave me immediately to understand I should not be hurt, holding me by the hand to show his property in me.

As we neither did nor could attempt any resistance, none of us at this time suffered any injury in our persons, but they began immediately to strip us; my companions were soon left almost without covering. Several attempts were made to strip me of my clothes, which were opposed by the Indian who held my hand. At length he acquiesced in the demands of one who began to be violent, and I lost my hat, coat and waistcoat. By this time we had gained the bank of the river, and were then led to a great fire, around which sat the war-chief, Nenessica, and about sixty Indians; their whole party was ninety. To the chief I was presented by his brother, the man who had held my hand. After examining me some time with attention, and conversing with those around him, who eyed me with no less complacency, the chief gave me his hand, and presented his pipe to me. He then made signs for me to sit down by him, which I did, when several chiefs introduced themselves and shook hands with me, in particular a Pottawatamie, exceedingly well dressed after their manner, and who was one of the finest figures I had ever beheld; he appeared to be about twenty-seven years of age, and to be upwards of six feet in height. No other prisoner received the civilities which I did

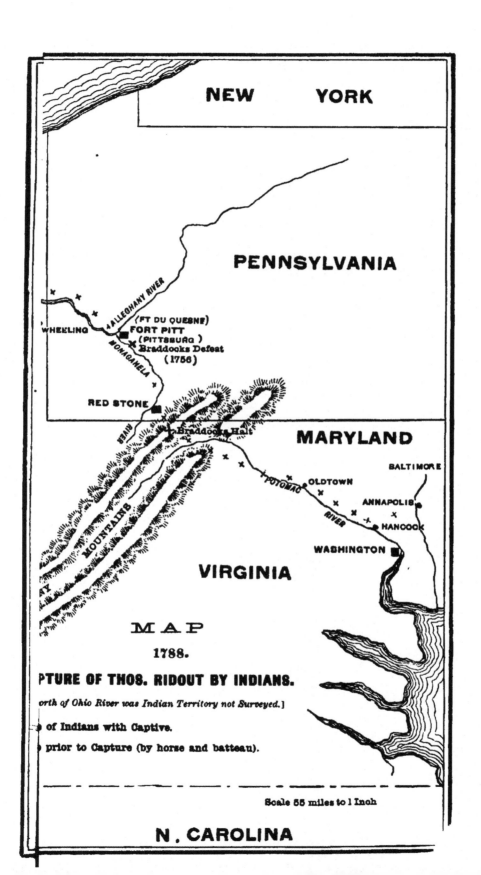

NEW YORK

PENNSYLVANIA

ALLEGHANY RIVER

WHEELING

(FT DU QUESNE)
FORT PITT
(PITTSBURG)
Braddocks Defeat
(1755)

MONONGAHELA

RED STONE

RIVER

Braddocks Hall

MARYLAND

BALTIMORE

POTOMAC

OLDTOWN

ANNAPOLIS

RIVER

HANCOCK

WASHINGTON

MOUNTAINS

VIRGINIA

M A P

1788.

PTURE OF THOS. RIDOUT BY INDIANS.

orth of Ohio River was Indian Territory not Surveyed.]

of Indians with Captive.

prior to Capture (by horse and batteau).

Scale 55 miles to 1 Inch

N. CAROLINA

Whilst I was sitting by the chief I heard myself called by name, and looking around saw two young men, tied and sitting at the foot of a tree; they had been taken early in the morning out of the boat which had sailed before us. They said a lock of hair had been taken from each of their heads,* and that they had been tied several hours in the manner they now were, and apprehended they were doomed to be put to death, and as I seemed to be taken into favour, they begged I would intercede for them. Upon my requesting this favour the Indians released them.

During the remainder of the day, the Indians, who were composed of Shawanese, Pottawatamies, Ottawas and Cherokees, but chiefly of the first, seemed to enjoy their good fortune, for their plunder exceeded £1,500 sterling, as I was afterwards informed. They gave us a portion of the provisions they had taken, and when night approached they renewed their fires. The chief, with the principal warriors, reposed on one side, the prisoners, amounting to ten men and one black woman, were placed on the other side. Some deer-skins were spread on the ground, on which we lay, and an old blanket was allotted for the covering of two people. I placed myself next to my old friend, Mr. Purviance, who was upwards of sixty years of age; he had been stripped of everything except his breeches and a thin flannel waistcoat; as the night was frosty, he suffered much by the cold. I endeavoured to keep the blanket over him. The Indian chief who had conducted me on shore placed himself by me on the outside, seemingly for my protection. During the night I felt the cold very sensibly, for I had very little covering, and my head was bare and exposed to the sky; it ached very much, but at length I was relieved by a bleeding at the nose. I slept but little, looking on the scene around me by the mild lustre of a full moon, and comparing my present situation with what it had been but a short time before. As soon as the sun rose, all were on foot and assembled around their great

* It is curious to note an old sacrificial ceremony of the Greeks and Romans practised by the Indians of North America.

23

chief, who divided the booty amongst them, apparently to every one's satisfaction.

Note from Mr. Ridout's Diary:—Memorandum of clothes, linen, and other apparel : 27 shirts ; 28 stocks ; 26 pocket-handkerchiefs ; 1 pair lace ruffles and bosom ruffles ; 6 pairs thread stockings ; 2 pairs black silk do ; 23 pairs white silk do ; 1 pair mild yarn do ; 4 pairs nankeen breeches ; 3 pairs cotton do ; a superfine cloth coat ; 3 linen and cotton night-caps ; 3 serre-têtes ; 2 linen dressing cloths ; 1 linen dressing apron ; 4 pairs black silk breeches ; 1 pair black everlasting do ; 1 white silk robe de chambre and waistcoat ; 5 silk waistcoats, embroidered ; 1 black satin do, plain ; 1 black silk do ; 1 dark purple silk coat ; 1 suit black silk, coat, waistcoat and breeches ; 1 suit dove colored, do ; 1 suit light brown, do ; 1 blue cloak, superfine broad cloth ; 1 dark green coat, do ; 1 lead-colored do, do ; 1 Prussian blue do, do ; 3 pairs shoes and 1 pair boots ; 2 pairs silver shoe buckles ; 1 pair silver knee do ; 2 pairs steel do ; 1 yellow metal stock do ; 1 gold repeating watch, double cased, and gold chain, key, etc., with arms, maker, Berthoud, Paris ; 1 gold-headed walking cane ; 1 ivory German flute ; 1 ebony German flute, with three middle pieces, and divers music books ; 2 pictures, engraved by Ryland and painted by F. A. Kaufman ; hair powder bag ; a portable writing desk, English ; do, French ; 3 large trunks, 1 small do, 1 portmanteau, containing my papers, clothes and books ; a Bath coating-coat ; a couteau de chasse, etc., etc. The above things, together with myself, were taken by the Shawanese near the falls of the Ohio.

A list of books belonging to me taken by the Indians : A Bible, once my mother's, and read by me in my earliest years ; Thompson's works, elegantly bound, four volumes ; Chesterfield's Letters, four volumes ; Posthlewaite's dictionary of Commerce, two volumes ; Lex Mercatoria ; Ainsworth's Latin and English dictionaries ; Italian, Latin and French dictionaries ; Chambaud's English and French dictionaries ; Life of Petrarque, three volumes , works of Montesquieu, three volume Plutarque's Lives in the old French of Amyot ; translation in French of Homer, eight volumes, elegantly bound ; Corneille's Tragedies, in French, elegantly bound, five volumes ; Essays of Montaigne, French, ten volumes ; Rochefoucaulds. Of these books the Bible alone was returned.

Among the prisoners was a decent looking man, of about forty-five years of age, by name Wm. Richardson Watson ; he had resided several years in the United States, but was said to be an Englishman. Immediately on our landing the Indians had taken from him 700 guineas ; he was of the party that was in the other boat. The Cherokees had him in charge, or rather

he had been given over to them. After the above distribution,
they arose and threw around his neck a broad belt of black
wampum, and a bundle, containing the toes of deer, in his hand
by way of a rattle. Two or three Indians placed themselves
before him and as many on each side, and began a song which
appeared to me an invocation, at first in a slow and solemn
manner, and soon after in a quick time, the poor man shaking
his rattles all the time. After the ceremony was over, he
passed near me and said to me, " I am led to think from the
ceremony which has passed that I am devoted to death, but as
you appear to be taken into favour, will you accept from me a
gold repeating watch, which our enemies have not yet taken
from me." I replied, that probably my life was in equal danger
with his own, and that should I accept the offered present it
would place me most likely in greater. I therefore declined
accepting it.

The prisoners were then ordered to seat themselves in a row,
fronting to the west, on the ground, having the woods immediately in their rear. On my left were two of my companions,
next to me on my right was my friend Mr. Purviance, and next
to him the other six; opposite us, to the south-east, was the
river. As soon as we were seated Mr. Purviance began to discourse with me of our present situation, and said that as
hitherto we had had not received any personal ill-treatment, he
hoped we were not in any great danger; it was evident, however, that some change was to take place in our situations; we
remained not long in suspense. A sturdy, thick-set Indian,
painted black, of a very fierce countenance, with a drawn
hanger in his right hand, came towards us, and addressing
himself to the outermost man on the left hand, who happened
to be the second from me, with a flourish of his weapon made
him get up, giving him a kick drove him into the woods to the
left of us.

We all remained silent, every one judging that his last
moment of life approached. In a few minutes this savage
returned and drove before him the man who had been sitting
next to me on the left. Mr. Purviance then said to me, " I

believe, my friend, that we draw near our end." These were my own sentiments also. I waited the return of the Indian for myself as his next victim; words cannot express what my feelings then were, and when I saw him approach. He came and stood before me, and, after a moment's pause, beckoned me to rise and follow him, and turned round into the woods which were behind us. I saw my friend no more. I understood some time after that he was not killed on the spot, but was taken into the interior of the country and there beat to death.

I followed the Indian step by step, expecting every moment that he would turn upon me and put me to death. After walking 300 or 400 yards, I perceived the smoke of a fire, and, presently, several Indians about it; my alarm was not diminished, but as we came nearer, a white man, about twenty-two years of age, who had been taken prisoner when a lad and had been adopted, and was now a chief among the Shawanese, stood up and said to me in English, "Don't be afraid, sir, you are in no danger, but are given to a good man, a chief of the Shawanese, who will not hurt you; but, after some time, will take you to Detroit, where you may ransom yourself. Come and take your breakfast." What a transition! passing from immediate danger and apparent certain death to a renovated life! I saw no more of my savage guide, but joined the party seated around the fire taking their breakfast, of which I partook, which consisted of chocolate and some flour cakes baked in the ashes, being part of the plunder they had taken from us. Whilst I breakfasted, an Indian, painted red and almost naked, had seated himself opposite to me and eyed me with fierceness of countenance inexpressible; his eyes glowed like fire, and the arteries of his neck were swollen and nearly bursting with rage; he said something to me in a tone of voice corresponding with his appearance, which was interpreted to me by the white man in the following words: "He says that you are his prisoner. and that it is more easy for him to put you to death than to tell you so." I answered, calmly, (for the extreme danger and situation from which I had just escaped had prepared me for every event,) that I acknowledged myself to be in his power, and that he could do with me as he pleased. This reply being made known to him, his rage seemed to subside, and he said no more to me.

The white man now informed me that in an hour or two we should begin our march, together with the other Indians and prisoners, to the village, which was about five days' journey from that place.

About noon we began our journey into the wood, in company with about ninety Indians. The weather was dark, gloomy and cold. We passed over a rapid river on the body of a tree, which had fallen over it at a considerable height from the water. In passing, my head became giddy, and I apprehended I should fall, but recollecting the yet greater dangers that beset me, I recovered a firmer step, About five in the afternoon, we came to a valley through which ran a rivulet, the land rising gently to the westward, full of large timber, but without under-wood. At this place, I understood, the Indians intended to pass the night in feasting and drinking a part of the spirituous liquors they had taken from us. As the Indians intended to regale themselves and drink to intoxication, a party of Cherokees, to the number of twelve, who had deserted from their own nation to reside amongst the Shawanese, were appointed to take charge of the prisoners during the feast, of which they, the Cherokees, were not to partake, but were to keep themselves sober. We were, therefore, committed to these Indians, who withdrew to a small eminence, a few hundred yards distant from the main body.

When they had kindled a fire they threw a few half-worn undressed deer-skins on the ground, for us to lie upon, on the west side of the fire, and then began to secure us from making an escape. They began with me, by passing a cord round my body, then between the legs, and under that part of the cord that surrounded the body, and forcing a stake six or seven feet into the ground, they fastened the cord to it, and on the top of the stake they fixed a small bell, so that I could not stir without its ringing. Lest I should make use of my hands, they put my fists into a small leather bag which they had tied round the wrist; then they drew the string round the wrists so tight, that I was instantly in an agony of pain. It was to no purpose to complain. I could not prevail upon them to slacken it, but ordering me to lie down, they threw over me a small, old blanket. My place was the outermost of the row, next to the drunken Indians, exposed to the weather, which was very cold and tempestuous. There fell much sleet, but the agony I suffered in my wrists, hands and arms, made me insensible almost to everything else.

About midnight, I was roused by the screams and whoops of an Indian from the other encampment, who seemed coming towards us. His yells and shouts became more and more loud and terrific; and turning my eyes towards the valley, I perceived, by the glimmering lights of the fires and of the moon, an Indian staggering with drunkenness, brandishing a knife in one hand and a tomahawk in the other, making all the haste he could towards us, and shrieking most horribly as he approached where I lay. I have, no doubt, but that he was bent upon murdering the prisoners, and that I should be his first victim. He had already come within one step of me, and his hand was lifted to give me the fatal blow, when one of the Cherokees sprang from the ground and caught him round the waist, and after some struggling mastered him and obliged him to retreat, which he did muttering.

As my sufferings were extreme from the strictures round my wrists, I entreated the Cherokee to loosen them, but giving me a look of savage fierceness, he laid himself down again unconcerned at the tortures I endured. In the space of about an hour the drunken Indian made a second attempt to execute his purpose; but as he approached, yelling and shouting, two Cherokees laid hold of him as soon as he came near the fire, and tying him neck and heels together, left him wallowing in the snow for the remainder of the night. At length the long-wished-for morning came, and my hands were set at liberty; but they were so swollen and black with the stoppage of circulation, that some hours elapsed before I could bend my fingers or use them. Soon after the sun had risen, the Indian chief to whom I had been given made his appearance. He seemed about fifty years of age, was a tall, slender man, and of a very pleasing and animated countenance. He, smiling, took me by the hand, called me "Nacanah," or his friend, and seeing my attention fixed on a wound, over one of his eyes, he, pointing to it, said, "Ah! matowesa whiskey," meaning he had got drunk with wicked whiskey or spirits, and that the wound was the bad consequence of it.

Perceiving that I had no covering on my head, he took about a yard of black silk mode (part of his share in the plunder) and tied it round my head. He then gave me an old blanket, which I fastened about my waist with a skewer. We then breakfasted, and began to prepare for our journey to the interior. My horse, which was a very good one and of an iron-gray colour, they loaded with as much as he could carry.

My friend, as I shall call the Indian to whom I belonged, and who never once forfeited the appellation, made up for himself a load of about fifty or sixty pounds, and another small bundle for myself, of about thirty pounds weight. Some of the prisoners had iron pots, and very heavy loads were put on them. A breech-cloth was given to me, instead of my breeches, and a pair of moccasins, or Indian shoes, in lieu of my leather ones. Our party now consisted of the seven prisoners, together with ten Indians. We marched on towards the first village, or their winter encampment, of which my friend was the principal chief. For two or three days we travelled together in company, at which time some of the Indians turned off with their prisoners to other villages, so that only another prisoner and myself were together for the rest of the journey. The residue of the Indians, to the number of eighty, returned to war against the Americans, which was continued from this period during seven years, without intermission. It is almost needless to say to those who are acquainted with the causes of disturbance between the Americans and natives, that the former are in general the aggressors, but in this war they were so in a more unjust degree than usual.

When the evening of our first day's journey drew nigh, I

dreaded lest I should be treated as I had been the preceding night; but when we lay down, which was before a good fire, my friend covered me with a blanket, and only fastened me round the body with a rope, which he drew under himself and lay upon. He never afterwards used this precaution, leaving me at perfect liberty, and frequently during the nights that were frosty and cold, I found his hand over me to examine whether or not I was covered. I think it was towards the third evening of our march that we came to the banks of the great Miami, a very rocky and rapid river, which empties itself into the Ohio, and whose waters were very high. My friend, another Indian, and myself begun to make a small raft to pass over this rapid stream, which was about 300 feet wide. I went awkwardly about my work. The Indian smiled, and allowed me to desist from working. They soon prepared a small raft, and we all three placed ourselves upon it, and with the help of a pole by way of paddle, we soon gained the opposite shore, having been carried a short distance down the stream. Soon after we encamped on the left bank of a small river, having a steep hill covered with woods on the left side. A good fire was kindled, and we supped heartily on some roasted venison, part of our day's sport—for these woods were full of the finest deer, buffalo and wild turkeys.

During the night I was much disturbed by the howling of a great number of wolves, that occupied the hill, but did not descend to the fire. In the morning we breakfasted, having being been joined by others of our party, among the rest was the great war chief Nenessica. When he killed any venison he always sent me the tongue as a compliment. Walking on the hard, frozen ground and over the roots of beech trees, which run horizontally along the surface of the ground, bruised my feet so much, that I could scarcely walk, having nothing but the thin moccasins to protect my feet, and although my load was but small, as I have before said, yet as it acted continually upon my loins, they had become so weak and painful, that I could scarcely stand upright. The Indians attempted to console me by observing that we should, on the morrow (the 5th day) reach their home by two in the afternoon, pointing to where the sun would be at that hour.

When the next morning came, I found myself so extremely weak and bruised, that upon making it known to my friend, he took my burthen upon his shoulders, in addition to his own, without making the least reproach. I was, however, so much exhausted, that I was but little relieved by this kind action, yet I advanced as well as I could till about ten o'clock.

My friend was then at some distance before us, not out of sight, and the great war chief immediately following me. I found my strength entirely gone, and turning around to the chief, made a sign that I wished to sit down.

He pushed me on very angrily. I found I could not proceed, and turning again, made another attempt to obtain his consent to sitting down. With great anger he again pushed me on, and made a stroke at me with his tomahawk, which I avoided by exerting all my strength, and springing forward.

At this critical moment I recollected that when they took my coat from me, I secured my pocket-handkerchief and half a guinea, which I put in a knot in one corner of it, and tied it around my waist, where it now was. With some difficulty and much agitation I loosened the knot, took the half guinea, and turning round, held it up between my finger and thumb. The savage smiled and beckoned me to seat myself on the ground, on which I fell and immediately fainted.

When I recovered, I found the great war-chief and my friend both sitting by me. They spoke kindly to me, and gave me to understand, by pointing to where the sun would be at two o'clock, that I should then arrive at the village. I signified my inability to walk, to which they replied by encouraging signs. However, we continued sitting, and soon after perceived some one on horseback galloping towards us. They soon explained to me that the horse had been sent for on my account. I mounted the horse and proceeded slowly towards the village. On our way thither we crossed a rapid and stony river, 300 or 400 feet broad, and about three feet deep. Without the horse I could not have passed it. When we came within a quarter of a mile of the village I was ordered to dismount, and myself and another prisoner, named Baffington, were painted red, and narrow ribbons of various colours (part of the plunder) tied to our hair.   The Indians began to fire their guns and to set up the war-whoop, and rattles being put into our hands, we were ordered to shake them and sing some words they repeated to us.   During this ceremony several of the Indians came from the village, and amongst them a black man, about twenty-five years of age, called Boatswain (or Boosini), who belonged to and was a servant of my friend.   He was exceedingly insolent and struck the other prisoner, but said nothing to me. Had he struck me I should have returned the blow, whatever might have been the consequence.   The other prisoner and myself were then marched in triumph to the village, shaking the rattles in our hands on entering it.   I had to cross a small rivulet, and in descending the bank an old woman came out of a wigwam or hut, and gave me a stroke on the neck with a small billet of wood.   However, it did not hurt me.   Immediately on entering the village we were conducted to the council-house, at the door whereof we were obliged to sing and shake the rattles for half an hour, and then entered the house (without suffering any ill-treatment), in the centre of which was a fire, and over it hung a kettle with venison and Indian corn boiling.

We sat down by the fire and were for some time left to our-selves.   At length, two or three women came into the house, and taking some meat and corn out of the kettle, put it into a bowl and gave us thereof to eat, with wooden spoons.   Salt they had not, but in lieu of that gave each of us a piece of sugar made of the sap extracted from the maple tree, in the making of which the women were now occupied in the adjoining forests.

As we had not seen any Indian for two or three hours, and night began to approach, I began to be uneasy.   At length the old chief to whom I belonged, and whose name was Kakina-thucca, appeared and led me to his own house.   This was about twenty feet long and fourteen feet wide, the sides and roof made of small poles and covered with bark.   The entrance was at the end, and an old blanket hung at the doorway. This man, besides being a war-chief, was also a great hunter and traded with people at Detroit, where he went annually with his furs and peltry, accompanied by his wife Metsigemewa, and the negro. He was owner of eight or ten horses, which he used in transporting his property, etc. Upon coming into the hut he presented me to his wife. She appeared to be forty years of age, and rather corpulent. Her looks were extremely savage, and she eyed me with a look of contempt, without speaking. The man, on the contrary, was of the most mild and intelligent countenance. I never once saw him out of humour, and as soon as he arose, which was early, he began to sing. As I was extremely bruised and fatigued, my feet being not only swollen exceedingly, but black with the bruises they had received from the rough ground and beech roots, the Indian planted four forked sticks at the entrance, on the left side, and laying other sticks on them, laid bark and skins upon it, and then gave me a blanket to cover me. I slept soundly all the night, and did not rise very early. The woman, at length, began to prepare for breakfast. She cut some venison (deer, wild turkeys, and other game being in abundance in this part of the country) into small pieces, and seasoning it with dry herbs, she put the whole into a frying-pan with bear's oil; she also boiled some water in a small copper kettle, with which she made some tea in a tea-pot, using cups and saucers of yellow ware. She began and finished her breakfast without noticing me in the least. When she had done she poured some tea in a saucer, which, with some fried meat on a pewter plate, she gave me.

This was a luxury I little expected to meet with, not only on account of the distance it must have come from, but being a prisoner, I could hardly expect such fare. The tea proved to be green tea, and was sweetened with maple sugar. The meat, also, was very savory and palatable. As soon as I breakfasted I returned to my bed, for I could scarcely stand. In the course of the morning a kettle was put on the fire and a quantity of venison put into it. When done, the Indian brought in two or three of his friends to treat them, and I had my share. My master or friend did not sit round the bowl with his guests, but behind them on the ground, smoking his pipe, entertaining them with diverting stories, which kept them in continual laughter. And this was his usual custom when he gave a treat.

In two or three days I was able to walk about. Upon my going into their huts (for there were fourteen or fifteen in the village), the Indian children would scream with terror, and cry out "Shemanthe," meaning Virginian, or the big knife. As soon as I understood the term, I desired them not to call me so, upon which I was named "Metticosea," viz., Englishman. My friend cautioned me not to go far into the woods, for I sometimes wandered about the village two or three hours at a time. From this circumstance I was also called "Laquiawaw," which signified "Where is he gone." One morning I felt my situation severely, it was, however, momentary, and I have since been surprised at my emotion at the time.

My mistress, upon putting the venison into a frying-pan as usual, and placing it on the fire, pushed the handle of the pan into my hand with such violence, that I felt I was a slave. As I took care, however, to pay attention to her orders in this matter, as well as in fetching water from the rivulet, which passed the house, sometimes making the fire, and at others, plucking turkeys, etc., I acquired her good graces. She permitted me to breakfast with her, and always afterwards behaved to me with complacency, for though her look was savage, her heart was naturally kind and tender.

To divert my solitary hours my Indian friend used to bring me books to read, some which had belonged to me. Amongst them was Postlethwaite's Dictionary, and the first edition of Telemachus in French, printed in Holland, with notes marking the living characters for whom the imaginary personages in that excellent work were intended. I was sorry I could not preserve this book. Some others were returned to me at the end of my captivity, particularly an old family Bible* I had read in when a child, and which is now in my possession in

* Now in the possession of Mr. D. C. Ridout, Toronto.

very good condition, and has the covering which my dear mother sewed on it about the year 1766.

I now learnt that the village we were in was the hunting place of this tribe of the Shawanese Indians, and that in the course of a fortnight they intended to set off with their furs, skins, etc., for Detroit, about 600 miles distant, taking the upper part of the Wabash on their way, at which place they were to plant their corn (called by us Indian corn). In the meantime the women and children of the village were mostly employed in making sugar from the maple tree, the spring of the year being the only time in which it can be made, about a mile from the village. To this place I was ordered, to assist in getting wood and attending the fires. I was for an hour or two employed in cutting wood for the sugar camp, but upon my showing how my hands were blistered, the Indian desired me to desist from cutting wood, and never afterwards imposed any service on me. Here I found the negro employed in this service for my mistress. He assumed great superiority over me, and though he acknowledged me to be a gentleman, he took delight in vexing and insulting me. I should have treated him with kindness had his manners been gentle, yet I now sturdily opposed him. Upon informing my friend of the negro's behaviour, he replied, "He is no more than a dog, why do you put up with him?" My greatest danger arose from this negro, by his lies and artifices, making all the young people inimical to me. By these means my life was often in imminent danger. The other prisoner was given to a family of the same name, and he was well treated, though made to work, which was not irksome to him, being used to labour.

My Indian friend had a principal share in the defeat of the American army under St. Clair, three or four years after this period. He had one daughter about eighteen years of age, called Altowesa, of a very agreeable form and manners. She lived with a family related to her father, and only visited him occasionally. Some time after my captivity, she and the woman in whose house she lived, saved me from the uplifted hand of an Indian, who had his hand over me ready to strike the fatal blow with his tomahawk. They struggled with him, and gave me time to escape and conceal myself. I shall, in this place, declare that during the whole of the time I was with the Indians, I never once witnessed an indecent or improper action amongst any of the Indians, whether young or old.

At the end of three weeks from my capture, the whole village having collected their horses and their peltry, began their journey towards the Wabash and Detroit. I travelled, at my ease, on foot, carrying an unbent bow in my hand. We seldom travelled more than fifteen or twenty miles a day, setting out after breakfast, about an hour after sunrise, and encamping about the same time before sunset, and if we came to good hunting ground, reposed ourselves for the day.

My dress consisted of a calico shirt, made by an Indian woman, without a collar, which reached below the waist; a blanket over my shoulders, tied round the waist with the bark of a tree; a pair of good buckskin leggings, which covered almost the thighs, given me by the great war-chief; a pair of moccasins, in which I had pieces of blue cloth to make my step easier; a breech-cloth between my legs; a girdle around my waist; and a small round hat, in which the Indian placed a black ostrich feather by way of ornament (the smaller the hat the more fashionable). If we encamped at an earlier hour than usual, or remained a whole day in one place, which we were obliged sometimes to do on account of the rain (this being a remarkably rainy spring), the Indian young men and women amused themselves at a game of chance, played by sitting in a circle, holding a blanket open in the centre, in which a certain number of bits of wood, black on one side and white on the other, were thrown up, and according to the number of black or white sides which fell uppermost, the game was reckoned.

I tasted bread made of Indian corn but once or twice after leaving the village, but lived entirely on boiled or roasted flesh, without salt, but sometimes with dried herbs. We also met with a root which was found near the surface of the ground, resembling ginger in appearance, and warm and pleasant in taste. Dried venison with bear's oil was reckoned a great dainty, and such I thought it. Sometimes we slept in the open air without any shelter, at other times under a bark covering. It was one continuous forest, at times pathless, and, at the best, but a path which none but an Indian could discern. But once, in the space of a month, did I see more of the heavens than was to be seen through the branches of the trees, and though the open space did not consist of more than twenty acres of natural meadow, I thought it a paradise. From the excessive rains that fell, I here caught cold with a fever, but my friend, in a day or two, restored me by some draught he gave me; he also endeavored to persuade me that my restoration was also owing a great deal to his blowing his breath upon my forehead with all his force, and repeating some words. Thus we travelled day after day towards the Wabash. We at length drew nigh to a village, where I was informed a great council was to be held concerning me, and for the examination of my papers and letters. We encamped within five or six miles of it, and the next day my friend the chief, accompanied by half a dozen more Indians and myself, all mounted on horseback, rode to the village where the council was to be held. On our way thither, we put up a flock of wild turkeys. Having no fire-arms, we hunted them down, and having caught a very large one, weighing about twenty-five pounds, it was tied, alive, to my back as I rode, and thus we galloped to the village.

Upon our arrival, several chiefs, to the number of fifty or upwards, opened the council. My papers were read by an interpreter, a white man, who several years before had been taken prisoner. After much sober discussion, in which it was declared that I was an Englishman and not an American, they broke up, after allowing my master to take me to Detroit, and there to receive my ransom. Towards the evening there was a dance of young women before the council-house, to the beat of a drum and their voices. They made signs to me to join them, but my friend advised me not to go. I had by this time acquired a tolerable knowledge of their language, and began to understand them, as well as to make myself intelligible. My mistress, as I have before mentioned, loved her dish of tea. With the tea paper I made a book,* stitched it with the bark of a tree, and with yellow ink of hickory ashes, mixed with a little water, and a pen made with a turkey quill, I wrote down the Indian names of visible objects. The negro, in his moments of good humour, used to explain to me that which was difficult to be understood. In this manner I wrote two little books, which I carried in a pocket I had torn from my breeches, and wore round my waist tied by a piece of bark; generally elm bark was used on such occasions, as it may be divided into numberless small strips, which are very strong. It was at this council I was informed that my gold repeating watch,† chain and seal were safe in the possession of a woman of this neighbourhood. Early next morning I went to her hut, about a mile distant; she showed it to me and promised to keep it in safety for me till I was liberated and could redeem it. This accordingly happened, for in the course of the ensuing winter, when I was at Montreal, my watch, chain, etc., were restored to me all in good condition (paying for the same about five guineas), and are now in my possession.

We remained a day or two longer in this village than we otherwise would have done, had it not been for a root found here somewhat resembling a potato. To me, who had but once tasted bread for six weeks, this root was a luxury. The bread I speak of had been made a few days before, out of the remains of a little wheat in their possession. To make it into cakes, baked in the hot ashes, it went through the following process, in which I bore a part. In a wooden mortar made of the sassafras tree—a tough wood—about a quart of wheat was put at a time; then, being moistened with a little warm water, it was pounded with a wooden pestle till the husk separated; it was then sifted in a tolerably fine sieve, made of small splits of wood; being then kneaded with a little water, it was placed upon the hot hearth and covered with hot ashes until baked.

* This book still remains in good preservation, to testify to Mr. Ridout's ingenuity. It is now in the possession of Mrs. Edgar, his granddaughter.

† This watch is now in the possession of Mr. Thomas Ridout, C.E., Ottawa.

We now resumed our journey, the party consisting of twenty men, thirty or forty women and children, and upwards of twenty horses, loaded. My master was the chief of this party, being all of his village. As the herbs began to cover the ground, the little path that there was was hidden by them, and the Indians, skilled as they are, missed the direct route to the Wabash, or to that part of it called the White river. We travelled a day or two out of the way. However, we recovered it. In general the weather was very rainy, which rose the rivulets higher than usual. One evening, as we were about to encamp, we came to a morass, 200 or 300 yards wide, and desirous to encamp on the opposite side, the horses were driven into it; but they were so entangled with the mire, roots of trees and water, that the Indians were compelled to unload them, and convey their baggage on their shoulders through the swamp. It was nearly midnight before we got over. The Indians were excessively enraged, uttering their wrath against the Americans, who were, they said, the cause of their misfortunes. They saw I was alarmed, and took every means to ease my mind, saying they were only enraged against the Americans, who had come to their village, on the Scito river (which empties itself into the Ohio), the preceding autumn, from Kentucky, and in time of profound peace, and by surprise, destroyed their village and many of their people, their cattle, grain, and everything they could meet with; which treatment was the cause, they said, that the hatchet was raised against them.

We continued to pursue our route, by easy journeys. I remarked that our numbers daily diminished, but was told that the reason was that provisions began to be scarce, the woods not affording the usual quantities of wild animals. The small party I was with bore a share of this scarcity. We had killed two wild cats, and though not esteemed by the Indians as good food, they were very acceptable at this time. At length our family, consisting of the chief, his wife, myself and negro, travelled alone. In the usual manner we encamped early in the evening, and set forth again in the morning after breakfast.

One delightful morning, as soon as the sun rose, my friend

24

walked a few paces from his tent (for occasionally he made use of a Russia sheeting one), and seemed to address himself to that glorious orb in a manner, style of words and accent, that I had not witnessed before. His manner was dignified and impressive.

Having arrived within half a mile from the village, situated on the White river, which empties itself, six or seven miles down, into the Wabash, he directed us to stop, and went himself to the village to prepare for me, as I afterwards learnt, a good reception. At the place we stopped there were two poles, fifteen or twenty feet high, standing upright, the bark stripped off, the one painted red and the other black. They were called war-poles, and indicated that prisoners had been brought to that village.

I should have mentioned that about a week after I had been made a prisoner, several rich suits of clothes were brought to this village, belonging to some French gentlemen, taken about the same part of the Ohio in which I had been captured. As they made resistance all were killed. They proved to be three gentlemen—agriculturist, botanist, and mineralogist—about to explore the country. They had wintered three or four miles above Fort Pitt. I was acquainted with them, and once had thought of joining their party. In the course of an hour, the chief returned and bade us follow him. He led me through the village. The Indians presented themselves at their doors to look at me, but did not speak. Having crossed a river about 200 yards wide, flowing in a gentle stream about three feet deep, over a fine gravelly bottom, we encamped on the other side, a small distance below the village. The rest of our village had arrived and encamped here before us. Amongst them was the white man, Baffington. The soil was very rich, and the scenery around delightful. A very large council-house was begun to be built at this place, in the construction of which the Indians had employed much skill, ingenuity and taste. Here we were to plant corn, pumpkins, etc., for their winter's food. After planting, we were to proceed, by the way of the Miami village, a journey of 400 or 500 miles. About sunset of the same day we arrived, I heard the Indian war-whoop on the other side of the river, at the village through which we had passed. The Indians of our party immediately concluded that a prisoner had been made and brought in. Some of our party went immediately to the village, and amongst them the negro. When he returned, some time after, he said it was a young man about twenty, of the name of Mitchell, who had been taken on the Ohio, together with his father, a Captain Mitchell, an American; that the father and son had been separated on the way, as they belonged to different nations, that it was probable the father would be liberated, but that the son had been given to a man who was determined to burn him, at a village five or six miles distant, where the White river unites with the Wabash. I was also informed that the war raged exceedingly; that many prisoners had been taken by the Indians, who began to be enraged at the loss of some of their friends. Two or three days elapsed before I heard anything further of the poor young man, till one morning, about break of day, I was awakened by an old woman, the same who had struck me with a billet of wood as before mentioned. She came to our hut and said the Virginian was to be burned Seeing that I was alarmed, as I thought I was alluded to, she said it was the prisoner taken a few days before, and not I, whom they loved much.

Immediately my friend, his wife, and the negro, left the hut and went to the opposite side of the river, and I was soon left alone in the camp. For some time I did not see any one moving, but about two hours after sunrise I perceived several Indians assembled at the door of a house near the water's side, opposite to where I was, and soon after I saw the young man run out of the house naked, his ears having been cut off, and his face painted black; the Indians following with the war-whoop and song, driving him before them, through a valley. They then ascended a hill, a little lower down the stream, distant about four or five hundred yards. As soon as they gained the summit of the hill, I heard the young man scream, and the Indians give a shout. I perceived a smoke, and judged that the fire was preparing. After a short interval I heard the poor victim utter a dreadful shriek. They were repeated without intermission for a few minutes. The Indians shouted during the interval of tortures. I heard the groans of the poor sufferer, and then his shrieks recommenced under new tortures. These tortures, with remissions, continued about three hours, when his cries ceased. The Indians then returned. To express my feelings during this scene would be impossible, and I began to think that my own fate might be similar.

The Indians did not return till the afternoon. At the approach of evening they fired their guns, and with large twigs beat their wigwams on the tops and sides, shouting. I inquired of the negro what that meant. He said that it was to drive away the spirit of the prisoner they had burnt. This ceremony continued for three succeeding nights. The tent or hut in which I slept, was covered with bark or poles; the sides were also covered in the same manner, but not the ends. The chief and his wife slept on a raised bed on one side of the fire-place, which was in the middle; I slept on the other side on a bear's skin, on a bench raised from the ground; and the negro wrapped in a blanket, slept on the ground by the fire. During the night I was roused by the shrieks of the negro. Calling to him, he said he had been dreaming that the young man they had burnt had come to him in a menacing manner, and I asked him what injury he had done him to have been tortured by him. I soon found that my situation became dangerous, and that the Indian to whom poor Mitchell had been given, wanted also to get me in his power. He used to beset the hut where I was, so that I was compelled to hide myself for many hours together under the banks of the river, among the weeds, to avoid him. I had crossed the river two or three times with my friend and his family to prepare a spot of ground for their corn, near the village. It was at one of these times that the bloody-minded savage had seen me. At one time I was obliged to cross the river, and fly for shelter to a house built of round logs, near the spot where Mitchell had suffered. There I obtained some protection from an Indian chief named

Papapaniwa. I was concealed from my enemies in this house by a curtain placed before me when they were in the house, for my friend was not sufficiently powerful to afford me protection. He was advised, if he wished to save me, to set off immediately for Detroit.

After three or four days my friend collected his horses and peltry, and with his wife and negro, set off with me for Detroit by way of the Miami villages, where, I understood, was a trading port; several traders, English and French, living there. I was on horseback; we all soon entered the woods. The mus-quitoes were so troublesome that we got no rest night or day, notwithstanding the smokes we made to drive them away. After, I think, four days' journey, we arrived at a branch of the Miami river, much swollen with rain. We crossed it with difficulty and encamped on a plain, where I saw several Indian huts scattered. I slept soundly that night, in the pleasing expectation that I was drawing near my deliverance. In the morning, as soon as it was day, my friend and his wife went out amongst their acquaintance. She returned in about an hour with the Indian who had burnt Mitchell, and who had followed me thither in the expectation of getting me into his power. I shuddered at seeing him. He and my mistress were each more than half drunk. They sat down upon the ground, fronting, and close to each other, relating their misfortunes, and crying and hugging one another as is their custom when drunk.

I was standing behind him, and I soon discovered that their discourse was concerning me; she said many things in my favour, but to no purpose, and seeing him grow angry, she had sufficient recollection and kindness, as her arms were about his neck, to beckon to me, unobserved by him, to get out of his way. I waited not a second bidding, but where to go I knew not. I perceived that every one I met with was drunk. However, I took shelter in a house. As soon as I entered I recognized my master's daughter, and the woman she lived with, and was relating to them my perilous situation, when, to my great sur-prise and terror, the young man who had first laid his hand upon me in the boat, now claimed me as his property by right of war. I endeavoured to escape, at which he lifted his tomahawk to kill me. The two women flew to my succour, and withheld his arm till I got out of the house. I immediately fled to the river, which was not far distant, and running under the bank, which was rather high, I perceived two sober Indians sitting. I ran and placed myself between them. They saw my terror. I related to them my situation as well as I was able. They were Delawares, whose village was in the neighbourhood. They said they would protect me. Whilst sitting between them I saw the Indian from whom I had last escaped, and who was called Black Fish, go down to the bank of the river, about 100 yards from where I was, apparently in quest of me. I pointed him out to the Indians, and sat still in great trepidation. At length, to my no small joy, he ascended the hill, and I saw him no more. In a few minutes after I perceived the white man who had announced to me my safety just after I had left the side of Mr. Purviance. I told him the danger I was in, upon which he promised he would get a horse and take me over the river to the house of a principal Shawanese chief, called the Great Snake, a mile or two down the river, and where I should be in safety. He left me for the purpose of getting a horse, and after some time, which to me appeared almost an age, I saw a man not far from where I was, on the same side, cross the river on horseback. To my great joy, I perceived it was the white man (his name was Nash).

Seeing him crossing, I was afraid he was going to leave me, but it was only to try the ford, for the river was hardly fordable. He soon returned and came to me with the horse. I mounted before him, and after passing two or three drunken parties of Indians, lying on the shore, we came to the ford and passed in safety. We then rode along on the other side and passed a fine plantation well stocked with cattle, belonging to a Shawanese chief, called Blue Jacket. He commanded the party, who afterwards vanquished the American general, St. Clair.* We soon came to the house of the Great Snake, who

* November, 1791.

received me with kindness and assured me of his protection. He was an elderly man, robust and rather corpulent. His wife, a pretty, well-looking woman, nearly his age, walked very stately with a handsome staff with a head to it. He ordered a bear's skin and blanket for me, alongside his own bed, and till my departure, three days after, he treated me with the greatest kindness. During this time I was informed that another council would be held upon me, in which it was to be determined whether I should be permitted to be taken to Detroit and ransomed. The day accordingly came in which the council was to be held. The Indians having assembled, I was also conducted thither. The council was under the authority of a Captain John, a Shawanese chief, before whom my case was to be decided. One Simon Girty, an Indian interpreter, now living on the Detroit river, was present. I perceived that my master and friend was much dejected, and did not speak to me. Several women endeavoured to cheer me by saying I should not be hurt. The council was at length opened, and the Indian who had burned Mitchell contended for me. He insisted that I was a spy and that I knew the whole country. Much was said, and my papers and letters were again brought forward, read, and explained. At length, after a cool and deliberate hearing, the chief pronounced my discharge, and told my friend that he might set out with me as soon as he chose. His eyes sparkled with joy when relating the result of the deliberations of the council. He would have deferred our departure till the morrow, for the Indian traders who lived on the other side of a river which also formed a junction here with the other two, had long expected me, but dared not intercede for me whilst my life was at issue. After urging with all my power to set off immediately, my friend got a canoe and took me over to the traders' village, called Fort Miami; and both the English and French gentlemen were waiting, with open arms to receive me, as they had been acquainted with the chief's decision in my favour. The names of the English gentlemen of this place were: Sharpe, Martin, Parkes and Ironside. Mr. Sharpe conducted me to his house, gave me a shirt, and Canadian frock and hat, trousers and shoes. I remained here three days. It was here I found my Bible, several books, a German flute, and some few other articles, but a tortoise-shell box inlaid with pearl, in which was my mother's wedding ring, and a gold coin of the Emperor Nero (weight about four pennyweights), and in great perfection, given me by a lady of Lisborne, in France, were lost to me forever. The coin had been found with many others at Saint Onge, in France. A French gentleman of the Miami, lent my friend, on my account, his large canoe to carry us, with the peltry, to Detroit, distance about 250 miles by water.

We embarked early on a Sunday morning, took in the peltry, his wife, myself and negro, and descended the Miami river, taking also two Indian women, whom we were to put on shore at an Indian village two miles down the river. We did so, and proceeded. After descending about fifteen miles, we stopped at a white man's house, who was an interpreter among the Indians. I naturally spoke of my deliverance in terms of joy, but I thought he seemed not much to encourage my hopes, for he knew the dangers which yet surrounded me, whilst I was happily ignorant of them. On our way to the mouth of the Miami river, which empties itself into Lake Erie, we passed several parties of Indians returning from Detroit. They were generally drunk, and I was in continual terror until we separated. At length we got to the falls, where there was a house belonging to a Captain McKee, Deputy Superintendent of Indian affairs, and of a Mr. Elliott. They were not there, but we received kind treatment and victuals from the Indians of their respective families. Soon after leaving these houses we reached the lake, and after coasting the west end of it for about thirty-eight miles, we entered the Detroit river. A few miles up this river there was another house of Mr. Elliott's. He did not happen to be at home, but we were kindly treated. The next day we descended the River Detroit, and passed the night upon an island, where there were several Indian families.

Early the next morning, being Sunday, we arrived at Detroit. My friend introduced and presented me to Captain McKee, who received me with civility, and with whom I breakfasted. He then accompanied me to the commanding officer, Captain Wiseman, of the 53rd regiment, and introduced me to him. By this gentleman, and by all the regiment, I was received as a brother. A bed was provided for me in the Government House. I messed with the officers, and every one strove to do me acts of kindness. A Mr. Hughes, lieutenant of the regiment, gave me ten guineas for my pocket; a Captain Haughton gave me clothes; and a Mr. Robinson, merchant, lent me 100 pounds in New York currency; and as the 53rd were, in a few days, to descend to Montreal, they offered me a passage with them, which I gratefully accepted.

Several gentlemen at Detroit invited me kindly to their houses, viz.: Commodore Grant, Mr. Macomb, Doctor Harfey. Mr. Askin, and others. I think it was the Sunday of my arrival that I dined at Mr. Macomb's. Whilst at dinner Mr. Parkes arrived from the Miami. His relation of what took place there after my departure, convinced me that the hand of an Almighty Protector had guided and preserved me in all my dangers. He said that I had just left Mr. Sharpe's house, when a party of young Indians, with Black Fish at their head, came to the house in quest of me. He immediately said that I was his property, and that he would have me. Mr. Sharpe and Mr. Parkes assured them I was not there. Black Fish insisted upon searching the house, which was permitted. Being disappointed in not finding me there, they searched other houses. Mr. Sharpe then told them I had gone away. "By which route?" said Black Fish, in a rage. He was answered that I had gone up the river to St. Joseph's. This delayed the time, and in the meanwhile God's good Providence conducted me in safety down the river, amongst unseen and unexpected dangers, for at the village we first landed at, to put the two Indian women ashore, Black Fish and his party resided. Between Miami village and this place, the river makes an angle, and the road is the chord of the angle. By this means we passed unobserved by Black Fish, who was on that road. The banks also at the lower village are steep.

In a few days I embarked with the 53rd regiment for Fort Erie. On my way to Niagara I saw the stupendous Falls of Niagara. At Niagara we continued two or three days, where I was kindly treated by Colonel Hunter, who then commanded a battalion of the 60th regiment. This officer was afterwards Lieutenant-Governor of Upper Canada and Commander-in Chief of both Canadas.

About the middle of July, 1788, I arrived at Montreal, where I received great civilities from Sir John Johnston, Captain Grant, and many other gentlemen; and from Lord Dorchester, at Quebec.

This adventure, joined with other vicissitudes I had experienced, induced me to fix my residence in Canada, and at the writing hereof * (29th May, 1811) I have the honour to serve His Majesty as Surveyor-General of Upper Canada.

THOMAS RIDOUT.

N.B.—In the year 1799 my friend Kakinathucca and three more Shawanese chiefs came to pay me a visit at my house in York.

They saw me and my family with pleasure, and my wife and children contemplated, with great satisfaction, the great and good qualities of this worthy Indian. He did not return home without bearing a testimony of my gratitude. He died about five years ago, under the hospitable care of Matthew Elliott, Esq., Superintendent of Indian affairs at Amherstburg, at the entrance of the Detroit river.

Amongst the many dangers I escaped, I ought to mention the repeated attempts made by an Indian, a young man, at the

* This narrative Mr. Ridout evidently compiled from his Diary,—a little book restored to him by the Indians, and now in the possession of Thomas Ridout, C.E., Ottawa.

instigation of the negro, to kill me. His behaviour to me kept me always upon my guard, but on my way from the Miami villages to Detroit, the negro informed me, without noticing the part he had taken in it, that the Indian had frequently attempted to kill me, but had so often been frustrated that he declared he could not execute his purpose, for that the Great Spirit protected me.

The idea the Indians had that I knew their country and the nations around, took its rise from my showing them, on the maps of North America in Postlesthwaite's Dictionary, that part where we then were, together with the different nations inhabiting the country; and having a small compass I noticed to them the direction which each respective nation bore from us.

This compass was now in the possession of my master, and not being able to comprehend its action, they called it a "Manitou," by which they mean "spirit," or something incomprehensible and powerful. This happened when we lay encamped at the natural meadow where I was attacked by fever.

Nash, the white man, told me that Mr. Purviance had been taken into the woods immediately after our sad parting, and there beat to death, whether because he had offered resistance I could not learn. I have, therefore, ample cause for adoring that all-powerful Being whose providence watched over me on all occasions during my perilous abode among savages, for sparing a life so often doomed to apparently inevitable destruction.

NOTE.—On the back of the diary is written this memorandum of the fate of the other prisoners: Samuel Purviance, killed; Garland, killed; Wm. Bassington Watson, burnt; James Black, beat to death; Symonds, burnt; Ferguson, sold for corn; a negro woman, unharmed.

FAC-SIMILE OF LETTER,

INTRODUCING THOS. RIDOUT TO COL. THOS. MARSHALL, KENTUCKY, WRITTEN BY GEORGE WASHINGTON, PRESIDENT OF THE UNITED STATES.

Mount Vernon Nov. 27th 1787.

Dear Sir

I take the liberty of introducing Mr Ridout, the bearer of this letter, to your civilities and attention. — He is spoken of in advantageous terms to me — which has induced me to give you this trouble. — Mr Ridout not only has it in contemplation to visit the Western Country but may, probably become a resident there which makes him more sollicitous of commencing an acquaintance with some of the principal characters of it. — My best wish attend you, and with esteem & regard

I am Dear Sir

Yr most obedt & hble Servt

G Washington

Col Marshall. —

This letter is endorsed by Mr. Ridout as having been returned to him by the Shawanese Indians after his release from captivity.

Among the other letters belonging to Mr. Ridout, taken by the Indians, and subsequently restored, were the following : The first in the packet is from the celebrated Marquis de Lafayette, whom he had met in France and who, the old diary says, had introduced him to the Baron de Montesquieu, the Baron de Secondat and the Marshal Duke de Mouchy, and other celebrated men of the time.

Lafayette's letter is dated

PARIS, *May* 12, 1785.

DEAR SIR,—Enclosed I have the honour to send you a letter of introduction to my uncle, Marechal de Mouchy, who is soon going to Bordeaux. I will be much obliged to you to let me know every opportunity there is going from that place to Alexandria.

There is, or will soon be, in Bordeaux, an Irish Major of volunteers called Mr. Lanier, to whom I beg you will deliver the enclosed. In case it was in my power ever to render you some service in this country, I beg you will not make ceremonies about it, because I will be truly happy to send you any letter or speak to any person that may promote your purposes.

With a sincere attachment and very good wishes, I have the honour to be your obedient, humble servant,

MR. RIDOUT.   LAFAYETTE.

This letter, written in English in a beautifully clear, though minute hand, is still in a good state of preservation.

Colonel Henry Lee writes to General Harmer, dated :—

NEW YORK, 24*th October*, 1787.

My friend, Mr. Ridout, will probably meet with you in his western tour. I cannot, therefore, refrain from recommending him to your particular civility, not only because his company will be pleasing to you, but because it may be in your power very much to assist him. In the full confidence that my introduction will ensure to him your warmest attention, I will only say that I remain unalterably yours, and am never more happy than when opportunity permits me to assure you of my regard and esteem.

This letter is addressed, Brigadier-General Harmer, commanding the Federal troops in the Western Territory.

Another letter of the same date, from Colonel Henry Lee to Judge Armstrong, is as follows :—

I commend to your civility my friend, Mr. Ridout ; treat him as such, and be assured that you will gratify me highly. The probability is that Mr. R. may settle himself among you. In this event, I wish he may become your neighbour, for your mutual satisfaction. I am, as when you left me, ever yours.

The address on cover is, The Hon. John Armstrong, Western Territory.

A third letter from Colonel Lee, the same date, is addressed to General Wilkinson, Kentucky :—

I beg to introduce to you Mr. Ridout, a gentleman who possesses every quality which commands esteem, and who visits your country with the design of establishing himself amongst you. Your ready civility renders it unnecessary for me to urge your attention to Mr. Ridout, and his merit will ensure to him the respect of all to whom he may be known. I will then not take up your time with a repetition of reasons on this subject, and only say that I shall consider myself specially obliged by every mark of attention which you may please to honour him with.

The last letter in the packet is from John Fitzgerald, dated Alexandria, November, 14th, 1787, addressed to Colonel Thomas Marshall, near Lexington, Fayette County ·—

The intention of this is to introduce to your polite and kindly attention Mr. Thomas Ridout, my much respected friend, who, enraptured with the general character of your fertile country, goes to explore and perhaps to settle in it. I have not a doubt of your affording him every friendly advice and assistance, of which you will find him extremely deserving.

A pen picture of Mr. Ridout, as he appeared during the last years of his life, is given by Dr. Scadding, in his " Toronto of Old " :—

Among the venerable heads and ancestral forms which recur to us, as we gaze down in imagination from the galleries of the old wooden St. James', of York, we will single out, in addition to those already spoken of, that of Mr. Ridout, some time

Surveyor-General of the Province, father of a numerous progeny, and tribal head, so to speak, of more than one family of connections settled here, bearing the same name. He was a perfect picture of a cheerful, benevolent-minded Englishman, of portly form, well advanced in years; his hair snowy-white naturally; his usual costume of antique style.

The old wooden church of St. James' has long passed away, but in its place has risen a noble pile which bears the same name, and under its shadow, in the old churchyard, Thomas Ridout sleeps.

A curious eye may still trace on the moss-covered stone the following inscription:

SACRED TO THE MEMORY

OF THE

HON. THOMAS RIDOUT,

of Sherbourne, Dorsetshire, England,

Late Surveyor-General of this Province, and member of His Majesty's Legislative Council, who departed this life on the 8th of February, 1829, in the 75th year of his age.

The kind and exemplary father of a numerous family, who loved and revered him and mourned his departure, the faithful servant of Government for nearly forty years, he endeared himself to the inhabitants of Upper Canada, and so won their affections by his unremitting attentions to their interests and unwearied courtesy to themselves, that they justly considered him an ornament to the colony. To a highly cultivated mind he added the most polished manners, and, what was far better, the meekness and the humility of a Christian looking forward in faith to a blessed immortality.

SUNDRY WORDS OF THE SHAWANESE LANGUAGE, THE ORTHOGRAPHY OF WHICH IS ACCORDING TO THE ENGLISH PRONUNCIATION.

Weisamanitoo .... God
Mutchamanitoo ...... the devil
Eleney .... a man
Quiawaw .... a woman
Queakee .... woman
Notha.............. a father
Neakea .... a mother
Theemeytha........ a brother
Eameetha........... a sister
Neawaw............. a wife
Neasit-chee....... a husband
Nealaw I
Kealaw.............. you
Yawmah .... he, or it
Wewawlee.......... my wife
Wessee-aw .... husband
Neaqueytha.......... my son
Tawneytha...... my daughter
Cheeakee .... we, or all
Meeaw-nelenee .. a young man
Meeaw-neequaw .. a young wo-
                    [man
Weela .... he, or him
Squeytheatha......... a girl
Skelouatheatha .... a boy
Passitotha........ an old man
Meakeybue-thetha ... an old
                    [woman
Scootee .... fire
Neepee .... water
Assiskee .... earth
Coonee............... snow

Secacoonee .... wind
Geemewawnee .... rain
Weapee .... cold
Awquaw-tegtee . heat of the sun
Kegsetee........ hot, as water
Quaw-ma............... ice
Quaw-melaw-nee .... hail
Melocaummee .... spring
Neabeakee .... summer
Teaquawko......... autumn
Pepokee .... winter
Nenimkee .... thunder
Pepapaunwey ..... lightning
Pouthquatee......... cloudy
Nenimkee-wanwee . loud thun-
                    [der
Seckthee .... a deer
Eyawpee........... a buck
Maaquaw........... a bear
Sea-a-way .... a horse
Thotho .... a cow
Thowthyaw........ a buffalo
Wyschchee .... a dog
Poosica.............. a cat
Pesseyywaw ...... a wild cat
Theepaatee......... a racoon
Wyeewaw.......... a wolf
Wawcouchee.......... a fox
Kittatee .... an otter
Wya-pe-tee-et........ an elk
Scoutelawmee ...... a tortoise
Kusko. Kuskokee... hog, hogs

Kawqua . . . . a porcupine
Seapessee . . . . a panther
Makeytha . . . . a sheep
Ameaqua . . . . a beaver
Macouteley-tha . . a fawn or colt
Wiskeloutha . . . . a bird
Poweatha . . . . a pigeon
Waw-wee . . . . an egg
Nawpeya . . . . a cock
Cockelamoutha . . . . a hen
Weynussee . . a turkey-buzzard,
[a vulture
Seaseepa . . . . a duck
Pealeywaw . . . . . . a turkey-hen
Awkitsee . . . . . a turkey-cock
Kakawkee . . . . a raven
Wawpatheea . . . . a swan
Leakaw . . . . a goose
Satewei . . . . a rattlesnake
Makalitou . . . . a frog
Pasquemei . . . . a musquito
Nameatha . . . . a fish
Teikou . . . . wood for fire
Mesisskee . . . . . . a leaf or herb
Teaquee . . . . a tree
Wawpaquemeysee . . white oak
Pawquanemeysee . . . . sassafras
Manitou-Wawquemeysee . . . . .
[buckeye tree
Popsquawsewaymeysee . beech
Skippeimeysee . . . . hickory
Squatawmeysee . shell-bark do
Cawwinakee . . . . thorny locust
[bean
Cawwimeysa . . . . thorny locust
[tree
Weilawnahai . . . . ginseng
Thenomeysee . . the sugar tree
Keisewaquata . . . the sycamore
Teatepawtaquey . . . . . the vine
Kitsetheynaweisa . . . . the bark
Mealawqua . . . . ash
Wei-coupee . . . bark to tie with
Sonlageysee . . . . a ship

Oulageysee . . . . a canoe
Papaqueymee . . . . . cranberries
Weewilsquee . . . . the capillaire
[plant
Sequaw . . . . cedar
Mutta . . . . no
Enee . . . . yes
A-a . . . . yes
Pea-atcho . . . . give me
Maw . . . . take
Muttalaqua . . not any—no more
Petsoie(Fr pronoun) . Wampum
Metticoseeah . . a white man, or
[Englishman
Toete . . . . a Frenchman
Spaniee . . . . a Spaniard
Shemanthee . . . . . . a Virginian
Catawelegnee . . . . a Negro
Leynowakee . . . . an Indian
Showanyaw . . . . . a Shawanese
Lenawpey . . . . a Delaware
Nottowei . . . . a Mohawk
Nottoweitha . . . . . . a Wyandot
Mosco . . . . a Creek Indian
Catawaypetheaway . . the head
Neleytha . . . . the hair
Skesuquey . . . . the eye
Tow-waaka . . . . the ear
Neetsawsee . . . . nose
Keelanee . . . . , . tongue
Keetawnenah . . . . mouth
Keepetsee . . . . teeth
Queekaca . . . . neck
Kenekee . . . . arm
Ketchena . . . . thumb
Peletsewah . . . . hand
Keletsee . . . . fingers
Keekaatsee . . . . the leg
Kethetena . . . . the foot
Squee . . . . blood
Outhaw-wee monie . . . gold, or
[yellow money
Wiapawkekee . . . silver dollars,
[or white money

25

Wiapawke-quaw......... tin
Withaw-waw-caquaw... brass
Coupelecou .... iron
Outhaw-wee......... yellow
Waw-connokee-wapea ..white
Squaw-wee............. red
Cuttey-waw.......... black
Oulamon .... vermilion
Methalui .... lead
Monathee............ a knife
Coquaw....... a pot, or kettle
Hamquaw.......... a spoon
Waupamoua...a looking-glass
Thequa.............. a comb
Goulaka...... a basin, or dish
Queg-awai .... a blanket
Poppea-awai .... a saddle
Thakoa....···· a shirt broach
Squathapeah .... a belt
Thya .... a skin
Elenaquey .... a bow
Elena lui........... an arrow
Peyteneekah.. a shirt, or jacket
Petacouah....... a hat, or cap
Teaquah.............. a gun
Pemqua Teaquah ...... a rifle
Alloley............. a bullet
Mecottey........ gunpowder
Sacouka.............. a flint
Weweyla...... a powder horn
Teekhauhka...... tomahawk
Sequawna .... a stone
Awsit-thekee.. crosses worn on
[the neck
Mecothey............ an awl
Theckthey....... deer sinews
Kethenequa .... soap
Masisskee .... tea
Melassey............. sugar
Tepthicah..... a cup, or teapot
Weeawthey .. venison, or meat
Weelenoix (Fr. pro.) ......fat
Pitssawkah... a rope, or halter
Setaquotha........... leather

Mokita .... leggings
Moketha .... moccasins
Macota.. the women's petticoat
They-amah .... tobacco
Quacah .... a pipe
Hattawa............. punk
Scoute-cagah... steel for strik-
[ing fire
Outatsica.... stem of the pipe
Peteyway.. smoke of a pipe or
[tobacco
Leewawtey.... smoke of a fire
Pemee............ bear's oil
Poutala.. a skin for carrying oil
Kawcoa .... a razor
Thawthicatsica .. a frying-pan
Quawnikee .... a chain
Petheawai... a breast-plate, or
[gorget
Wythaw-quawkey-quaw .....
[a bottle
Thepee .... a river
Speleawee-thepee.. Ohio river
Wawkitomica-thepee .. Musk-
[ingum river
Quass-quetuckkee.. a cataract,
[or falls
Chepcock.. Port St. Vincent, on
[the Wabash
Ta-winikee.......... a town
Weykeewaw......... a house
Wythaw-wicommikee.... Fort
[Pitt
Kikawka-mackee ..... Detroit
Kitsecommey. the sea, or a lake
Mine-athey........ an island
Poconuey............ a wave
Oucahounie.......... a fort
Wessitic .... a mountain
Spemme-kee ...... on the top
Ou-ecawteke.. a book, letter, or
[map
Meeawee ...... a path, or road
Skeaquee .... a pond of water

Nounouconwey......a swamp
Tike comnee..a spring of water
Simmenachkee ......an apple
Tawmey.........Indian corn
Ouskipemee.......sweet corn
Nepepemee ....salt
Squimenuckee..........haws
Meeasathucckee.Irish potatoes
Peneeakee......wild potatoes
Cowasquee............wheat
Weethuckapee ....rum
Loucanah ....flour
Meleynawpee..........milk
Scoutseathawpou ......coffee
.... pepper
Saw-wee ....big
Squawthee............little
Monspethey............ tall
Spemmekee........on the top
Nepey-waw...........sleep
Tat-chimokee ....a council
Kikenecaw ....a prisoner
Notob-oley .... war
Wanesucca ....a fool
Ka-anah..............friend
Nekaanah.........my friend
Kesekee-kasothwaw...the sun
Allotheka....... the sunshine
Tepeykee kasothwaw .... the
[moon
Metsemee ....moon
Ala-aqua ....the stars
Nonolaweisky..the north star
Quala-aqua ...... Ursa Major
Teypatuca ....Orion's Belt
Peaquelineykee'... the Pleiads
Keisekelaqua.Venus, the planet
Kessekee ....day
Wawpauwey ....daylight
Tepeykee............. night
Oulacon...........yesterday
Enoukee ....to-day
Leykuckee.........last night
Nenesacou......two days ago

Wawpackee ....to-morrow
Necounakikee. two days hence
Thecounakikee.... three days
[hence
Kesothwa...a moon, or month
Kicotto...............a year
Metsemee..........no moon
Thawkee ..new moon, or come
[out
Peliko ....once
Neseeno............ twice
Nicoutee 1
Nisswee 2
Theywe 3
Neawee 4
Nealanawey 5
Necotothwey.............6
Nesothwey 7
Thyawsicthewy 8
Chagathwey 9
Metaghthwey 10
Metaghtheney   keteneycoutey
[11
id   keteneyswee.12
id   ketenthwea..13
id   keteneawey .14
id   keteneallauwey
[15
id   ketenecoutoth-
wey 16
Metaghtheney ketenesoythwey
[17
id   ketensoyuricoth-
wey..................18
Metaghtheney ketenchawgath-
thwea 19
Necoutothwey, or... } 20
Neaswawpeatatache . }
Thyawpeytockkee 30
Newawpetockkee 40
Nea allanwawpetockkee....50
Neekatyawsee 60
Neesyawsee 70
Thyawsee................80

Chawa-ka 90
Tepea-away 100
Neasinee tepea-away 200
Thenee tepea-away......300
Neawee tepea-away 400
Neallany tepea-away 500
Necoutoyththeni tepea-away..
[600
Nessoyththeni tepea-away.700
Chawaka tepea-away.....800
Metagththeney tepea-away...
[1,000
Memeaquee...........to run
Nemenee ....to drink
Theaquee............to kill
Menealapee ....to dance
Nacommo...........to sing
Atchsemo..........to speak
Neuatchsemo....to speak false
Kitellee ....to tell
Pemoutee..........to walk
Kipscawquee.......to choke
Neapouthou.........to burn
Nepaalo...........lie down
Hoosstou...........to make
Nensweleymaw }
Jackqueleymaw } .I love you
Kataqueleymawtee....do you
[love me
Alequenenthequa....will they
[kill me
Squawlawey ....I am hungry
Tawqueloukee......I am sick
Awkitawkeloukee. are you sick
Yawmawqueloukee..he is sick
Chiakee....we, or all are sick
Wanatho ....he is drunk
Nawacouta ....I know it
Mutta-nawacouta......I don't
[know it
Pawpiachee ....I will
Netessatahai.......I think so
Coqueo.........I don't care
Wetheneto.........eat some

Eleckhaalee ....go away
Peealo ....come here
Neawai.........I thank you
Awquiloukee..............sick
Mattapelou ....sit down
Keweeakouah ..are you angry
Taa-neweikata..where are you
[going
Scothakeweitamee ...will you
[be my wife
Tawney ....where is it
Nepouah ....dead
Wetchewai Scup-qua ...'tis so
Neteibois (Fr. pro.)..I tell true
Mutta teibois (Fr.pro.)..'tis not
[true
Teneetsup..........it is true
Teaque matta nemeta....don't
[give it
Teaquea-atchsimo ...don't tell
Teaque-weitemaha ..don't tell
[him of it
Tawneweicoomah...where do
[you come from
Peeawaw ....they are coming
Pesalo.............take care
Alla-luey.'tis very unfortunate
Enou Kee-mehee..a little while
[ago
Allicaw Paw keeta ...throw it
[away
Pyawaw..................here
Mawweeachee ......that way
Pealouee......a great way off
Tawnewee.........let me see
Pete keneth pia..when will he
[come back
Sweagetissetha ..what is your
[name
Laquyawaw..where is he gone
Wetchewai........let it be so
Kalipatchehee ..never mind it
Matow-e-hahee ......nothing
Neloutsy ....for nothing

Key Kenethucca ⎫
Metsigynewaw ⎬ Names of
Nenessica   some
Atowssee   ⎬ Shawanese
Wessketou   ⎭ Indians

Peccouai ....town
Olethey ....pretty
Lamyolethey .....very pretty
Lami.................very
Olethey quiawa.pretty woman
Ouey........done, or dressed
Ouesa ....good
Lamyouesa or Lamouesa .very
            [good
Matowessa..............bad
Metsy ....many

Kincapethou.......a bracelet
Keletsapethou ....a ring
Okemah ....a king
Nelowto. ....a captain
Peloutsyhea ....presently
Peloutsy..........by and by
Neheewey.how do you call that
Kethwee..........how many
Ketheney ....to wash
Pakitchee.........gone away
Winussey...........a scalp
Seeaway ....a horse
Seeaway kee.........horses
Papiache..............I will
Oucahounie.... Fort Mattawa

INDEX.

Buffalo, 162, 261, 262, 263, 269, 283, 315, 328.
Burlington Heights, 132, 188, 191, 192, 205, 211, 226, 237, 241, 284, 289, 291, 292, 334.
Burr, Aaron, 24.
Butler, Lieut., 157.
Butler, Lieut.-Col., 157.
Button, Captain John, 184.

CALAIS, 37.
Cambray, 35.
Cameron, Capt. Duncan, 130, 149, 151, 154, 157, 184, 185.
Cameron, Mr., 44.
Campbell, Alexander, 12.
Campbell, Judge, 288, 311, 312.
Campbell, Lieut.-Col., 330.
Campbell, Mary, 12.
Canada Company, 41.
Canvas House, 18.
Carey, S., 312.
Cartwright, Hon. Richard, 26, 43.
Cartwright, James, 54.
Caughnawaga, 250.
Chambers, Capt., 239, 331.
Chambly, 256.
Champlain, 319.
Champlain Lake, 249, 274, 277, 317, 318, 319, 321, 327, 334.
Chandler, Capt., 215.
Chandler, Gen., 187, 191, 196, 266.
Chapin, Col., 270, 271.
Charlotte, Princess, 120, 124.
Chateauguay, 178, 244-247.
Chatham, 231.
Chauncey, Commodore Isaac, 169, 179, 181, 187, 188, 189, 205, 208, 209, 211, 213, 223, 224, 242, 279, 284, 291, 299, 310.
Chazy River, 319.
Chewett, James, 185.
Chewett, Lieut.-Col., 13, 130, 184.
Chilicothe Journal, 173.
Chippewa, 189, 201, 226, 261, 283, 285, 286, 287, 288, 290, 292, 294, 332, 333, 335.
Chrysler's Field, 248, 252, 255, 256, 317.
Clark, Lieut.-Col., 157, 162, 198, 201.
Clark, Thomas, 131.
Claus, Col., 157.

Claus, Lieut., 254, 255.
Clay, Gen., 215.
Clayton, 242.
Clergy Reserves, 13.
Cleveland, 222.
Clifford, Major, 279, 282.
Cockburn, Admiral, 315.
Coffin, Col., 227.
Cook, Capt., 18.
Cooper, Capt., 157.
Cornwall, 13, 16, 18, 19, 21, 25, 26, 243, 251, 255, 256, 269, 270, 274, 275, 277, 279, 318.
Coteau du Lac, 255.
Couche, 225, 239, 243, 256, 268, 269.
Covent Garden, 72, 109.
Covington, Gen., 256.
Crawford, Wm., 65,
Croghan, Col., 314, 315.
Crooks, Capt., 149, 157.
Crookshank, 206.
Crossings, The, 334.
Cumberland Head, 322.

DALY, Capt., 247.
Dance, 226.
Davis, Gen., 329.
Dawson, Capt., 288.
Dearborn, Gen., 132, 147, 148, 157, 164, 165, 169, 172, 179, 185, 187, 188, 197, 266.
Decatur, 213.
De Cew, 199.
Defiance, Fort, 215.
Delaware Town, 276.
De Lorimier, Lieut., 254.
Denison, Charles, 185.
Derby, Col., 51.
De Rottenburg, Gen., 134, 226, 238, 242, 258, 270.
De Salaberry, Major, 128, 164, 198, 244-248.
Detroit, 11, 132-147, 188, 214, 229, 272, 312, 314, 315, 334.
De Watteville, 211, 213, 265, 280, 303, 305, 330, 332.
Dickson, 204.
Dickson, Mr., 20, 34.
Dixon, Capt., 141.
Dobbs, Capt., 304, 305.
Dorchester, Lord, 12.
Downey, Capt., 321, 322, 325.
Downs, The, 10.

14

Lightning Source UK Ltd.
Milton Keynes UK
UKOW07f1836100917
308942UK00004B/89/P